EXPLORING ———————
PARALLEL ———————
PROCESSING ———————

The Advanced Programming Technology Series

Exploring Natural Language Processing:
Writing BASIC Programs that Understand English

by David Leithauser

Exploring the Geometry of Nature:
Computer Modeling of Chaos, Fractals, Cellular Automata and Neural Networks

by Edward Rietman

Exploring Hypertext Programming:
Writing Knowledge Representation and Problem-Solving Programs

by Safaa H. Hashim

Exploring Parallel Processing

by Edward Rietman

EXPLORING PARALLEL PROCESSING

Edward Rietman

 WINDCREST®

Published by **Windcrest Books**
FIRST EDITION/FIRST PRINTING

Library of Congress Cataloging-in-Publication Data

Rietman, Ed.
    Exploring parallel processing / by Edward Rietman.
      p.   cm.
    ISBN 0-8306-3367-7
    1. Parallel processing (Electronic computers) I. Title.
QA76.5.R4843   1990
004'.35—dc20   90-30387
                                                       CIP

TAB BOOKS offers software for sale. For information and a catalog, please contact TAB
Software Department, Blue Ridge Summit, PA 17294-0850.

Questions regarding the content of this book should be addressed to:

Windcrest Books
An Imprint of TAB BOOKS
Blue Ridge Summit, PA 17294-0850

Acquisitions Editor: Ron Powers
Technical Editor: David M. Harter
Production: Katherine Brown

Notices

To S.
I couldn't have done it without you.

Contents

Preface

This is an introductory book on parallel processing in the PC environment. There are examples, in this book, of parallel processing cards for PC-clones and examples of simulations of parallel processing in BASIC and C. To read this book, you should be an advanced computer hacker, or have a strong interest in parallel processing.

Acknowledgments

I thank Joe Griffith for many helpful conversations and assistance In learning C in a short time. I thank Iain Bason for teaching me about the message passing language for the Parallon 2 and Oren Clark for many helpful conversations on the architecture of the Parallon 2. I owe a "thanks" to Reed Spotten, of CSA, for reading the Transputer chapter. I thank Matthew Marcus for helping me with the ideas of scaling used in CHAPTER 3. I couldn't have finished the cellular automata chapter if it wasn't for the helpfulness of Norman Margolus, Bob Tatar and Steve McClure. I thank Bob Frye for help on the neural network chapter, and I couldn't have completed this book without the assistance of Ron Powers and the editorial staff of TAB BOOKS.

Finally I thank my wife, Suzanne Harvey, for reading the entire manuscript. Love and blisses to her.

Introduction

Parallel processing has been developed to circumvent the von Neumann bottleneck. The main thrust of this research has been to increase the processing speed of computers. There are many approaches to parallel processing. These include multitasking with a single processor, message passing on a LAN, special-purpose vector processors, small clusters of tightly coupled CPUs, and massive parallel systems with hundreds to tens of thousands of processors.

Parallel processing in the PC environment is a rather new idea. In this book, I discuss several approaches using parallel processing boards that plug into the PC and simulations of massive parallel processing systems. After an introduction to the mathematical methods of complex dynamics (because parallel processors are complex systems), I discuss, in a general way, most of the existing parallel computer architectures in CHAPTER 2.

CHAPTER 3 is a discussion of an MIMD parallel processing card (now orphanware) for IBM-PC, XT, AT, and 386 clones. The main section of this chapter is a discussion of parallel processing in a real message-passing environment. There are many ways to simulate virtual message passing systems, but this is an actual hardware environment not vaporware.

CHAPTER 4 is a discussion of the popular Transputer. This is a 32-bit RISC processor with on-chip links so that the chip can be considered as a LEGO for building blocks of parallel systems. In this chapter, I discuss programming a transputer board plugged into a PC-XT clone. The chapter includes simulation of parallel processing on the transputer, and message passing in this environment.

CHAPTER 5 describes in some detail the dynamics of cellular automata. Included are several BASIC and C programs. These allow you to simulate massively parallel systems in which each processor is a one-bit automaton. In the last part of the chapter, I describe a cellular automata machine that plugs into the PC and allows you to do cellular automata computations faster than a Cray computer.

Neural networks are discussed in CHAPTER 6. This discussion covers all the major network types and includes programs written in BASIC and C. There are PC plug-in boards to speed up neural network simulations, but these are very expensive and are really just simulation accelerators—most based on DSP chips. The general-purpose neural network chip is still being researched by many groups.

In CHAPTER 7 I discuss applications and algorithms for parallel processors, and in CHAPTER 8 I describe some commercial supercomputers and the technologies for the next several generations of parallel and supercomputers.

1

Mathematical Techniques

In this first chapter I discuss some of the mathematical techniques used to study complex systems. I review the elements of set theory and graph theory. Then, I review differential equations and difference equations, and solve systems of differential equations using a Taylor series expansion. The final part of the chapter is concerned with vector and matrix operations.

SET THEORY

This section on set theory will be little more than a review of the introductory aspects, and will include examples from dynamical systems similar to mappings of chaotic dynamical systems. This is included primarily so you can understand some of the terminology used in research journals and books on complex dynamical systems.

Much of the following is similar to that found in Lin and Lin (1974). I will represent logical statements symbolically by lowercase letters, such as p, q, and r. These can be combined to form compound statements. There are only five common connectives, all of which are shown in Table 1-1.

Table 1-1 shows the common Boolean logic connectives with which computer programmers are familiar. The phrase "if and only if" is sometimes written as "iff." As I stated above, you can make compound statements with these connectives. If p is a statement, then ~p reads "not p" or the negative of p. Table 1-2 is a simple truth table for this example.

Table 1-1.

Connective Word	Connective Symbol
NOT	$\sim$
AND	$\wedge$
OR	$\vee$
IF....THEN...	$\rightarrow$
...IF AND ONLY IF...	$\leftrightarrow$

Table 1-2.

p	$\sim$p
T	F
F	T

Another example is p q. This is read "p and q" or the "conjunctive of p and q." This is an example of a compound statement. The truth table for this example is given in Table 1-3.

Table 1-3.

p	q	p $\wedge$ q
T	T	T
T	F	F
F	T	F
F	F	F

A more complex statement truth table can be constructed, such as that in Table 1-4.

Table 1-4.

p	p	$\sim$p $\vee$ $\sim$p
T	F	T
F		T

For any given discussion concerning a set or group of objects it is common to see a statement such as, "for all x in the set . . . ." This is a universal quantifier and is symbolized as ($\forall$x). Another common phrase is, "there exists at least one x such that . . . ." This is called an *existential quantifier* and is symbolized as ($\exists$x). Now you can take these two definitions and make more complex statements.

If you are given a domain, U, or a collection of objects under consideration and a general statement p(x), called a *propositional predicate*, whose variable x ranges over U, then you can make the following statement:

($\forall$x) (P(x))

This says that for all x in U, the statement p(x) about x is true. Another example is:

$$(\exists\ x)\ (P(x))$$

This means that there exists at least one x in U such that p(x) is true. In summary, the statement "f(x) = 0 for all x" is just the same as:

$$(\forall\ x)\ (f(x)) = 0$$

I will now cover some more definitions. A *set* is any collection of distinguishable objects, called *elements*. A set that contains a limited number of elements is called a *finite* set; an *infinite* set is one that is not a finite set. Sets are frequently designated by enclosing symbols representing their elements in braces. The empty set is called a *null* set and is denoted by the symbol {∅}. If item a is an element of set A, you write a ∈ A which is read: "a is an element of A" or "a belongs to A." Similarly b ∉ A means that b is not an element of A.

Two identical sets are represented as

$$(\forall\ x)\ [(x \in A) \leftrightarrow (x \in B)]$$

The order of elements of a set is irrelevant. Set {a,b,c} is the same as {b,c,a} or {c,b,a}.

Another important concept is subsets. If every element of a set A is also contained in a set B, then A is a *subset* of B. In symbols this is written A ⊆ B or B ⊇ A. Of course, if A is a subset of B then B is a *superset* of A.

$$(A \subseteq B) \equiv (\forall\ x)\ [(x \in A) \rightarrow (x \in B)]$$

Naturally, every set is a subset and superset of itself. When A ⊆ B, and A ≠ B, you write A ⊂ B or B ⊃ A, which reads A is a proper subset of B, or B is a proper superset of A. The empty set is a subset of every set.

$$(x \in \varnothing) \rightarrow (x \in A)$$

I would like to now introduce set-builder notation. To every set A, and to every statement p(x) about x ∈ A, there exists a set:

$$\{x \in A | P(x)\}$$

whose elements are those elements x of A for which the statement p(x) is true. The symbols

$$\{x \in A | P(x)\}$$

are read: "the set of all x in A such that p(x) is true." This notation is the *set-builder* notation.

Additions, multiplications and subtractions are all operations on numbers. The analogous operations can be performed on sets. The union of two sets is represented by $A \cup B$. This results in a set of all elements x, such that x belongs to at least one of the two sets A and B. That is:

$$x \in A \cup B$$

if and only if

$$(x \in A) \lor (x \in B)$$

The intersection of two sets A and B is represented by $A \cap B$. It results in a set of all elements x which belong to both A and B. In symbols:

$$A \cap B = \{x | (x \in A) \land (x \in B)\}$$

or

$$\{x \in A | x \in B\}$$

As an example, let

$$A = \{1,2,3,4\}$$
$$B = \{3,4,5\}$$

then

$$A \cup B = \{1,2,3,4,5\}$$
$$A \cap B = \{3,4\}$$

The complement of B in A is the set $A - B$ symbolized by

$$A - B = \{x \in A | x \not\in B\}$$

As an example, let

A = {a,b,c,d}
B = {c,d,e,f}

then

A − B = {a,b,c,d} − {c,d,e,f} = {a,b}
A − (A ∪ B) = {a,b,c,d} − {c,d} = {a,b}

You should note that

A − B ≠ B − A

Now look at some examples of set theory notation used in non-linear dynamics system theory. In one-dimensional iterated maps of chaotic dynamical systems, you will often see the relation:

$$x_{n+1} = f(x_n), \quad x_n \in [0,1], \quad n = 0, 1, 2, \ldots$$

This is a difference equation of a unimodal map, i.e. the mapping is contained in the unit interval.

Another example from dynamical systems theory in the Cantor Middle-Thirds set. Start with the unit interval and remove the middle third. Next, remove the two middle thirds from what remains again. Continue removing middle thirds in this fashion. At the nth stage, 2^n open intervals are removed. Figure 1-1 graphically demonstrates this

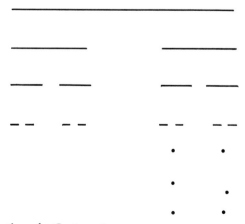

Fig. 1-1. Construction of a Cantor set.

procedure. The Cantor Middle-Thirds set is an example of a fractal. A *fractal* is a set that is self-similar under magnification.

GRAPH THEORY

In this section I discuss a few points of graph theory. This section is also included as an introduction and review so you will understand the terminology used in research journals and advanced books. Later in this section I give an example of graph theory in application to neural networks and parallel processing. Much of this section is similar to Maxwell and Reed (1971).

A *graph* is a set of points. The points are called *vertices*, and they are connected by lines called *edges*. These graphs have no properties other than the visual. Graph theory is a study of the interrelationships between vertices and edges. Graphs have many applications including: game theory, networks, flow diagrams, molecular structure, and family trees. Network applications are used in the study of iterated maps.

For a network containing a number of elements, e, it is necessary to solve a system of 2e equations. Later in this section I show how to construct a graph from a matrix; but first, I would like to cover a few basic definitions. A subgraph, G_S of a graph G, is a subset of the set G.

$$G_S \subset G$$

Also important is the definition for a connected graph. These graphs are called *circuits* if each vertex is of degree two. In other words, each element is a two-terminal device. Several circuit examples are given in Fig. 1-2.

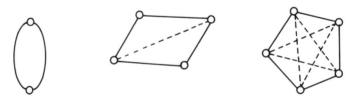

Fig. 1-2. Examples of circuit graphs.

In the three examples pictured in Fig. 1-2, the subgraphs are also circuits shown by dotted lines. Circuits are distinguished by several properties. A circuit contains no end elements, and it contains only interior vertices. A circuit contains at least two elements and is always a connected planar graph.

Another important graph, in addition to the circuit, is the tree. A *tree* is a subgraph of a point P, such that it contains no circuits, is connected, and contains all the vertices of point P.

Figure 1-3 is an example of a tree graph. Tree graphs are models for interconnection of parallel processing computers, and are used in algorithms for artificial intelligence solutions to games.

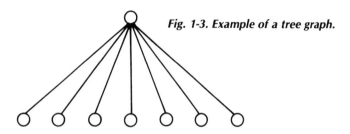

Fig. 1-3. Example of a tree graph.

I would now like to show how to construct a graph from a matrix. A directed graph is a graph in which an arrowhead is assigned to each element of the graph. Given the matrix M, you can construct a directed graph. The matrix is given as

$$M = \begin{bmatrix} 0 & 1 & 0 & 0 & 0 \\ 0 & 0 & 1 & 0 & 0 \\ 0 & 0 & 0 & 1 & 0 \\ 0 & 0 & 0 & 0 & 1 \\ 1 & 0 & 0 & 0 & 0 \end{bmatrix}$$

This matrix is described by the mapping:

$M(1,1)=0$	$M(2,1)=0$	$M(3,1)=0$	$M(4,1)=0$	$M(5,1)=1$
$M(1,2)=1$	$M(2,2)=0$	$M(3,2)=0$	$M(4,2)=0$	$M(5,2)=0$
$M(1,3)=0$	$M(2,3)=1$	$M(3,3)=0$	$M(4,3)=0$	$M(5,3)=0$
$M(1,4)=0$	$M(2,4)=0$	$M(3,4)=1$	$M(4,4)=0$	$M(5,4)=0$
$M(1,5)=0$	$M(2,5)=0$	$M(3,5)=0$	$M(4,5)=1$	$M(5,5)=0$

From this mapping you can construct the two equivalent graphs shown in Fig. 1-4. You should note that the spatial arrangement of the points is irrelevent.

Another interesting example of graph theory is in discrete iterations. Dewdney (1986) wrote an introduction to this model and Robert (1986) has gone into far more detail on discrete iterations. Pick any number at random between 0 and 99. Find its square and take the last two digits of this result and square this number. Repeat this pro-

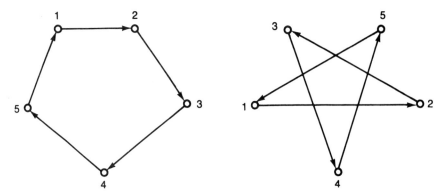

Fig. 1-4. Example of two equivalent graphs.

cess and eventually you will encounter a number you have already encountered. As an example take 81 and square it.

$$81^2 = 6561$$
$$61^2 = 3721$$
$$21^2 = 441$$
$$41^2 = 1681$$
$$81^2 = 6561$$
$$\cdot \;\; = \;\; \cdot$$
$$\cdot \;\; = \;\; \cdot$$
$$\cdot \;\; = \;\; \cdot$$

This leads to a cycle of period four. From this graph you could produce the graph shown in Fig. 1-5.

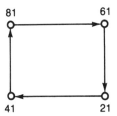

Fig. 1-5. Graphical example of a period-four cycle.

DIFFERENTIAL EQUATIONS

The opening few paragraphs of this section are a review of calculus, which is followed by a discussion of differential equations and difference equations. The final part of this section will describe an algorithm and computer program to solve systems of differential equations using a Taylor series expansion.

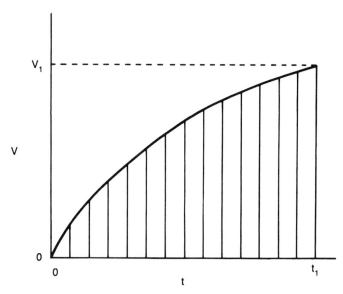

Fig. 1-6. Plot of a simple function. The area under this curve is the integral of the function from zero to t_1.

I will first begin with the integral because this is easy to grasp graphically as an area under a curve. Given a curve such as Fig. 1-6, describing the function $v(t)$, the area under the curve is given by

$$I = \int_0^{t_1} v\,dt$$

where dt is an infinitesimally small interval of time. The integral symbol $\int$ is known as a lazy "s" and represents the summation of the product of v dt from zero to t_1.

Differentiation is the opposite of integration. A small change in v, represented by dv, is divided by an infinitesimally small time interval dt. The symbol dv/dt is known as the derivative of v with respect to t. These infinitesimally small changes can be represented as small changes in v with respect to a small change in t.

$$\frac{dv}{dt} \approx \frac{\Delta v}{\Delta t}$$

The derivative is given as the slope to the curve $v(t)$ evaluated at the point of interest. This is an important concept that is used in the solution of differential equations, and in evaluating the critical properties of chaotic systems.

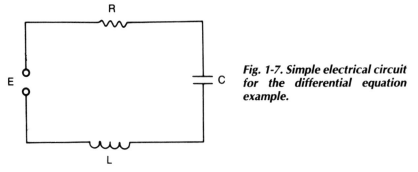

Fig. 1-7. Simple electrical circuit
for the differential equation
example.

An example of a simple differential equation is for a series circuit shown in Fig. 1-7.

For resistance R, capacitance C, inductance L, and voltage source E, the current flowing around the circuit I(t) at time t is given by:

$$L\frac{dI}{dt} + RI + \frac{q}{C} = E$$

where RI is the voltage across R, and the voltage across C is given by q/C. The voltage across the inductance L is given by L dI/dt. If you differentiate this equation with respect to time and substitute dq/dt = I then you get

$$L\frac{d^2I}{dt^2} + R\frac{dI}{dt} + \frac{I}{C} = \frac{dE}{dt}$$

Now that I have reviewed the introductory concepts of calculus, and have shown how differential equations are built up from derivatives, I would like to show how to solve a differential equation.

For a simple example of solving differential equations, I would like to start with what is known as a first order differential equation. Given the simple equation:

$$\frac{dy}{dx} = \sin(x)$$

This can be solved by separation of variables

$$dy = \sin(x)\,dx$$
$$\int dy = \int \sin(x)\,dx$$
$$y = -\cos(x) + c$$

where c is the constant of integration.

An example of a non-linear differential equation in dynamics is the motion of a damped pendulum. The equation for this system is:

$$ml^2 \frac{d^2\Theta}{dt^2} + cl \frac{d\Theta}{dt} + mgl \sin(\Theta) = 0$$

From Fig. 1-8, the angle Θ is the angular displacement of the pendulum from the vertical.

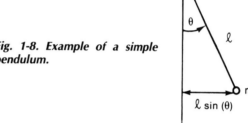

Fig. 1-8. Example of a simple pendulum.

The damping constant is given by c and is always greater than zero. The mass is given by m and the length and gravitational constant are given by l and g, respectively. This equation can be solved by substitution.

Let $\quad x = 0$

$$y = \frac{d\Theta}{dt}$$

then $\quad \dfrac{dx}{dt} = y$

$$\frac{dy}{dt} = -\frac{g}{l} \sin(x) - \frac{c}{ml} y$$

This gives a system of differential equations. This is an example of a two-dimensional system. Rather than actually solving this system analytically, I will now introduce a computer algorithm for the solution.

ALGORITHMS FOR SOLUTION OF DIFFERENTIAL EQUATIONS

After this discussion of computer algorithms for solutions of differential equations, I present a computer program and give a line-by-line discussion of the program. There are many books that discuss computer solutions to differential equations. There is an excellent chapter in Boyce and DiPrima (1977). Shoup (1983) has written an excellent book for numerical methods with a personal computer; and Danby (1985) has written a small book with hundreds of examples of differential equations for solving with a personal computer. I should also mention the advanced book by Potter (1973) which is devoted to computer modeling in physics.

The simplest method for the solution of differential equations is a one-step technique known as Euler's method. The method is illustrated in Fig. 1-9.

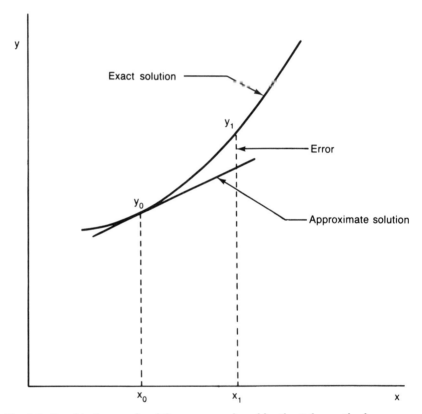

Fig. 1-9. Graphical example of the error produced by the Euler method.

The principle of the method involves a Taylor series expansion of the form:

$$y (x_o + h) = y (x_o) + hy' (x_o) + \frac{1}{2} h^2 y'' (x_o) + \ldots$$

Taking a small step h from the initial value, you can see that if h is indeed small, then h^2 is even smaller, and so the equation can be approximated by

$$y(x_o + h) = y(x_o) + hy'(x_o)$$

This can be written as a difference equation.

$$y_{n+1} = y_n + hf(x_n, y_n), \qquad n = 1, 2, \ldots$$

In the Euler method, the slope at the curve for the initial value is exact. The slope changes at the step value $x_o + h$ giving an error. In the modified Euler method, a better solution is found by taking an average value of the derivatives at the beginning and end of the interval. This average value is then used to calculate the derivative at the end of the interval. There are other methods to solve differential equations; these include the Ruge-Kutta method, Gill's method, Milne's method and the Adams-Bashforth method. These methods are not discussed here. If you are interested, you should check out Shoup (1983), or Boyce and DiPrima (1977). These other methods can give very high accuracy with good speed for the computer solution. I selected the simple Euler method for the computer program because it is very easy to modify the program for a system of n equations, but the method is slow.

COMPUTER SOLUTION OF DIFFERENTIAL EQUATIONS

I would now like to describe a computer program to solve systems of differential equations. The example I use is the damped pendulum. The system, as derived earlier in this chapter, is:

$$\frac{dx}{dt} = y$$

$$\frac{dy}{dt} = -\frac{g}{l}\sin(x) - \frac{c}{ml}y$$

The program is written in BASIC, and should run on any system. This program, SDEQ1, shown in Fig. 1-10, solves a system of differential equations using the Euler method.

Now look at the program, line by line. Line 30 allows the operator to input the initial and final time t_1 and t_2. In line 40 the operator enters the time increment. This has the variable name D. I usually select a value of about 0.1 for the time increment. Smaller values can be used, but computation time increases, and the number of data

```
10 REM DEFINE DX/DT=D2=F(T,X,Y,Z) IN LINE 130
20 REM DEFINE DY/DT=D1=F(T,X,Y,Z) IN LINE 140
30 INPUT "INPUT INITIAL AND FINAL VALUES OF T ";T1,T2
40 INPUT "INPUT DELTA T ";D
50 INPUT "INPUT INITIAL CONDITIONS X,Y ";X,Y
60 INPUT "INPUT NUMBER OF CALCULATIONS FOR EACH DELTA T ";N
70 INPUT "INPUT FILE NAME ";FILE$
80 OPEN "O",#1,FILE$
90 FOR T9=T1 TO T2 STEP D
100 PRINT T9,X,Y
110 PRINT #1,X,Y
120 FOR T=T9 TO T9+D STEP D/N
130 D1=Y
140 D2=-6*SIN(X)-5*Y
150 X=X+D1*D/N
160 Y=Y+D2*D/N
170 NEXT T
180 NEXT T9
190 CLOSE #1
200 END
```

Fig. 1-10. 5DEQ1.BAS

points generated increases rapidly. In line 50 the initial conditions are entered. These are the initial conditions for the x and y values. In line 60 the number of calculations for each time increment is entered. I usually enter 50. Some explanation might be needed as to what this number represents. Earlier in this chapter I showed that the Euler method can be written as a truncated difference equation derived from a Taylor series expansion. The difference equations for the two equation systems in the example can be written as:

$$x_{n+1} = x_n + hf(x_n, y_n, t_n)$$
$$y_{n+1} = y_n + hg(x_n, y_n, t_n)$$

In this system the function $f(x_n, y_n, t_n)$ is the derivative dy/dt, which in this example is:

$$f(x_n, y_n, t_n) = \frac{dx}{dt} = y$$

Similarly, the function $g(x_n, y_n, t_n)$ is

$$g(x_n, y_n, t_n) = \frac{dy}{dt} = -\frac{g}{l}\sin(x) - \frac{c}{ml}y$$

The parameter h is directly related to the error. If h is very small, the error is also very small (but the computation time increases quickly).

This h value is given by the relation:

$$h = \frac{\Delta t}{N}$$

where Δt is the time increment (in the program this is named D) and N is the number of calculations per time increment.

Because I am giving a line-by-line discussion, I will get back to the discussion of the calculation after a few more comments. Line 70 asks the user to enter a filename. The computed data points are stored on this file and then plotted or manipulated with a separate program. This will be discussed later in this chapter. Line 80 opens the file.

In line 90 the calculation begins. The loop is set up to increment from T_1, the initial time to the final time T_2 in a step size D or delta time. Line 100 prints the x,y values to the computer display, and line 110 prints these values to the file. The first time through the loop the initial values are printed. In line 120 the calculation begins. A loop is started to calculate the derivative using the difference equation and incrementing the step size D/N, as defined above. This is the time increment divided by the number of calculations per increment. Line 130 and 140 define the differential equation and the difference equation. The loops are repeated until the end. Then the file is closed in line 190 and the program ends.

Now run the program. First notice that the program is set up for the pendulum example. By changing the differential equations in lines 130 and 140 you could investigate a different system. For this system I selected the values of the constants as follows:

$$g/l = 6$$
$$c/ml = 5$$

After entering RUN, I selected the initial time as 0 and the final time as 100 with a time increment of 0.1. The initial condition I chose was the point (5,5) on the x,y plane. I selected the number of calculations between each time step to be 25. Once you have the data file you can then graph the data. My plot of this file for the pendulum example is given in Fig. 1-11.

Notice that the curve starts at the point $y = 3.0$ and quickly falls to $y = 0$ at $t = 4.2$. The quick relaxation of this pendulum is due to the damping coefficient, c. In this example c is divided by mass and length to give a new constant with a value of 5.

I would like to reiterate that this is a general purpose program and can be easily modified to solve a system of n differential equations.

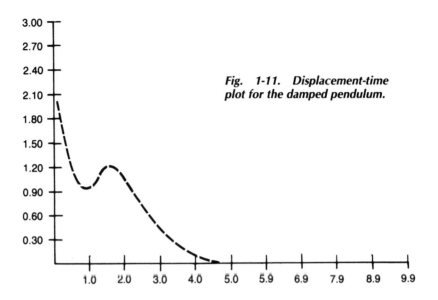

Fig. 1-11. Displacement-time plot for the damped pendulum.

DATA-FILE PLOTTING PROGRAM——————————————

The following program is for an IBM PC clone. This graphic program would require extensive modification for non-IBM clones. By making the majority of programs generate data files rather than plotting simultaneously, a larger number of readers can experiment with these dynamical systems. Of course, if you do not have an IBM PC clone, you will have to write your own graphics module.

The program PLOT1 (see Fig. 1-12) can be used to plot two-dimensional data files, or the program can be modified to plot three-dimensional data files by selecting a two-dimensional slice through three-dimensional space. Here, I will only discuss some of the program highlights rather than a line-by-line description.

```
10 CLS
20 INPUT "INPUT NUMBER OF POINTS ";NPTS
30 DIM X(5001),Y(5001)
40 CLS
50 INPUT "what is the name of the disk file you want to plot";FILENAME$
60 OPEN "I",2,FILENAME$
70 FOR I=1 TO NPTS
80 IF EOF(2) THEN 110
90 INPUT#2,X(I),Y(I)
100 NEXT I
110 NPTS=I-1
120 XMAX=-1E+20 :XMIN=-XMAX
130 YMAX=-1E+20
140 YMIN=-YMAX
150 FOR I=1 TO NPTS
160 IF YMIN>Y(I) THEN YMIN=Y(I)
170 IF YMAX<Y(I) THEN YMAX=Y(I)
```

Fig. 1-12. PLOT1.BAS

Fig. 1-12. Continued.

```
180 IF XMAX<X(I) THEN XMAX=X(I)
190 IF XMIN>X(I) THEN XMIN=X(I)
200 NEXT I
210 CLS
220 NXTIC=10:NYTIC=10
230 XMN=XMIN:XMX=XMAX:YMN=YMIN:YMX=YMAX
240 CLS
250 SCREEN 2
260 DSX=ABS(XMX-XMN):DSY=ABS(YMX-YMN)
270 SX=.1:SY=.1
280 AXMN=XMN-DSX*SX:AXMX=XMX+DSX*SX
290 AYMX=YMX+DSY*SY:AYMN=YMN-DSY*SY
300 WINDOW (AXMN,AYMN)-(AXMX,AYMX)
310 LINE (XMN,YMN)-(XMX,YMN)
320 LINE (XMN,YMN)-(XMN,YMX)
330 DXTIC=DSX*.02:DYTIC=DSY*.025
340 XTIC=DSX/NXTIC:YTIC=DSY/NYTIC
350 FOR I=1 TO NXTIC
360 XP=XMN+XTIC*I
370 LINE (XP,YMN)-(XP,YMN+DYTIC)
380 ROW=24
390 NEXT I
400 FOR I= 1 TO NYTIC
410 YP=YMN+I*YTIC
420 LINE (XMN,YP)-(XMN+DXTIC,YP)
430 NEXT I
440 FOR I=1 TO NPTS-1
450 J=I+1
460 IF Y(I)>YMX OR Y(J)>YMX OR Y(J)<YMN OR X(I)<XMN THEN 480
470 CIRCLE (X(I),Y(I)),0
480 NEXT I
490 FOR I=1 TO NXTIC
500 XP=XMN+XTIC*I
510 XC=PMAP(XP,0)
520 COL=INT(80*XC/640)-1
530 LOCATE 24,COL
540 PRINT USING "###.#"; XP;
550 NEXT I
560 FOR I=1 TO NYTIC
570 YP=YMN+I*YTIC
580 YR=PMAP(YP,1)
590 ROW=CINT(24*YR/199)+1
600 LOCATE ROW,1
610 PRINT USING "###.##"; YP
620 NEXT I
630 GOTO 630
```

After clearing the screen, the program prompts the user for the number of data points in the file, and for the filename. The file is then read into a matrix that has been dimensioned in line 30. After reading the entire file, the minimum and maximum value for both the abscissa and ordinate is found. The screen is then cleared in line 210, and axes and tic marks are drawn on the computer display. The data points from the matrix are then plotted on the display. After displaying the numerical values for the tic marks on the axes, the program enters an infinite loop to prevent the cursor from appearing on the display. The user can now press the print graphics keys for a hardcopy of the graph.

VECTOR ALGEBRA

A vector can be represented on an x-y coordinate system, as shown in Fig. 1-13. This vector has components $x = 3$ and $y = 4$ which can be represented by $v = (3, 4)$.

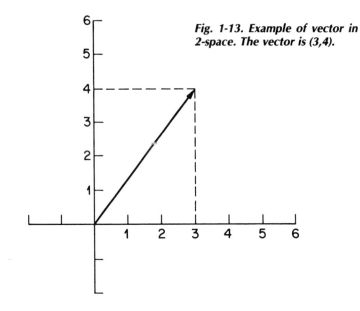

Fig. 1-13. Example of vector in 2-space. The vector is (3,4).

A three-dimensional vector would have three components, $v = (x\ y\ z)$ and an n-dimensional vector would have n components, $v = (v_1\ v_2\ v_3\ \ldots\ v_n)$. Where the v_i's represent the component for the dimension i up to n dimensions. The vector $v = (3\ 4)$, can be multiplied by a number, A, as follows:

$$A*v = (A*3, A*4)$$

and for an n-dimensional vector you get:

$$A*v = (A*v_1, A*v_2, A*v_3, \ldots, A*v_n).$$

Vector addition is done by adding the components. For example: Given two vectors, $a = (12, 4)$ and $b = (-6, 1)$, then their sum is $a+b = (12-6, 4+1) = (6, 5)$.

Multiplication of two vectors is a little less obvious. Vectors can be multiplied in two ways. One is called the *dot product* $a \cdot b$. The other is called the *cross* product a x b. The dot product is also called the *scalar* product or the *inner* product.

The inner product is given by the relation

$$a \cdot b = (a_1b_1, a_2b_2, a_3b_3, \ldots)$$

The magnitude of vector a is represented by $|a|$ and similarly for vector b. The magnitude of a vector is found by taking the square root of the sum of the squares of the components of the vector. For example:

$$|a| = (a_1^2 + a_2^2 + \ldots a_n^2)^{1/2}$$

in n dimensions:

$$|a| = \left(\sum_i a_i^2 \right)^{1/2}$$

The angle between the two vectors can be found by the relation

$$\cos \Theta = \frac{a \cdot b}{|a| \; |b|}$$

This equation can be written in terms of the components as

$$\cos\theta = \frac{\sum_i v_i \, w_i}{\left(\sum_i v_i^2 \right)^{1/2} \left(\sum_i w_i^2 \right)^{1/2}}$$

An example of the use of this relation in parallel distributed processing is shown in Fig. 1-14. Given a processor, u, it receives its input from n processors v_i. This output process u is given by the inner product of the input process v_i and the strength of the weight of each process w_i.

$$u = w \cdot v$$

In the dot product, the commutative law holds.

$$w \cdot v = v \cdot w$$

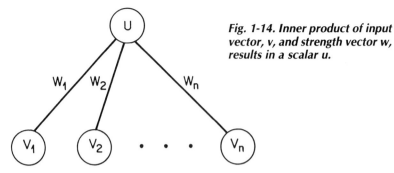

Fig. 1-14. Inner product of input vector, v, and strength vector w, results in a scalar u.

The cross product, also called the *outer* product, results in a vector. The vector product in three-dimensional space can be represented by

$$a \times b = ((a_2b_3 - a_3b_2), (a_3b_1 - a_1b_3), (a_1b_2 - a_2b_1))$$

MATRICES

A matrix is an array of elements or real numbers. For example

$$M = \begin{bmatrix} 3 & 2 & 9 \\ 7 & 6 & 0 \\ 1 & 4 & 2 \end{bmatrix}$$

M is a three-dimensional matrix, or a 3 × 3 matrix. Matrices need not be square. For example:

$$P = \begin{bmatrix} 2 & 0 \\ 7 & 1 \\ 5 & 4 \end{bmatrix} \quad N = \begin{bmatrix} 1 \\ 0 \\ 1 \end{bmatrix}$$

P is a 3 × 2 matrix and N is a 3 × 1 matrix.

It is sometimes convenient to think of a vector as a one-dimensional matrix:

$$V = [3\ 1\ 0]$$

Multiplication of a matrix by a scalar is the same as multiplication of a vector by a scalar. Each element in the matrix is multiplied by the scalar.

$$3 \cdot P = \begin{bmatrix} 3 \cdot 2 & 3 \cdot 0 \\ 3 \cdot 7 & 3 \cdot 1 \\ 3 \cdot 5 & 3 \cdot 4 \end{bmatrix} = \begin{bmatrix} 6 & 0 \\ 21 & 3 \\ 15 & 12 \end{bmatrix}$$

Addition of matrices is similar to addition of vectors. For example:

$$M1 = \begin{bmatrix} 1 & 0 & 5 \\ 0 & 7 & 2 \\ 4 & 6 & 6 \end{bmatrix} \quad M2 = \begin{bmatrix} 6 & 9 & -3 \\ 5 & 2 & 0 \\ -8 & 4 & 4 \end{bmatrix}$$

then

$$M1 + M2 = \begin{bmatrix} 1+6 & 0+9 & 5-3 \\ 0+5 & 7+2 & 2+0 \\ 4-8 & 3+4 & 6+4 \end{bmatrix} = \begin{bmatrix} 7 & 9 & 2 \\ 5 & 9 & 2 \\ -4 & 7 & 10 \end{bmatrix}$$

This has application in memory storage. If each matrix represents one memory, then the sum of the two matrices results in a storage matrix for the two memory states.

A very important concept is the multiplication of a vector by a matrix. This can be used in pattern recognition and memory recall. For example given a vector:

$$v = \begin{bmatrix} 2 \\ 9 \\ 7 \end{bmatrix}$$

and a matrix:

$$M = \begin{bmatrix} 1 & 0 & 5 \\ 0 & 7 & 2 \\ 4 & 3 & 6 \end{bmatrix}$$

the inner product is found as follows:

$$u = Mv = \begin{bmatrix} 1 & 0 & 5 \\ 0 & 7 & 2 \\ 4 & 3 & 6 \end{bmatrix} \begin{bmatrix} 2 \\ 9 \\ 7 \end{bmatrix}$$

$$u = \begin{bmatrix} 1 \cdot 2 + 0 \cdot 9 + 5 \cdot 7 \\ 0 \cdot 2 + 7 \cdot 9 + 2 \cdot 7 \\ 4 \cdot 2 + 3 \cdot 9 + 6 \cdot 7 \end{bmatrix} = \begin{bmatrix} 37 \\ 77 \\ 77 \end{bmatrix}$$

Notice that the inner product of a matrix with a vector is a vector. The matrix need not be square, as shown in the following example.

$$K = \begin{bmatrix} 3 & 7 & 1 \\ 0 & 1 & 2 \end{bmatrix} \qquad t = \begin{bmatrix} 1 \\ 0 \\ 3 \end{bmatrix}$$

$$q = Kt = \begin{bmatrix} 3 & 7 & 1 \\ 0 & 1 & 2 \end{bmatrix} \begin{bmatrix} 1 \\ 0 \\ 3 \end{bmatrix} = \begin{bmatrix} 3 \cdot 1 + 7 \cdot 0 + 1 \cdot 3 \\ 0 \cdot 1 + 1 \cdot 0 + 2 \cdot 3 \end{bmatrix} = \begin{bmatrix} 6 \\ 6 \end{bmatrix} = 6 \begin{bmatrix} 1 \\ 1 \end{bmatrix}$$

This is sufficiently important to be written in symbolic terms.

$$u = M v$$

$$(i_{th} \text{ component of } u) = (i_{th} \text{ row of } M) (v)$$

A convenient way of thinking of this operation is as a mapping, where v is mapped to u by the operation M (see Fig. 1-15).

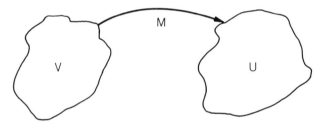

Fig. 1-15. Map of v to u, by process, M.

This mapping of one state into another is analogous to a one layer parallel distributed processing system. In Fig. 1-16 there are n input units and p output units. Each input processor is connected to each output processor by a connection strength, M_{pn}. Where M_{pn} represents the pn^{th} element in the matrix M. Each output unit computes the inner product of its weight vector and the input vector. In other words the output at the ith output processor is found by computing the inner product of the input vector with the weight vector for the ith processor.

The components of the input vector are the values of the input units. The weight vector for the ith process is the ith row of the strength matrix M.

This technique can be extended to multilayered systems where the output of one layer becomes the input of the next layer. In Fig. 1-17, the processors at a are connected to each of the processors at b. These are, in turn, connected to each of the c processors. An input vector at a is mapped to b by the connection strength matrix Y. Vector b is then mapped to vector c by connection strength matrix Z. This can be represented symbolically as:

c = Z(Ya)

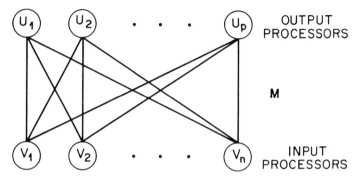

Fig. 1-16. *Two layer process. All processors at v are connected to all processors at u.*

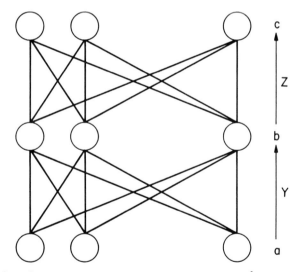

Fig. 1-17. *Three layer process. Processors at a are connected to processors at b, by the matrix, Y. Processors at b are connected to those at c, by matrix, Z.*

In other words, the matrix vector product of Ya results in the vector b, and the matrix vector product Zb results in c.

A very important mathematical technique in parallel distributed processing theory is the transpose and outer product of a vector. The transpose of a $n \times m$ matrix is a $m \times n$ matrix. If the matrix is a one-dimensional matrix, i.e. a vector, then the transpose is found as demonstrated in the following example. Given a vector:

$$v = (3\ 7\ 9\ 2)$$

then the transpose of v is given by:

$$v^t = \begin{bmatrix} 3 \\ 7 \\ 9 \\ 2 \end{bmatrix}$$

Notice the superscript t. This indicates the transpose operation.

The inner product of a vector with a transposed vector gives a scalar as shown in the following example:

$$v = [9\ 7\ 3]$$
$$u = [5\ 2\ 0]$$

$$vu^t = [9\ 7\ 3] \begin{bmatrix} 5 \\ 2 \\ 0 \end{bmatrix} = 9 \cdot 5 + 7 \cdot 2 + 3 \cdot 0 = 59$$

The outer product of a vector with a transposed vector gives a matrix:

$$v^t u = \begin{bmatrix} 9 \\ 7 \\ 3 \end{bmatrix} [5\ 2\ 0] = \begin{bmatrix} 45 & 18 & 0 \\ 35 & 14 & 0 \\ 15 & 6 & 0 \end{bmatrix}$$

The outer product concept can be applied to learning in a neural network. This is called the Hebb learning rule (Rumelhart, et. al. 1986). A particular matrix can be generated by associating an input vector with an output vector. This is known as associative learning. The technique will be used in an example program in Chapter 6 on associative memories for neural networks.

For any given vector v, when the outer product of v with its transpose vt is found, a memory matrix unique for that memory state is generated. If the inner product of this memory state and the memory matrix is found, then the result is the memory. The input vector need not be the pure memory state, but only a partial memory. When this partial memory state is operated on by the memory matrix, the inner product will give the complete and correct memory state.

What is not obvious from the above is that a given memory matrix can store more than one memory state. The actual number of memories depends on the size of the matrix.

2

Parallel Processing Architectures

In this chapter, I introduce the major parallel processing architectures. Parallel processing was developed to circumvent the von Neumann bottleneck—a concept I will develop later in this chapter. The main purpose of the research and development into parallel processing was to increase the processing speed of computers. In order to handle such tasks as real-time speech, visual and signal processing computers must be much faster. Processing speed is also required in scientific computing and social system modeling. Not only are faster computers needed but also more efficient software. In short, what is needed are smarter computers.

The first generation of digital computers were the vacuum tube-based systems. Arithmetic was done on a bit-by-bit, fixed-point basis and the system was programmed in binary machine code. The ENIAC (Electronic Numerical, Integrator and Computer) in 1946 was the most famous computer from this generation.

In 1954, Bell Laboratories built the TRADIC (Transistorized Digital Computer). This marked the beginning of the second generation. The third generation (1962–1975) used small-scale integrated and medium-scale integrated circuits.The IBM 360/91 is a famous model from this generation. The fourth generation to the present is marked by use of large-scale integrated circuits.

In each of the generations, a move has been made from simple data processing to information processing. Now, with expanding knowledge bases, the world is moving from fifth-generation knowledge processing to sixth-generation intelligence processing. The current parallel processors are the beginning of the fifth-generation computers. These systems use a few processors, composed of very large-scale integration, in parallel, such as the Cray X-MP, along with sophisticated software to process large knowledge bases. These parallel processors are also used for information processing, such as huge spreadsheets, and the data processing, such as scientific number crunching.

Sixth-generation and massively parallel computers are just beginning to appear. Architecture and design for these machines are under extensive investigation in many research laboratories. These machines will have applications in intelligence processing, real-time speech recognition and synthesis, visual pattern recognition, robotics, scientific computing, social modeling and artificial intelligence—to name just a few. The human brain contains about 10^{11} neurons or small threshold logic devices interconnected with resistive interconnections called *synapses*. Some of the sixth-generation architecture being developed have only a few orders of magnitude fewer processors than the human brain. As the digital computer approach ever more closely approximates the complexity of the human brain, you can expect these machines to become your friends and servants.

FINITE STATE MACHINES AND VON NEUMANN MACHINES————

Both the finite state machine and the von Neumann machine are information processing machines. They receive a set of input signals and generate a set of output signals. All digital computers are derived from the finite state machine. Liu (1985) states that a finite state machine is specified by a finite set of states $S = \{s_0, s_1, s_2, \ldots\}$. The first element in this set is called the *initial state*. There is also an input set I and an output set O. A transition function, f, is defined as:

$$f = S*I$$

At any instant in time a finite state machine is in one of its states. For every input there is an output state. This can be shown diagramatically in Fig. 2-1.

In this figure, state A gives rise to state G. In other words, if the machine is put in state A it will be attracted to state G. Similarly state B, D, and F also settle to state G. State B can also settle to state C. State B is said to be able to flow to two states depending on state H. State C can also flow to two states: It can settle into state D, or into itself, depending on its two inputs B and I. State C is also an input for itself. Without further detailed analysis of this state diagram, I would like to mention that state G is the most stable or global attractor, and C is a local attractor. Once the machine is placed in a state, it will naturally

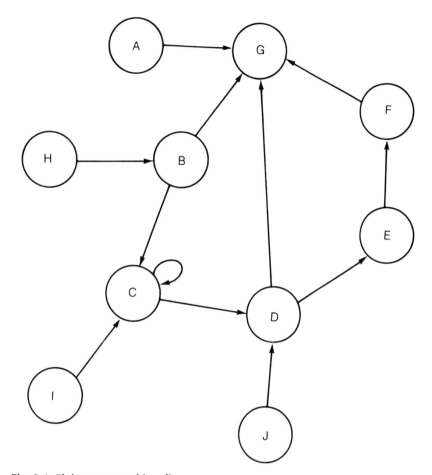

Fig. 2-1. Finite state machine diagram.

run until it settles to the local attractor C or the global attractor G. What relevance does this have with digital computers? Digital computers can be thought of as reconfigurable (programmed) finite state machines.

Modern sequential (non-parallel) digital computers are all derived from the von Neumann machine. These sequential processing architectures give rise to a bottleneck that hinders the flow of signals between the central processing unit (CPU) and the memory, thus limiting the speed of the entire system. A schematic diagram of this bottleneck, known as the von Neumann bottleneck, is shown in Fig. 2-2.

The CPU is surrounded by input, output, and memory for storage of intermediate results and program steps. The stored results are retrieved as needed, and the first result is sent to the output unit. The

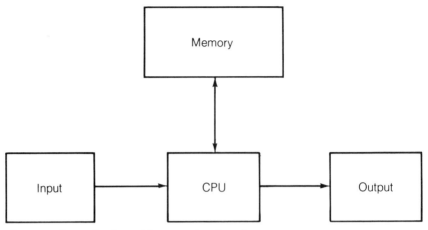

Fig. 2-2. Schematic of von Neumann bottleneck.

bottleneck is clearly illustrated in a simple program such as

    x = 5
    y = z + x.

Most of the program is involved with where to put, or get, something rather than actual computation. From Fig. 2-2 it is clear that a finite state machine is a part of a von Neumann machine. The machine depicted in Fig. 2-2 is also known as a uniprocessor.

UNIPROCESSORS AND VIRTUAL PARALLEL PROCESSING

Figure 2-2 is a simple block diagram of a uniprocessor architecture. It contains a central processor, a memory and input/output units. Very often the architecture of the uniprocessor is similar to that shown in Fig. 2-3.

The bottleneck in this case occurs because only one unit such as the CPU, memory, input or output can have access to the bus at a time. Otherwise a data conflict of some sort will result. The bottleneck effect can be minimized by increased speed of the computer bus and increased width. For example, the bus can be increased to 10MHz and 32-bits, and memory access could be reduced and speed of access increased by placing local memory on chip with the CPU.

The CPU is about 1000 times faster than memory access. To close this speed gap, local memory (often of the cache type) is included on chip. Several authors, including Stone (1987), Desrochers (1987), and Hwang and Briggs (1984), have discussed cache memories.

Cache memories consist of two parts: the cache directory and the random-access memory (RAM). The directory is usually an associative

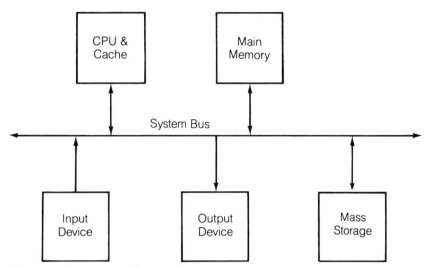

Fig. 2-3. Uniprocessor schematic.

memory. In Chapter 6 I discuss associative memories in terms of massive neural networks. For now, the associative memory consists of address bits and control bits. The control bits are used for cache management and access control. The cache contains a set of address-data pairs, each of which contains a main memory block address and a copy of the contents at that corresponding address. The cache directory can be a simple look-up table.

In the design of a cache memory there are a number of parameters to consider. *Fetch policy* is the method the CPU uses to access data from the cache memory. *Replacement policy* is the algorithm the system uses to replace data in the cache with new data. In general, the cache memory operates by a statistical algorithm. Data that is most often needed is stored in the cache, and data that is seldom used is sent back to the main memory (RAM).

When the CPU needs a data item, it first searches the cache memory. If the item isn't there it is said to be a *miss* and the data is retrieved from the main memory and stored in the cache. The number of misses decreases with increasing cache memory size, as shown in Fig. 2-4. Naturally there is a size to number-of-misses ratio to be minimized by the cache designer.

Earlier I hinted at the concept of bandwidth and how it can be increased to increase the performance of a uniprocessor such as that depicted in Fig. 2-3. The bandwidth of the system is defined as the number of operations performed per unit of time. If the processor cycle time is defined as t_p, in tens of nanoseconds (10^{-9}), the memory cycle time, t_m, is hundreds of nanoseconds and the I/O device

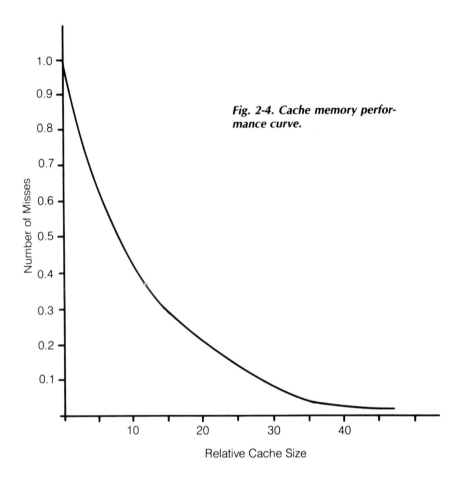

Fig. 2-4. Cache memory performance curve.

cycle time, t_d, is a few milliseconds then we can write

$$t_d > t_m > t_p$$

If W is the number of bytes delivered per memory cycle time, then using the above definition of bandwidth you can write the bandwidth as

$$B_m = \frac{W}{t_m}$$

The data transfer rate of the I/O device, such as the mass storage disk, is given in bytes per unit of time, B_d. Similarly the CPU rate is the number of instructions executed per second. For example, MIPS is millions of instructions per second. The bandwidth of the CPU is given by:

$$B_p = \frac{R_w}{T_p}$$

where R_w is the number of byte results, and T_p is the time required to generate the results. Based on the present technology, the relationship between the subsystems bandwidth is given by:

$$B_m > B_p > B_d$$

Because of the bandwidth difference, computations in the CPU can be taking place while the devices are accessing the bus. Thus with a multiprogramming operating system, like UNIX, it is possible to do virtual parallel processing.

A time-sharing operating system is ideal for virtual parallel processing. A local area network (LAN) could have several terminals all connected to one mainframe CPU. While one terminal is being used to input data, the CPU can be used to crunch data from another user. The time it takes for even a fast typist to enter the data is much longer than the CPU time. So the CPU can easily be utilized in processing data from one user while waiting for the keyboard to send another byte from another user. The outward appearance is that each user is connected to a separate computer—but in fact it is a virtual processor and virtual parallel processing.

PARALLEL PROCESSOR PERFORMANCE

In this section I discuss parallel processor performance. These analyses concern real parallel processors with multiple processor elements rather than virtual parallel processors like those discussed in the last section.

The size of the processing elements or nodes in a parallel architecture is usually referred to as the *grain size*. You can choose either a small or large node as the basic element for the parallel processing machine; these are referred to as *fine-grain* or *large-grain* machines, respectively. *Granularity* refers to the power of each processing element in the architecture ranging from one-bit processors to 32- or 64-bit processors.

Other important elements, besides granularity, to consider for parallel processor performance is the topology of the interconnection between the processing elements and distribution of control across the processing elements. Topology refers to the pattern and density of the communication connections that exist between the processing elements. Control distribution is concerned with allocating tasks to the processing elements and synchronizing their interaction. Control distribution is also concerned with load balancing. Each processor should spend about the same amount of time on computation and communication. With parallel processing, communication is more than memory access or I/O; it also involves message-passing between nodes in the machine.

Much of the following performance analysis is after Fox, et al (1988) and Hwang and Briggs (1984). In the ideal case you could expect linear speedup as shown in Fig. 2-5. For eight processors the speedup is a factor of eight. For 64 processors you get a speedup of 64 times better. Minsky's conjecture that the speedup scales as $\log_2 n$ is so pessimistic it is seldom observed, and I will not discuss it. In order to get the performance speculated by Minsky, you almost have to go out of your way to write bad code and use bad algorithms and a poorly designed architecture. The linear speedup of the ideal case is hard to reach, but it can be reached with good hardware, algorithms, software, and communication design. I show a situation in Chapter 3 in which it is possible to approximate the ideal case by using the par-

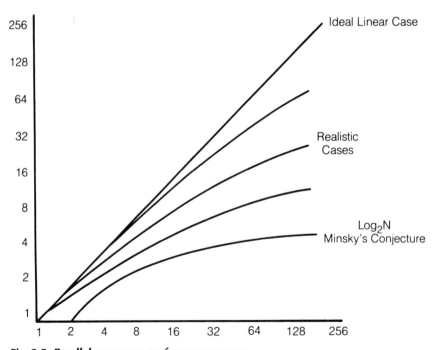

Fig. 2-5. Parallel processor performance curves.

allel processing machine as a task farm with little to no internode communication. In most situations the actual speedup of parallel processing is somewhere between the ideal, as the upper limit, and Minsky's conjecture, as the lower limit.

As a framework for the discussion of performance analysis, consider the example of computing the evolution of a galaxy from a giant gas nebula. This is shown schematically in Fig. 2-6.

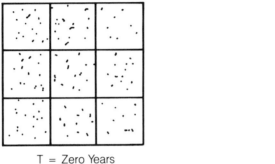

T = Zero Years   T = Ziga Years

Fig. 2-6. Evolution of a galaxy from a gas nebula.

In this figure, the space is discretized into nine elements. Each processor, in a nine-element machine, is assigned to one of the small squares of space in the figure. In this example you will not need to consider the algorithm except to say that the major force causing the formation of the galaxy is gravity. In this example, it is clear that each of the processors must communicate with its neighbor to pass a message about the gravitational force, and particle position and momentum. Also notice that at time $t = 0$ there is more-or-less equal load for each processor. Each processor has about the same number of particles to use in its computation; but as time progresses, some of the processors are not even in use and only three processors are finally being used after ziga years in computer time units. This means that after a time the load is no longer balanced. Each node, in this example, runs identical code but at any given time different nodes will typically be executing different instructions, because of data-dependent branches. The overall problem is therefore being computed asynchronously.

Another point to note about this example is that there are a large number of particles per processor. Each of the nine processors must compute the trajectory for a large number of particles. This is called large-grain size. If each particle was assigned to only one node and you had 64K nodes you would then have a fine-grained problem. It is obvious that as the number of particles each processor must keep track of increases, then the interprocessor communication decreases. Likewise, in a fine-grained approach to this problem, each node would compute the trajectory for only a small number of particles, but the internode communication time would increase. Now look at some of these issues from a more analytical approach.

Defining t_{comm} as the time spent by each node in internode communication and t_{calc} as the time spent by each node in calculation, then we can define the fractional communication overhead as:

$$f_c \propto \frac{t_{comm}}{t_{calc}}$$

The constant of proportionality is made up of two parts.

$$f_c = \frac{c \, t_{comm}}{n^{1,d} t_{calc}}$$

The first part c is on the order of unity:

$$0.1 \leq c \leq 10.$$

The second part is really made up from the grain size n. The parameter d is the topological dimension of the system. From this equation it is clear that fractional communication overhead, f_c, is dependent on the hardware only through the ratio, t_{comm}/t_{calc} and f_c depends on the size of the domain through the grain size, n. The fractional communication overhead does not grow with increasing number of processors. You can therefore see that massive artificial parallel systems are a possibility. Your own brain is an existent proof for this also.

In calculating the speedup I will define two parameters. Let t_{seq} be the time required for a sequential computer to solve a particular problem, and t_{conc} the time for a concurrent, parallel computer to solve the same problem. Speedup, S, depends on N, the number of nodes.

$$S(N) = \frac{t_{seq}}{t_{conc}(N)}$$

The efficiency of a parallel machine in solving a particular problem is given by:

$$\epsilon = \frac{S}{N}$$

The speedup is reduced from its ideal value of N for several reasons. These reasons include non-optimal algorithms, software overhead, poor load balancing and communication overhead. If calculation and communication cannot be overlapped, as is often the case, then the effect of communication overhead on the speedup is given as:

$$t_{conc}(N) = \frac{t_{seq}}{N}(1 - f_c)$$

or

$$S = \frac{N}{1 + f_c}$$

and

$$\epsilon = \frac{1}{1 + f_c}$$

If you regard ϵ as efficiency per node, it is clear that speedup per node is independent of N the number of nodes. This implies that parallel processing machines with large numbers of nodes can be used efficiently, and that large problems can be solved with greater efficiency as the number of nodes N increases. Minsky's conjecture is simply false. It is a lower limit, and often the upper limit can be reached. This is part of the driving force for the development of massive parallel machines for sixth-generation computers. Already machines have been built with tens of thousands of processors. In the following section you will see how to configure such massive parallel machines.

PIPELINES AND VECTOR PROCESSORS

The process of executing an instruction in a digital computer involves four major steps. These include: the instruction fetch (IF) from the main memory; instruction decoding (ID) to identify the operation to be performed; and operand fetch (OF) which might be needed in the execution (EX) of the decoded arithmetic logic operation. At the completion of these four steps, the next instruction can be issued. Figure 2-7 shows schematically in a space-time diagram the steps involved in executing an instruction.

Each instruction, I_i, requires four time steps. If the IF operation for the second instruction I_2 can be fetched while I_1 is executing, you have a simple pipeline processor. A schematic diagram for a pipelined processor is shown in Fig. 2-8.

This diagram represents a pipeline. While the instruction cycle is at ID, a new cycle can start at IF. This sequential-pipeline process is

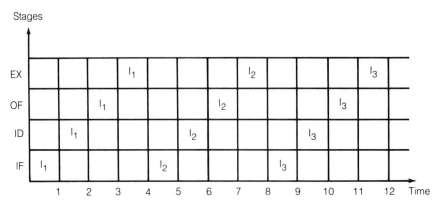

Fig. 2-7. Nonpipelined processor space-time diagram.

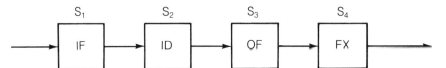

Fig. 2-8. Pipelined processor block diagram.

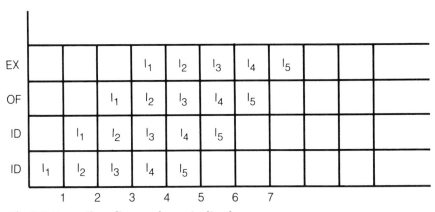

Fig. 2-9. Space-time diagram for a pipelined processor.

more easily shown in the space time diagram of Fig. 2-9. From this diagram it can be seen that in six clock cycles three instructions have been executed. For a non-pipelined processor this would take 12 clock cycles.

There are several commercially available pipelined processors. The Transputer is a pipelined processor. This processor is the basic building block for many parallel processing systems and is the subject of Chapter 4. The NEC V20, which makes up the board discussed in Chapter 3, is also a pipelined processor. The 8086 and 8087 can be operated in parallel by a pipelined fashion. Vector processors also operate in a pipelined mode. Pipelined computers are discussed at length by Kogge (1981).

Vector processors, as the name implies, perform operations on vector data. Vector parallelism is characterized by performing the same operation on all elements of the vector at once. Vector processors usually have an attached host computer/controller. Short vectors are best operated on with a normal sequential computer because of the overhead of loading data and initiating the vector arithmetic operation.

ARRAY PROCESSORS

Much of the following is from Desrochers (1987), Hwang and Briggs (1984), and Ducksburg (1986). An array processor is a grid of simple processing elements often in a rectangular pattern. Each node in the array consists of a conventional sequential processor complete with its own memory and I/O ports either of the serial or parallel type connected in a point-to-point link configuration. The array processor is connected to a host processor either at the corners or as a vector on one edge. The edges of the array can be unrouted. That is, the edges are connected to registers that contain constant values. (See Fig. 2-10.)

The edges can also be connected to form cylinders, spirals or tori. The type of edge connection depends on the application. In operation, the processing elements are synchronized to a system clock in the host processor. Similarly, data transfer to and from the array is all simultaneous to avoid conflict. The machine is said to be a single instruction, multiple data stream machine. Each processor executes the same instruction in synchrony with its neighboring processors, producing a vector or matrix of data from a vector or matrix of input data. A *cellular automata array* is a type of array processor. In Chapter 5 I discuss a cellular automata board that plugs into a PC. These array processors are often used for vector-matrix multiplication and image processing such as Fourier transform operations.

Systolic arrays are another type of array processor. A single issue of the journal *Computer* (July, 1987) was devoted to systolic arrays. All computation can be classified as compute bound or I/O bound. In I/O-bound applications, there is not enough I/O bandwidth to keep the processing elements busy. For compute-bound problems there are not enough computational resources to process the data at the incoming rate. One approach to solving these problems is systolic arrays. These are extensions of the pipeline processor. Operands are pumped in one end, operated on for a while, and then pumped out. This

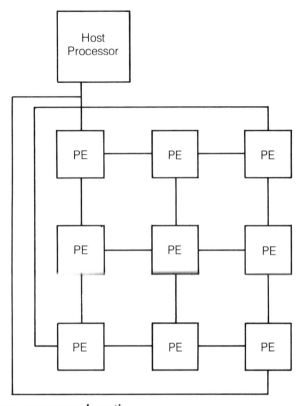

Fig. 2-10. Array processor schematic.

pumping action is similar to that of a heart, and thus the term systolic arrays.

Figure 2-11 shows a systolic array configured for matrix multiplication. The input matrix A is operated on by matrix B stored in the array to generate the matrix C. At each cycle of the array, a row of products is generated.

These systolic architectures readily lend themselves to VLSI and wafer-scale integration. Little and Grainberg (1988) have described a wafer-scale three-dimensional 128×128 array processor they have constructed. McCanny and McWhirter (1987) also describe a systolic array processor they have built. Their system is a VLSI wavefront array processor designed for signal processing. A number of cellular and array processing chips and wafer-scale integrated circuits are described by Legendi, et al (1987). Loucks, et al (1982) describe a vector array processor based on the Motorola MC14500B. This is a one-bit processor. Signal processing chips like the Texas Instruments TMS32010 are closely related to array processors and can be used for

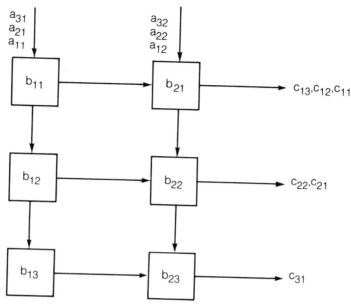

Fig. 2-11. Systolic array processing.

very fast vector matrix computation. I will discuss the use of this type of chip to implement massive neural networks in Chapter 6.

I should not leave this section on systolic array processors without mentioning two classic papers on systolic architectures. H.T. Kung (1982) presents an excellent introduction to the basic ideas and advantages of systolic arrays. S.Y. Kung (1984) has discussed at great length a variety of applications including fast Fourier transform, digital filters, and signal-flow and data-flow graphs.

TAXONOMY OF PARALLEL PROCESSORS

Flynn (1972) has written the first taxonomy paper on parallel processing architectures. He has classified parallel architecture into four types:

1) SISD   Single Instruction Single Data stream
2) SIMD   Single Instruction Multiple Data stream
3) MISD   Multiple Instruction Single Data stream
4) MIMD   Multiple Instruction Multiple Data stream

The first, SISD, represents the typical sequential computer. The second, SIMD, is represented by array processors. The third type, MISD, is a pipelined processor. The fourth type, MIMD, is a multiprocessor and is the most general type of parallel machine. In Chapters 3 and 4 I describe MIMD processing with plug-in boards for a PC.

Fathi and Krieger (1983) have constructed a taxonomy tree similar to that shown in Fig. 2-12. In this figure, all the major processor types are classified into one of Flynn's four types. Basu (1987) has described an entirely different parallel taxonomy tree based on the type of algorithm and control structure. Flynn's is probably adequate for most uses, and further taxonomical classification will not be discussed.

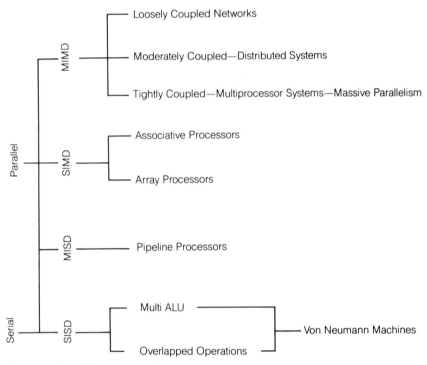

Fig. 2-12. Parallel taxonomy tree.

INTERCONNECTION NETWORKS FOR PARALLEL PROCESSING————

The real meat of parallel processing architecture is the interconnection network of the processing nodes and memory nodes. A very simple parallel processor is shown in Fig. 2-13.

In this configuration there are several processors, all of which share the same memory. The operating system must avoid using the same memory cells for more than one processor. Furthermore, the operating system must synchronize use of the memory bus. This memory bus can lead to a bottleneck, and suggests the next type of architecture shown in Fig. 2-14.

In this system the operating system would control flow between the processors and the memory unit. Obviously the complexity of the

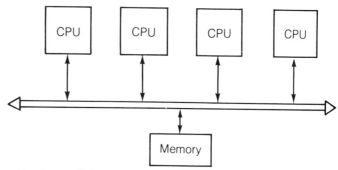

Fig. 2-13. Simple parallel processing computer.

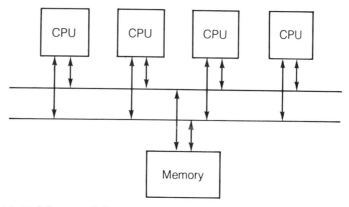

Fig. 2-14. Multibus parallel system.

code can grow much faster than the system. As a result, the system might appear to easily be expandable to large numbers of processors; but the system bandwidth, fanout on the bus, and operating code would prohibit large systems. By *fanout* I mean the number of processors and electrical load the bus can support.

A switching network such as that shown in Fig. 2-15 avoids the bottleneck and bus loading, but it isn't easily expandable to large numbers of processors. Later in this chapter I will give some relationships for switch size and number of processors. This system does not offer the advantage that any processor can communicate with any memory module.

If each processor contains enough memory for its own needs and only messages need to be passed between processors, then there are a number of interconnection network topologies. These are classified into two major types: Static and dynamic networks. Feng (1981) and Hwang and Briggs (1984) have written about static and dynamic networks and much of the following is derived from these sources. Figure 2-16 shows several one- and two-dimensional static networks of

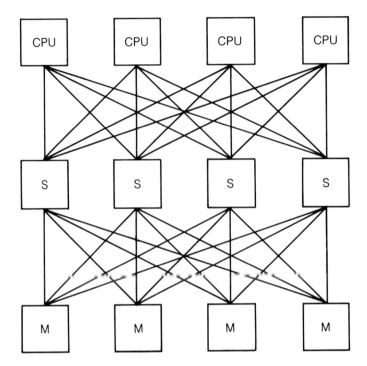

Fig. 2-15. Switchable network of processors.

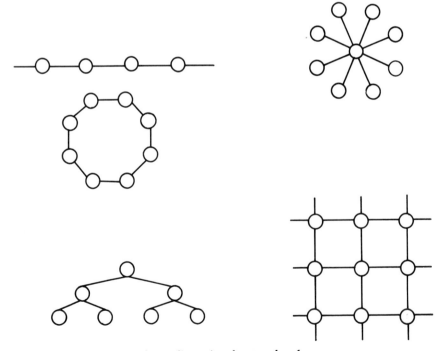

Fig. 2-16. Static, one- and two-dimensional networks of processors.

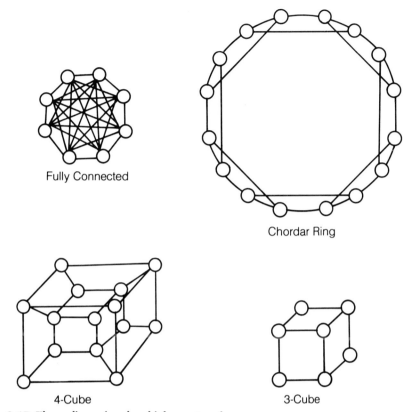

Fig. 2-17. Three-dimensional or higher networks.

processors. Figure 2-17 shows several static networks of three-dimensional or higher. In the ring network messages pass from node-to-node one way around the loop. Message delay and message density increase linearly with N, the number of nodes in the loop. Clearly the average distance a message must travel in a ring is N/2. So the delay is said to be N/2.

For the global bus system shown in Fig. 2-13 and Fig. 2-14, message density increases linearly with N. In addition, N must be small because of electrical overload of the bus. On average a message will have to delay N/2 time units to access the bus—and a bus failure will disable the entire system. A bus failure on the linear or ring network will also disable the entire system. This is not the case for the other networks, which are said to be fault tolerant.

In star networks the size is limited to small N because of queuing at the hub. If a bus fails, only one processor is taken out of the system; but if the hub fails, the entire system is disabled. In a completely connected network there is a dedicated link between each node. N is usually small because links grow as N^2. In Chapter 6 I discuss fully connected networks and hypercube neural networks.

Tree networks have limited traffic density because messages must pass through other nodes. Line connections increase linearly with N, and queuing delays develop near the root of the tree. In Chapter 3 I discuss a virtual tree processing system that avoids many of these problems and easily expands to a massively parallel system.

If the nearest neighbor mesh is extended to any dimension D, and is W wide with N processors, then:

$$N = W^D$$

If W is increased then N is also. If D is fixed at 2

$$N = W^2$$

and W might grow as $\sqrt{N}$. In this case the number of connections per node is constant, but message delay and message density also increase as $\sqrt{N}$. In general for a D dimensional mesh, message delay and traffic density is given as $N^{1/D}$. If you fix W, in the above examples, as N increases you get a hypercube. The average message delay and message density increases as log N, but connection costs grow as N(log N) and the number of connections per node grows as log N. With log N growth in message overhead, allocation of tasks to nodes is easier because the nearness of communicating nodes is not a critical factor in very large networks. Hypercubes, which have been studied extensively by Fox, et al (1988), cannot be expanded arbitrarily.

Much of the above I have summarized in Table 2-1. The table is not complete and I have left out some numbers. In general the entries represent the scaling relation with respect to N—the number of processing nodes. Agrawal, et al (1986) give a more complete table of network performance. Now look at some dynamic interconnected networks.

Dynamic networks are networks in which the processing nodes interconnection is software configurable, or at least easily configured with jumpers. Figure 2-15 is an example of a dynamic network. All of the dynamic networks to be discussed are easily configurable, but the networks are not easily expandable to massively parallel systems. The system shown in Fig. 2-15 is a single-stage system because it has one layer of switch boxes.

A basic switch box, and the types of exchanges in which it can be used, is shown in Fig. 2-18. From the four basic switching interconnections shown in this figure it is possible to build up more complex

Table 2-1.

	Message Delay	Message Density	No. of Connections
Global	N/2	N	N
Linear	N/2	N	N
Ring	N/2	N	N
Star	1	- -	N
Mesh	$N^{I/D}$	$N^{I/D}$	- -
Tree	- -	- -	N
Hypercube	log N	log N	N log N
Fully connected	1	- -	N^2

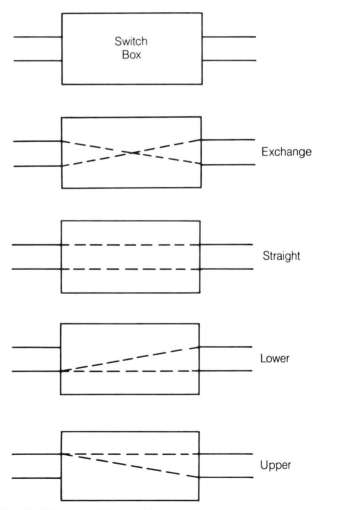

Fig. 2-18. Two-by-Two switch box and basic exchange.

switching networks for parallel processing nodes. Figure 2-19 is known as a 8 × 8 shuffel exchange, and Fig. 2-20 is an 8 × 8 multistage baseline network.

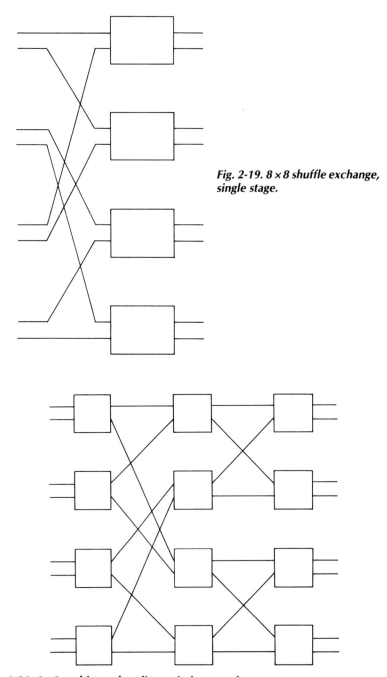

Fig. 2-19. 8 × 8 shuffle exchange, single stage.

Fig. 2-20. 8 × 8 multistage baseline switch network.

The most useful switch, in providing full interconnection to any node in the system, is the crossbar switch shown in Fig. 2-21. This is similar to the C004, a 32-point crossbar switch made by INMOS Ltd. I will discuss this switch in more detail in Chapter 4. Both the basic switch box and the crosspoint switch can be used as building blocks to build a massively parallel system.

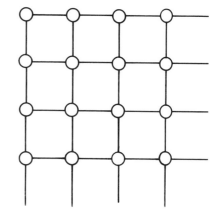

Fig. 2-21. Cross bar switch.

DATA-FLOW COMPUTERS AND SPECIAL-PURPOSE COMPUTERS———

Conventional computers are called *control-flow* computers because the program controls the entire operation. An all-new concept is known as the data-flow computer. The execution of an instruction is enabled whenever the operands are available. It is therefore called a *data-flow* machine. To see how these computers operate, consider the following expression:

$$Z = 2 (x + y)$$

Each instruction in a data-flow computer is implemented as a template that consists of the operator and its input and output. This is shown in a data-flow graph in Fig. 2-22. These ideas are easily made in VLSI adders, multipliers, etcetera—and are simply assembled in the appropriate arrangement to give the desired result.

Besides the data-flow computer, there are many other special-purpose computers designed for the solution of a single problem. The one problem that has occupied more CPU time than any other is the simulation of quantum chromodynamics (QCD). This is the theory of how quarks and other subatomic particles bind together to form particles known as *hadrons*. Brown and Christ (1988) have written about several special-purpose supercomputers designed for simulation of QCD.

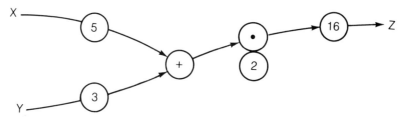

Fig. 2-22. Data-flow graph.

Another important physics problem is the Ising model of ferro-magnetism. In this problem a set of N variables S_i each taking on the value of $+1$ or -1 is used to represent the set of spins. The energy of these interacting spins is given by:

$$E(\{S_i\}) = -k \sum_{\langle i,j \rangle} S_i S_j - H \sum_i S_i$$

Without going into any more detail of this energy relation, or the Ising model, I will say that this relation is very closely related to some neural network relations that I will cover in detail in Chapter 6. Condon and Ogielski (1985) have described an Ising machine they built. This machine has been especially effective in these calculations. Hilhorst, et al (1984) have described several other types of special-purpose computers for physics and a more recent review of special-purpose computers for physics can be found in the special issue of *Computers in Physics* (Jan/Feb, 1989).

Nash and his coworkers (Derra 1984) have assembled a special-purpose computer for collecting data from high-energy physics experiments at Fermi National Laboratory. Another interesting special-purpose computer to play chess has been described by Bernstein (1984).

Connectionist architectures—such as those summarized by Shastri (1986), for artificial intelligence, and the Connection Machine described by Hillis (1985)—can be classified as cellular automata machines. Cellular automata are covered in Chapter 5. Connectionist architectures, often associated with neural networks, are discussed in Chapter 6.

3
Programming a
MIMD Parallel Processor

In this chapter I discuss MIMD programming. In particular I discuss programming a parallel processing MIMD board. The Parallon 2 board from Human Devices, New York, NY, was a prototype MIMD machine designed for the PC, XT, AT, and 386 clones. The company is currently marketing Transputer-based products for the Macintosh computer. (I will discuss the Transputer in detail in Chapter 4.) The decision to discontinue the Parallon 2 is understandable from only a speed consideration. One Transputer chip can outperform the entire Parallon 2. The chief advantage of the Parallon is that it is a true MIMD machine with eight nodes and is an excellent machine for parallel program development at a low level of programming. The user can, with low-level function calls, write and design high-level languages for parallel processing. This type of software development cannot be done with other parallel processing cards for the PC. There are now several parallel processing languages that are almost user-friendly, and only a hacker would desire to develop his own language from low-level functions. The Parallon 2 would be excellent for development of a parallel Prolog, for example. Later in this chapter I discuss two parallel languages, and in Chapter 4 I discuss another parallel language.

   The Parallon 2 is an eight-node parallel machine that is compatible within the IBM PC, XT, AT and 386 clones. In the first part of this chapter I discuss the Parallon 2 architecture and programming. Then I discuss, in some detail, several programs and the commands used for communication with the nodes. In the last part of this chapter I discuss two languages that have been developed for MIMD message-passing computer systems.

Before starting on the Parallon 2 architecture I would like to discuss some ideas about message passing. The classic paper on the subject of communication in sequential processes is by Hoare (1978). Landers (1988) has extended some of Hoare's ideas into what is known as bidirectional I/O. There are two basic mechanisms for message-passing communication between processing nodes: synchronous and asynchronous. In synchronous communication the sender and receiver processes must synchronize to exchange a message. This is also known as zero-buffered communication. Zero-buffered communication eliminates the need for message buffers and queues. In synchronous communication the sender must wait for the receiver to acknowledge. In asynchronous communication the message is sent by the sender nodes but it does not wait for the receiver to acknowledge it. Asynchronous communication requires buffers and queues. Communication with the Parallon 2 is by synchronous message passing.

PARALLON 2 ARCHITECTURE

Oren Clark, while at Human Devices, was the primary design engineer of the Parallon 2. The Parallon message passing architecture has been described by Bogoch and Bason (1988). Figure 3-1 is a rough sketch of the Parallon 2 architecture.

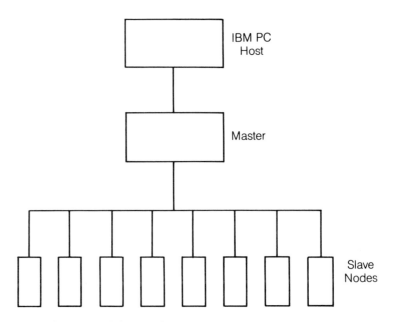

IBM PC
Host

Master

Slave
Nodes

Fig. 3-1. Architecture of the Parallon 2.

From the figure it can be seen that this is an MIMD tree architecture, but it has features that a real tree architecture does not have. The host, for example, can communicate directly with a single slave node without first asking the master to communicate the message to the slave. Furthermore the node can communicate directly with the host without asking the master. This virtual-tree architecture is much more flexible than a normal-tree architecture. In a typical tree architecture, each node in a level can communicate only with the levels directly above and below. This is not true with the Parallon 2 virtual tree. The developers of the Parallon achieved this flexibility through direct memory mapping. The Parallon also can easily be expanded to a massively parallel system, and the host can communicate with any node. Figure 3-2 shows how a massively parallel system can be assembled from Parallon 2 boards. Using this arrangement with eight Parallon boards in one host, it would be possible to build up a system with 128 nodes. If eight such systems were connected to a super host, you could assemble a system with 1024 nodes.

The hardware of the Parallon 2 consists of the following: There are eight slave processors, each consisting of an Intel-compatible

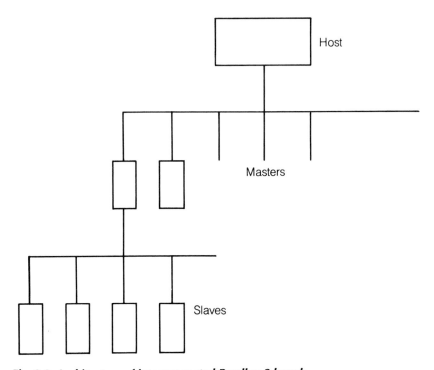

Fig. 3-2. Architecture of interconnected Parallon 2 boards.

be expanded to 128K. The board also contains another V20 and 32K (or 128K) memory and acts as the master processor. This processor can be used to control communication between the nodes of that board and the host processor. The Parallon 2 board also contains a Zilog Z8536 programmable I/O chip that is mapped to the bottom half of the master's I/O. This allows the possibility of building a massively parallel system on board a mobile robot and using the I/O ports from the Parallon boards for signal processing and stepper motor control.

The nodes of the Parallon 2 do all the computing, and the master and host are used in communication. This communication is synchronous or non-buffered. The master processor has a window mapped to each node's full memory address space. Any combination of nodes can easily be accessed through this window by peeking or poking at specific memory locations in the tree. The host can easily access any node in the tree through this window in the master. The nodes cannot directly communicate with each other but they can ask the master or host to pick up a message and send it to another node. Because all the nodes are memory mapped to the master and the actual data is sent over a high-speed parallel bus, this indirect communication between nodes is actually quite fast in the Parallon.

Now look at the memory-mapped window in a little more detail. Each node contains 32K (or 128K) of RAM starting at 0000 (all addresses are in hexadecimal). The same 32K (or 128K) is mapped redundantly into the one-megabyte address space of the V20 node. There is no ROM. In other words, each node is a pure 8086 clone processor with 32K of RAM and no operating system or ROM. In theory any high-level language can be used to write code for the nodes. The code needs to be compiled to an executable level (i.e., pure ROMable code). In practice this is a little more difficult as I will show later in this chapter. The only action a node can take, besides accessing its own RAM, is to signal the master that it has a message. The attention request flag is memory-mapped into the top of the nodes' RAM. A peek from any address between 80000 and BFFFF will set the attention request flag and a peek between C0000 and FFFFF will reset the flag.

The Master node has I/O capability through the Zilog Z8536. The RAM is mapped at the bottom 512K with some of this space for RAM expansion. Memory between 80000 and BFFFF is reserved and mapped to a node's entire 32K of RAM. Which node is determined by the hold node register beginning at C0000.

Low-Level Programming

In this section I will discuss low-level programming of the Parallon 2 board. Before actually discussing a program, I'd like to catalog all the low-level functions provided as software to accompany the Parallon. In all cases it is assumed that MicroSoft C or MS Quick C is used for the program development. The following are functions that can be used on the master or nodes and attached as functions in C programs. Much of the following is derived from the Parallon 2 operating manual. I have simply rewritten it in a clearer format and alphabetized the functions.

Global Low-Level Functions: Used at all levels in the tree.

clri( )
Arguments: none
Returned values: none
Function: Used to disable external processor interrupts.

csreg( )
Arguments: none
Returned values: [AX] Address copied from the processor's code segment register.
Function: Used to return the processor's current code segment address.

dsreg( )
Arguments: none
Returned values: [AX] Address copied from the processor's data segment register.
Function: Used to return the processor's current data segment address.

halt( )
Arguments: none
Returned values: none
Function: Used to halt a processor and wait for an external interrupt.

peek(segment,offset)
Arguments: Segment address and offset address of desired memory. These two values are separated by a comma.
Returned values: Returns a byte of memory from the address.
Function: Used to read a byte of memory.

poke(segment,offset,byte)
Arguments: Segment address, offset address of desired memory location and byte of data to be poked. Arguments are separated by a comma.

Returned values: none
Function: Used to write a byte of data at a particular memory address.

psreg( )
Arguments: none
Returned values: [AX] Data copied from processor's status register.
Function: Used to return the processor's current status register.

wpeek(segment,offset)
Arguments: Segment address and offset address of desired memory.
    These two values are separated by a comma.
Returned values: Returns a word of memory from the address.
Function: Used to read a word of memory.

wpoke(segment,offset,word)
Arguments: Segment address, offset addresses of desired memory
    location and word of data to be written to the desired memory loca-
    tion. Arguments separated by commas.
Returned values: none
Function: Used to write a word of data at a particular memory
    address.

Other Low-Level Functions: Level in tree specified for each function.

atr( )
Arguments: none
Returned values: none
Function: Used to set the attention request flag for a processing node.

atroff( )
Arguments: none
Returned values: none
Function: Used to turn off an attention request flag.

holdm(masternum)
Arguments: Number of master to be held. The master must be held for
    addressing it or any of its slave nodes for I/O.
Returned values: 0 indicates master processor successfully held. − 1
    indicates a timeout occurred.
Function: Used to hold a master processor for I/O to it or its nodes.

holdm_vec(mastermap)
Arguments: The hexadecimal value of an 8-bit vector representation
    of the master processors to be held for data I/O.
Returned values: 0 indicates master processors successfully held. − 1

indicates a bad master map vector was passed. -2 indicates a timeout occurred.

Function: Used in massively parallel systems to hold many board's masters for data I/O.

holdn(nodenum,boardnum)

Arguments: Requires two arguments separated by a comma. The first is the node number (0 - 7). The second is the board number in hex.

Returned values: 0 indicates processing node successfully held for data I/O. -1 indicates master on board not held. -2 indicates a timeout occurred.

Function: Used to hold or halt a processing node for data I/O.

holdn_vec(nodemap,boardnum)

Arguments: Requires two arguments separated by a comma. The first is the hexadecimal value of an 8-bit vector representation of the nodes to be held for I/O. The second is the board number in hex.

Returned values: 0 indicates processing nodes successfully held. -1 indicates master processor not held. -2 indicates a bad map vector was passed. -3 indicates a timeout occurred.

Function: Used to hold several processing nodes on one board for data I/O.

hpollm( )

Arguments: none

Returned values: The hexadecimal value of an 8-bit vector reflecting the hold acknowledge signal from each master.

Function: Used by the host system to ascertain which master processors are being held for data I/O.

hpolln(boardnum)

Arguments: Board number in hex. (0 - F)

Returned values: An 8-bit vector reflecting which processing nodes on the board are being held for I/O.

Function: Used to ascertain which nodes are held for I/O.

intrm(masternum)

Arguments: Number of master processor to interrupt.

Returned values: 0 indicates master processor successfully interrupted.

Function: Used to interrupt a master processor.

intrm_vec(mastermap)

Arguments: Hexadecimal value of an 8-bit vector representing the master processors to be interrupted.

Returned values: 0 indicates master processors successfully interrupted. −1 indicates a bad master argument was passed.

Function: Used to interrupt the masters in a massively parallel system with more than one Parallon 2 board.

intern(nodenum,boardnum)

Arguments: Two arguments separated by a comma are required. The first is node number and the second is the board number.

Returned values: 0 indicates processing node successfully interrupted. −1 indicates master processor not held on the requested board.

Function: This function is used to interrupt a single processing node.

intrn_vec(nodemap,boardnum)

Arguments: Two arguments separated by a comma are required. The first is a hexadecimal value of an 8-bit vector indicating the nodes, and the second argument is the board.

Returned values: 0 indicates processing nodes successfully interrupted. −1 indicates master processor on the board was not held. −2 indicates bad mode map parameter passed.

Function: Used to interrupt more than one node on a single board.

loadfile(filename.exe,startaddress,flag)

Arguments: Three arguments separated by a comma are required. The first is the name of the exe file to be run on the node processor. The second argument is the start address for this file to be down loaded and the third argument is a flag to represent if the code loaded is executable or not. If the code is executable then the flag is set to 1. Otherwise the flag is set to 0.

Returned values: none

Function: Used to down-load code from the host system to a node processor for execution.

pollm( )

Arguments: none

Returned values: Returns a hexadecimal value of an 8-bit vector reflecting which master processors are requesting attention.

Function: Used to ascertain which master processors are requesting service.

pollnode(boardnum)

Arguments: Board number in hex.

Returned values: Returns a hexadecimal value of an 8-bit vector representing which processing nodes are requesting attention.

Function: Used to ascertain which nodes on a board are requesting attention.

resetm(masternum)
Arguments: Master number to be reset.
Returned values: 0 indicates requested master processor successfully reset.
Function: Used by the host to reset the master processor.

resetn(boardnum)
Arguments: Board number in hex.
Returned values: 0 indicates requested processing nodes have successfully been reset. Note that this reset does not clear the values in the RAM or clear the program.
Function: Used to reset the nodes on a requested board.

rlsm(masternum)
Arguments: Number of master processor to be released for program execution.
Returned values: none
Function: Used to release a master processor for program execution.

rlsm_vec(mastermap)
Arguments: Requires a hexadecimal value representing an 8-bit vector reflecting the master processors to be released for program execution.
Returned values: 0 indicates the master processors have been successfully released. − 1 indicates a bad master map was passed.
Function: Used to release one or more master processors in a massively parallel system with more than one parallon board.

rlsn(nodenum,boardnum)
Arguments: Takes two arguments separated by a comma. The first argument is the node number to be released for program execution, and the second argument is the board number in hex.
Returned values: 0 indicates the node has successfully been released for program execution. − 1 indicates master processor on requested board is not held.
Function: Used to release an individual node on a board for program execution.

rlsn_vec(nodemap,boardnum)
Arguments: Takes two arguments separated by a comma. The first is a hexadecimal value representing an 8-bit vector reflecting the node numbers to be released for program execution. The second is the board number in hexadecimal.

Returned values: 0 indicates nodes successfully released for program execution. − 1 indicates master processor on board was not held. − 2 indicates a bad node map was passed. − 3 indicates a timeout occurred.
Function: Used to release nodes on a board for program execution.

sysreset( )
Arguments: none
Returned values: 0 indicates success.
Function: Used to reset all nodes and masters in the system.

I use many of the above functions in several example programs. I used low-level programming for two reasons: It allows the programmer to experience all the details involved in programming a synchronous message-passing concurrent computer system; and it is conceptually easier to understand the C functions and program construction than using the POS operating system that came with the Parallon 2 board. Later in this chapter I discuss the POS operating system. Another advantage with programming in low-level functions is that the user can develop new parallel processing languages. As I stated earlier the chief advantage of the Parallon 2 is that it allows the user to develop new parallel languages. I would like to reiterate that Human Devices developed the Parallon 2 as a prototype board but it is no longer being marketed. Here I include several programs to show the basic ideas in program development and message passing on a MIMD machine.

In programming any parallel computer that has many nodes and a control processor, it is necessary to write program code for the nodes and the control processor. The Parallon is no exception. The program nodlow.c (shown in Fig. 3-3) was written for a node on a Parallon 2, and hstlow.c (see Fig. 3-4) was written for the host computer to control message passing and execution of the node program.

Now do a line-by-line analysis of the programs. The program nodlow.c starts with the function main( ), followed by declarations for two int values, and one far int pointer. This far pointer points to a "safe" address. By safe I mean one that is far enough away from program code. The program nodlow.exe occupies 279H bytes starting at 400 (hexadecimal). Below 400 are interrupt vectors for the V20 processor. The V20 is a pipelined CMOS 8086 clone. To see what these interrupt vectors are, I recommend *The 8086 Book* by Rector and Alexy (1980). Because the Parallon 2 has 32K of memory you see that poking at 7000 (hexadecimal) is safe with the top of memory at 8000 (hexadecimal).

```
/*
 * low-level access example for Parallon.  The program on the node
 * (this file) adds two numbers together, puts them in a pre-defined
 * memory location, sets the atr flag, and halts.  The program on the host
 * waits for the node's atr flag, then picks up the result and prints
 * it.
 */

main()
{
        int far *a, sum;
        int i;

        a = (int far *)0x7000L; /* pick an address to use */
        a[0] = 2;
        a[1] = 3;
        sum = *a++;
        sum += *a++;
        *a = sum;          /* or wpoke(0,0x7004,sum) */
        atr();             /* turn on attention request flag -- we're
                                ready for the host to pick up answer */
        while(1);
}
```

Fig. 3-3. nodlow.c is a program written for a node on a Parallon 2.

```
/*
 * see the comment for nodlow.c
 */

unsigned BRDADDR = 0xd000;

main()
{
        int sum;
        unsigned u;

        sysreset();
        hold(0);
        holdn_vec(0xff,0);
        peek(0xd000,0x8080);
        loadfile("nodlow.exe",0xd0000400,1);
        resetn(0);
        rlsn_vec(0xfe,0);
        peek(0xd000,0x8080);
        poke(0xd000,0x7ff0,0xea);
        rlsn(0,0);
        while(!((u = poll_nodes(0)) & 1)) printf("%x\n",u);
        holdn(0,0);
        peek(0xd000,0x8080);                    /* set window to node's RAM */
        sum = wpeek(0xd000,0x7004);
        printf("The magic number is %x\n", sum);
}
```

Fig. 3-4. hstlow.c is a program written for the host computer.

The next line of code in nodlow.c essentially pokes the int value 2 into memory position 7000 and the following line pokes int value 3 into 7002. The next two lines amount to summing the values at addresses 7000 and 7002. This sum is then poked into 7004 in the following line. The attention request flag is then set by the atn( ) function. An endless while loop is used to keep the CPU busy as a way of gracefully ending the program. The whole nodlow.c program is involved in just adding the value at two addresses and poking that sum into a third address. It is a very simple program.

The host program, hstlow.c, is the control program for nodlow.c which does the computation. The first line in hstlow.c sets the board address to D000. Main( ) then starts, and two variables are declared. The first thing to notice about the rest of the program is that it is built up entirely from low-level functions. This program must be linked with host.lib and loader.obj. The host.lib contains all the appropriate functions.

The first function, sysreset( ), resets all nodes and masters in the system. This reset does not clear or affect any RAM on the board. The next function, hold(0), performs a hold operation on the master processor on board number 0. The function holdn_vec( ) is used to hold the nodes with the map vector FF. The value FF is a hexadecimal conversion of the binary vector representing the nodes to be held. In this case the vector is: (1 1 1 1 1 1 1 1), i.e., all nodes are held. It will, in effect, broadcast the executable code to all nodes. Later I show why this does not create a problem even though the program is running on only one node.

The next function, peek(0XD000,0X8080), opens the window in the master to allow the host to look at the nodes. The arguments are segment and offset. The segment is, of course, the board address and the offset 8080 is an address in the appropriate area of memory to open the window.

The next function, loadfile( ), is used to load the executable code to the node(s). In this program the executable code, nodlow.exe, is down-loaded to all the nodes. The start address is D0000400, i.e., the code is loaded starting at 400 (hexadecimal) in all the nodes. Below 400 are CPU interrupts as discussed by Rector and Alexy (1980). The third argument in the function is a flag. The 1 represents that the code is executable and will soon be run. Summarizing heretofore: The system is reset, all processors are held for data/program I/O, and a window is opened to broadcast the program to all the nodes. This broadcast is not a problem because, in the next function, after loadfile( ), you have resetn(0). This function resets node 0 only. This can be thought of as resetting the program counter to the beginning of this node only.

The next function, rlsn_vec, releases all the nodes except node 0. The node must be released in order for the program to execute. The first argument in the function, 0XFE, is a hexadecimal conversion of the binary vector (1 1 1 1 1 1 1 0). This vector indicates that all the nodes except node zero are released. The second argument to the function is the board number. The function peek( ) is again used to open the window. When the resetn( ) was done the window was "closed." After opening the window you poke a jump vector to signal the program to execute. The arguments to the poke function are segment and offset location of the vector, and the value EA is poked to set the vector. The next function, rlsn(0,0), is used to release the node and the program begins. The first argument is the node number and the second argument is the board number.

The while statement in the next line is used to poll the nodes on board 0. This result is bit-wise ANDed with the node number. Actually the node number is not used but rather $2^{nodenumber}$. It is important to keep in mind that the function, poll_nodes, returns a hexadecimal value of an 8-bit vector representing which processing nodes are requesting attention. Later, in another program, I show another application of the poll_nodes function.

After the while statement is finished, the processing node 0 on board 0 is held for data I/O. The window in the master is opened again and a word is peeked at in location 7004. This word is the value of sum from the nodlow.c program. The final result is printed with the printf function.

An interesting observation is that executable code was loaded to all the nodes using a general broadcast. Then all the nodes except the node selected to run the code was released. This node was then set with a jump vector to begin program execution and then released.

Before I continue with other programs I should mention how to compile and link C programs for the Parallon. Compile as follows:

    qcl /c /Gs /Od /FPi *filename*.c
    (Host programs do not need to be compiled this way.)

The /c option is to compile only to object code. The /Gs option is to disable stack checking and possible error printing. This disables some DOS interrupts—which, of course, would not exist on the V20 nodes. The /Od option disables code optimization. This again is to prevent calling MS-DOS interrupts. You are not loading the entire DOS to each node, but only executable code. That is the purpose for all this disabling. The last thing to be disabled is the 8087 optimization and code loading. Because an 8087 does not exist at each node, the option /FPi must also be included.

To link the code for the host you must link with the appropriate object code the loader.obj file and then the library file host.lib. To link code for nodes, you must link with the appropriate object code the libraries node.lib and newrt0.lib.

The above technique for executing code on one node can be extended to all nodes. The programs nodlowx.c have been written as an extension of nodlow.c (see Fig. 3-5 through Fig. 3-12). The x in the name represents node numbers 0-7. Most of the node program is a straightforward derivative of nodlow.c. Each node program adds two numbers and pokes the result in address 7004. The attention request flag is then set by atr( ) and a while loop is executed peeking into

```
main()
{
        int far *a, sum;
        int i;

        a = (int far *)0x7000L; /* pick an address to use */
        a[0] = 3;
        a[1] = 0;
        sum = *a++;
        sum += *a++;
        *a = sum;          /* or wpoke(0,0x7004,sum) */
        atr();             /* turn on attention request flag -- we're
                              ready for the host to pick up answer */
        while(peek(0,0x7050) != 0x1)
        {
                ; /* peek until flag is set by host */
        }
        wpoke(0,0x7050,sum);
        atroff();
        while(1);
}
```

Fig. 3-5. nodlow0.c

```
main()
{
        int far *a, sum;
        int i;

        a = (int far *)0x7000L; /* pick an address to use */
        a[0] = 3;
        a[1] = 1;
        sum = *a++;
        sum += *a++;
        *a = sum;          /* or wpoke(0,0x7004,sum) */
        atr();             /* turn on attention request flag -- we're
                              ready for the host to pick up answer */
        while(peek(0,0x7050) != 0x1)
        {
                ; /* peek until flag is set by host */
        }
        wpoke(0,0x7050,sum);
        atroff();

        while(1);
}
```

Fig. 3-6. nodlow1.c

```
main()
{
        int far *a, sum;
        int i;

        a = (int far *)0x7000L; /* pick an address to use */
        a[0] = 3;
        a[1] = 2;
        sum = *a++;
        sum += *a++;
        *a = sum;             /* or wpoke(0,0x7004,sum) */
        atr();                /* turn on attention request flag -- we're
                                     ready for the host to pick up answer */
        while(peek(0,0x7050) != 0x1)
        {
                ; /* peek until flag is set by host */
        }
        wpoke(0,0x7050,sum);
        atroff();

        while(1);
}
```

Fig. 3-7. nodlow2.c

```
main()
{
        int far *a, sum;
        int i;

        a = (int far *)0x7000L; /* pick an address to use */
        a[0] = 3;
        a[1] = 3;
        sum = *a++;
        sum += *a++;
        *a = sum;             /* or wpoke(0,0x7004,sum) */
        atr();                /* turn on attention request flag -- we're
                                     ready for the host to pick up answer */
        while(peek(0,0x7050) != 0x1)
        {
                ; /* peek until flag is set by host */
        }
        wpoke(0,0x7050,sum);
        atroff();

        while(1);
}
```

Fig. 3-8. nodlow3.c

address 7050. If this address contains the value 1 then the content of 7004 is also set to 7050 and the attention request flag is turned off, and the program gracefully ends with an endless while loop.

Most of the host program hstalpl1.c should be self-explanatory hstalp1.c (Fig. 3-13). The program is designed to be an example of how to use low-level function calls from the host. The program loads

```
main()
{
        int far *a, sum;
        int i;

        a = (int far *)0x7000L; /* pick an address to use */
        a[0] = 3;
        a[1] = 4;
        sum = *a++;
        sum += *a++;
        *a = sum;          /* or wpoke(0,0x7004,sum) */
        atr();             /* turn on attention request flag -- we're
                              ready for the host to pick up answer */
        while(peek(0,0x7050) != 0x1)
        {
                ; /* peek until flag is set by host */
        }
        wpoke(0,0x7050,sum);
        atroff();

        while(1);
}
```

Fig. 3-9. nodlow4.c

```
main()
{
        int far *a, sum;
        int i;

        a = (int far *)0x7000L; /* pick an address to use */
        a[0] = 3;
        a[1] = 5;
        sum = *a++;
        sum += *a++;
        *a = sum;          /* or wpoke(0,0x7004,sum) */
        atr();             /* turn on attention request flag -- we're
                              ready for the host to pick up answer */
        while(peek(0,0x7050) != 0x1)
        {
                ; /* peek until flag is set by host */
        }
        wpoke(0,0x7050,sum);
        atroff();

        while(1);
}
```

Fig 3-10. nodlow5.c

processes into each of the nodes and then instructs the nodes to execute the processes. The nodes add two numbers and poke the sum
into 7004. The node program then sets the attention request flag. The
host program then polls all nodes. If the return code from this polling
is FF then all nodes are asking attention and are therefore finished
with the calculation. The host then services each of the nodes sequentially. This consists of reading the memory address 7004 and printing

```
main()
{
        int far *a, sum;
        int i;

        a = (int far *)0x7000L; /* pick an address to use */
        a[0] = 3;
        a[1] = 6;
        sum = *a++;
        sum += *a++;
        *a = sum;         /* or wpoke(0,0x7004,sum) */
        atr();            /* turn on attention request flag -- we're
                             ready for the host to pick up answer */
        while(peek(0,0x7050) != 0x1)
        {
                ; /* peek until flag is set by host */
        }
        wpoke(0,0x7050,sum);
        atroff();

        while(1);
}
```

Fig. 3-11. nodlow6.c

```
main()
{
        int far *a, sum;
        int i;

        a = (int far *)0x7000L; /* pick an address to use */
        a[0] = 3;
        a[1] = 7;
        sum = *a++;
        sum += *a++;
        *a = sum;         /* or wpoke(0,0x7004,sum) */
        atr();            /* turn on attention request flag -- we're
                             ready for the host to pick up answer */
        while(peek(0,0x7050) != 0x1)
        {
                ; /* peek until flag is set by host */
        }
        wpoke(0,0x7050,sum);
        atroff();

        while(1);
}
```

Fig. 3-12. nodlow7.c

the result to the display device. After printing, the host pokes a flag in 7050. This flag is the value 1. The node then reads this flag at 7050. If the result is 1 then it is set to the same value as 7004 and the attention request flag is turned off. Although this program is quite simple, it shows all the basic steps involved in message passing. The host did not have to poll all the nodes, for example. It could have polled only one or two and then poked a value into a third node based on the results of this polling.

```
/*      The program is designed to be an example of how to use
        low level function calls from the host.  The program loads
        programs on each of the nodes and then instructs the nodes
        to execute the programs.  The programs add two numbers and pokes
        the sum in 0x7004.  The node programs then set an atn flag.
        The host program, this program, then polls all nodes.  If
        the return code is 0xff then all nodes are asking attention.
        The host then services each of the nodes sequentially.  This
        consists of reading the memory 0x7004 and printing the result
        to the CRT.  After 'servicing' a node the host pokes a flag in
        0x7050.  This flag is 0x1.  The node then reads this flag at
        0x7050.  If 0x7050 is 0x1 then it is set to the same value
        as 0x7004 and the atn flag is turned off with atnoff().
*/


unsigned BRDADDR = 0xd000;

void main()
{
        int u,n;
        int sum;

        sysreset();
        hold(0);

        holdn_vec(0xff,0);

        /* node 0 */
        peek (0xd000,0x8080);
        loadfile("nodlow0.exe",0xd0000400,1);
        resetn(0);
        peek(0xd000,0x8080);
        poke(0xd000,0x7ff0,0xea);
        resetn(0);
        rlsn(0,0);

        /* node 1 */
        peek(0xd000,0x8080);
        loadfile("nodlow1.exe",0xd0000400,1);
        resetn(0);
        peek(0xd000,0x8080);
        poke(0xd000,0x7ff0,0xea);
        resetn(0);
        rlsn(1,0);

        /* node 2 */
        peek(0xd000,0x8080);
        loadfile("nodlow2.exe",0xd0000400,1);
        resetn(0);
        peek(0xd000,0x8080);
        poke(0xd000,0x7ff0,0xea);
        resetn(0);
        rlsn(2,0);

        /* node 3 */
        peek(0xd000,0x8080);
        loadfile("nodlow3.exe",0xd0000400,1);
        resetn(0);
        peek(0xd000,0x8080);
        poke(0xd000,0x7ff0,0xea);
        resetn(0);
        rlsn(3,0);
```

Fig. 3-13. hstalpl1.c, an example of how to use low-level function calls from the host.

Fig. 3-13. Continued.

```
/* node 4 */
peek(0xd000,0x8080);
loadfile("nodlow4.exe",0xd0000400,1);
resetn(0);
peek(0xd000,0x8080);
poke(0xd000,0x7ff0,0xea);
resetn(0);
rlsn(4,0);

/* node 5 */
peek(0xd000,0x8080);
loadfile("nodlow5.exe",0xd0000400,1);
resetn(0);
peek(0xd000,0x8080);
poke(0xd000,0x7ff0,0xea);
resetn(0);
rlsn(5,0);

/* node 6 */
peek(0xd000,0x8080);
loadfile("nodlow6.exe",0xd0000400,1);
resetn(0);
peek(0xd000,0x8080);
poke(0xd000,0x7ff0,0xea);
resetn(0);
rlsn(6,0);

/* node 7 */
peek(0xd000,0x8080);
loadfile("nodlow7.exe",0xd0000400,1);
resetn(0);
peek(0xd000,0x8080);
poke(0xd000,0x7ff0,0xea);
resetn(0);
rlsn(7,0);

rlsn_vec(0xff,0);

while(0xff != poll_nodes(0))
{
        ; /* keep polling untill all nodes have set the atn flag */
}

/* service each node */

/* node 0 */
holdn(0,0);
peek(0xd000,0x8080);
sum = wpeek(0xd000,0x7004);
printf("node 0, sum %x\n",sum);
poke(0xd000,0x7050,0x1); /* flag to indicate atten. observed */
peek(0xd000,0x8080);
sum = wpeek(0xd000,0x7004);
printf("node 1, sum %x\n",sum);
poke(0xd000,0x7050,0x1);
rlsn(1,0);

/* node 2 */
holdn(2,0);
peek(0xd000,0x8080);
```

Fig. 3-13. Continued.

```
sum = wpeek(0xd000,0x7004);
printf("node 2, sum %x\n",sum);
poke(0xd000,0x7050,0x1);
rlsn(2,0);

/* node 3 */
holdn(3,0);
peek(0xd000,0x8080);
sum = wpeek(0xd000,0x7004);
printf("node 3, sum %x\n",sum);
poke(0xd000,0x7050,0x1);
rlsn(3,0);

/* node 4 */
holdn(4,0);
peek(0xd000,0x8080);
sum = wpeek(0xd000,0x7004);
printf("node 4, sum %x\n",sum);
poke(0xd000,0x7050,0x1);
rlsn(4,0);

/* node 5 */
holdn(5,0);
peek(0xd000,0x8080);
sum = wpeek(0xd000,0x7004);
printf("node 5, sum %x\n",sum);
poke(0xd000,0x7050,0x1);
rlsn(5,0);

/* node 6 */
holdn(6,0);
peek(0xd000,0x8080);
sum = wpeek(0xd000,0x7004);
printf("node 6, sum %x\n",sum);
poke(0xd000,0x7050,0x1);
rlsn(6,0);

/* node 7 */
holdn(7,0);
peek(0xd000,0x8080);
sum = wpeek(0xd000,0x7004);
printf("node 7, sum %x\n",sum);
poke(0xd000,0x7050,0x1);
rlsn(7,0);
```

The program nodsort1.c (see Fig. 3-14) is a little less useless, from an applications point of view, than nodlowx.c. The program name is a misnomer. The program actually sorts through 100 random numbers looking for the maximum value. After main is opened and some variables and pointers are declared, the program begins by setting a random seed that was supplied by the host. 100 random integers are then put in the b array, and the maximum value in that array is poked into memory address 7004. The attention request flag is then set until the host pokes a flag value at address 7050. The value max is then poked in 7050 and the program gracefully ends with an endless while loop. The same node process runs on each node—so you will have eight "maximum" numbers printed to the display.

```
/* sorting program for nodes of Parallon 2
                01/15/89                          */

void main()
{
        int far *a;
        int seed,i,max = 0;
        long int b[100];

        seed = peek(0,0x6ffe);
        srand(seed);

        a = (int far *)0x6000L;

        for(i=0;i<100;i++)
        {
                b[i] = (long int)(rand());
        }
        for(i=0;i<100;i++)
        {
                if(max < b[i])
                {
                        max = b[i];
                }
        }
        wpoke(0,0x7004,max);
        atr();
        while(peek(0,0x7050) != 0x1)
        {
                ; /* peek until flag is set by host */
        }
        wpoke(0,0x7050,max);
        atroff();

        while(1);

}
```

Fig. 3-14. nodsort1.c is a program that sorts through 100 random numbers looking for the maximum value.

The host program, hstsort1.c, is almost a copy of hstalpl1.c except that it also includes the user-entered seed being sent to the node. Notice that this is done eight times, so each node gets a new seed for the pseudorandom number generator. Also notice that the master window is opened and the seed is then poked into address 6FFE.

```
/* Sort program for the Parallon 2.  This is the
            host program.  01/15/89    */

#include "\c\quick\include\stdio.h"
#include "\c\quick\include\stdlib.h"

unsigned BRDADDR = 0xd000;

void main()
{
```

Fig. 3-15. hstsort1.c includes the seed being sent to the node.

Fig. 3-15. Continued.

```
/* declarations */
long int i,seed;
long int max[7];

/* set up */
sysreset();
hold(0);

holdn_vec(0xff,0);

/* node 0 */
printf("input a random seed \t");
scanf("%d",&seed);
printf("Node 0\t");
peek(0xd000,0x8080);
poke(0xd000,0x6ffe,seed);
peek(0xd000,0x8080);
loadfile("nodsort1.exe",0xd0000400,1);
resetn(0);
peek(0xd000,0x8080);
poke(0xd000,0x7ff0,0xea);
resetn(0);
rlsn(0,0);

/* node 1 */
printf("input a random seed \t");
scanf("%d",&seed);
printf("Node 1\t");
peek(0xd000,0x8080);
poke(0xd000,0x6ffe,seed);
peek(0xd000,0x8080);
loadfile("nodsort1.exe",0xd0000400,1);
resetn(0);
peek(0xd000,0x8080);
poke(0xd000,0x7ff0,0xea);
resetn(0);
rlsn(1,0);

/* node 2 */
printf("input a random seed \t");
scanf("%d",&seed);
printf("Node 2\t");
peek(0xd000,0x8080);
poke(0xd000,0x6ffe,seed);
peek(0xd000,0x8080);
loadfile("nodsort1.exe",0xd0000400,1);
resetn(0);
peek(0xd000,0x8080);
poke(0xd000,0x7ff0,0xea);
resetn(0);
rlsn(2,0);

/* node 3 */
printf("input a random seed \t");
scanf("%d",&seed);
printf("Node 3\t");
peek(0xd000,0x8080);
poke(0xd000,0x6ffe,seed);
peek(0xd000,0x8080);
loadfile("nodsort1.exe",0xd0000400,1);
resetn(0);
peek(0xd000,0x8080);
poke(0xd000,0x7ff0,0xea);
resetn(0);
rlsn(3,0);
```

Fig. 3-15. Continued.

```
/* node 4 */
printf("input a random seed \t");
scanf("%d",&seed);
printf("Node 4\t");
peek(0xd000,0x8080);
poke(0xd000,0x6ffe,seed);
peek(0xd000,0x8080);
loadfile("nodsort1.exe",0xd0000400,1);
resetn(0);
peek(0xd000,0x8080);
poke(0xd000,0x7ff0,0xea);
resetn(0);
rlsn(4,0);

/* node 5 */
printf("input a random seed \t");
scanf("%d",&seed);
printf("Node 5\t");
peek(0xd000,0x8080);
poke(0xd000,0x6ffe,seed);
peek(0xd000,0x8080);
loadfile("nodsort1.exe",0xd0000400,1);
resetn(0);
peek(0xd000,0x8080);
poke(0xd000,0x7ff0,0xea);
resetn(0);
rlsn(5,0);

/* node 6 */
printf("input a random seed \t");
scanf("%d",&seed);
printf("Node 6\t");
peek(0xd000,0x8080);
poke(0xd000,0x6ffe,seed);
peek(0xd000,0x8080);
loadfile("nodsort1.exe",0xd0000400,1);
resetn(0);
peek(0xd000,0x8080);
poke(0xd000,0x7ff0,0xea);
resetn(0);
rlsn(6,0);

/* node 7 */
printf("input a random seed \t");
scanf("%d",&seed);
printf("Node 7\t");
peek(0xd000,0x8080);
poke(0xd000,0x6ffe,seed);
peek(0xd000,0x8080);
loadfile("nodsort1.exe",0xd0000400,1);
resetn(0);
peek(0xd000,0x8080);
poke(0xd000,0x7ff0,0xea);
resetn(0);
rlsn(7,0);

rlsn_vec(0xff,0);

while(0xff != poll_nodes(0))
{
        ; /* keep polling until all nodes have set the atn flag */
}

/* service the nodes */
```

Fig. 3-15. Continued.

```
/* node 0 */
holdn(0,0);
peek(0xd000,0x8080);
max[0] = wpeek(0xd000,0x7004);
poke(0xd000,0x7050,0x1); /* flag to indicate atten. observed */
rlsn(0,0);

/* node 1 */
holdn(1,0);
peek(0xd000,0x8080);
max[1] = wpeek(0xd000,0x7004);
poke(0xd000,0x7050,0x1);
rlsn(1,0);

/* node 2 */
holdn(2,0);
peek(0xd000,0x8080);
max[2] = wpeek(0xd000,0x7004);
poke(0xd000,0x7050,0x1);
rlsn(2,0);

/* node 3 */
holdn(3,0);
peek(0xd000,0x8080);
max[3] = wpeek(0xd000,0x7004);
poke(0xd000,0x7050,0x1);
rlsn(3,0);

/* node 4 */
holdn(4,0);
peek(0xd000,0x8080);
max[4] = wpeek(0xd000,0x7004);
poke(0xd000,0x7050,0x1);
rlsn(4,0);

/* node 5 */
holdn(5,0);
peek(0xd000,0x8080);
max[5] = wpeek(0xd000,0x7004);
poke(0xd000,0x7050,0x1);
rlsn(5,0);

/* node 6 */
holdn(6,0);
peek(0xd000,0x8080);
max[6] = wpeek(0xd000,0x7004);
poke(0xd000,0x7050,0x1);
rlsn(6,0);

/* node 7 */
holdn(7,0);
peek(0xd000,0x8080);
max[7] = wpeek(0xd000,0x7004);
poke(0xd000,0x7050,0x1);
rlsn(7,0);


for(i=0;i<=7;i++)
{
        printf("node %d\tmax value %ld\n",i,max[i]);
}


}
```

The program bsort.c is a simple bubblesort program that could be easily modified to run on a node. The host-level program takes a huge array to be sorted, and breaks it into eight sections of more or less equal length. Each of these sections are then farmed out to a single node. The basic bubble sort is shown in Fig. 3-16 as bsort.c. The host program also needs to poll the activity of each node and take care of message passing between nodes. This type of message passing activity is similar to the seed being sent to each node in the previous program, and the polling of the nodes by using attention request flags set at a memory location (7050 in the last program). Harel (1987) gives an excellent description of parallel sorting for MIMD machines.

A good scientific application for parallel processors is Monte Carlo integration, as suggested by Fox, et al (1988). This consists of

```
#include "\c\quick\include\math.h"
#include "\c\quick\include\stdio.h"

static int array[100];

void main()
{
        int i,j;
        int temp;

        /* fill random array */
        for(i=0;i<100;i++)
        {
                array[i] = rand();
                printf("%d\t",array[i]);
        }
        printf("\n");

        /* sort random array */
        for(i=0;i<100;i++)
        {
                for(j=0;j<100;j++)
                {
                        if(array[i] < array[j])
                        {
                                temp = array[i];
                                array[i] = array[j];
                                array[j] = temp;
                        }

                }
        }

        /* print sorted array */
        for(i=0;i<100;i++)
        {
                printf("%d\t",array[i]);
        }

}
```

Fig. 3-16. bsort.c is the basic bubble sort.

evaluation of the integral:

$$I = \int_0^1 f(x)\, dx$$

If you let $f(x) = x^2$, as an example, then:

$$I = \int_0^1 x^2\, dx$$

To evaluate this integral by the Monte Carlo method you select random numbers r_i between 0 and 1. This integral is then:

$$I = \lim_{L \to \infty} \frac{1}{L} \sum_{i=1}^{L} f(r_i)$$

For the Monte Carlo simulation it is assumed that events are independent; therefore, by choosing a huge L and letting each node span $1/8$ of the L-space no message passing is required while computation is taking place. The speedup is almost linear. Each node will have as its end result one number. This number can then be passed to the host and the host can compute the final answer.

The Parallon 2 is best used for integer processing because there is no floating point coprocessor associated with each node. (Also keep in mind that there is no clock and therefore the time( ) function cannot be called.) In order to do scientific computation or simulations it is necessary to scale floating point numbers or to do fixed-point arithmetic. Leeds and Weinberg (1961), Klerer and Korn (1967), Booth and Chien (1974), Cheney and Kincaid (1980) all discuss fixed- and floating-point numbers. Knuth (1969) is the diffinitive source on the subject.

As an example of scaling take the function:

$$y = e^x.$$

Then substitute

$$y = \frac{I_y}{S}$$

and

$$x = \frac{I_x}{S}$$

where S is the scale factor and I is an integer values. Let x be in the range $-1 < = x < = 1$. Then you have:

$$I_y = S e^{I_x/S}$$

Because

$$e^x = 1 + x + \frac{x^2}{2!} + \frac{x^3}{3!} + \frac{x^4}{4!} + \frac{x^5}{5!} + \frac{x^6}{6!} + \cdot \cdot \cdot$$

then using the substitutions

$$I_y = S\left(1 + \frac{I_x}{S} + \frac{I_x I_x}{2! SS} + \frac{I_x I_x I_x}{3! SSS} + \frac{I_x I_x I_x I_x}{4! SSSS} + \cdot \cdot \cdot\right)$$

Multiplying through by S

$$I_y = S + I_x + \frac{I_x I_x}{2! S} + \frac{I_x I_x I_x}{3! SS} + \frac{I_x I_x I_x I_x}{4! SSS} + \cdot \cdot \cdot$$

It is important to notice that I_x cannot be larger than S, by definition, and therefore the numerator in each term is larger than the denominator—so you will never have numbers that are less than one.

The program iscale3.c (see Fig. 3-17) computes the exp(x) of small s in the range $-1 < = x < = 1$ by the above scaling technique. Here a small scale factor was used (S = 32). By sacrificing apparent accuracy and using a smaller number of bits, the actual accuracy for exp goes up because you can compute the sixth order. Otherwise you can only compute the third order, for example, with a scale factor of S = 1024. These results are shown in Fig. 3-18 and Fig. 3-19. Each figure also has a plot of the double exp( ) version to compare with the scaled int (exp( ) function. Notice that in Fig. 3-18 the double exp( ) function is almost the same as the int exp( ) function. This is not the case with that shown in Fig. 3-19. In Fig. 3-18 the scale factor is 32 and the computation is carried out to the sixth order, whereas in Fig. 3-19 the scale factor is 1024 and the computation is carried out to only the third order before the computation "blows up" past long int range. The program iscale3.c dumps the data to a disk file and another program was used to plot the data. Each function, even functions as simple as x*x, should be looked at as an individual case considering such factors as range of x and range of the result to make sure that the function does not blow up past the long int limit.

```
#include "\c\quick\include\float.h"
#include "\c\quick\include\math.h"
#include "\c\quick\include\stdio.h"


#define S (long int )32

void main()
{
        FILE *fe;
        char datafile[80];

        long int iy;
        long int ix;
        int counter=0;
        double y;

        printf("input datafile name\n");
        scanf("%s",datafile);
        if((fe=fopen(datafile,"w"))==NULL)
        {
                printf("\007ERROR can't open file");
                exit(0);
        }


        for(ix = -S; ix <= S; ix = ix + 1)
        {

                iy = ix - ix*ix/(2*S) +
                        ix*ix*ix/(3*S*S) -
                        ix*ix*ix*ix/(4*S*S*S) +
                        ix*ix*ix*ix*ix/(5*S*S*S*S) -
                        ix*ix*ix*ix*ix*ix/(6*S*S*S*S*S);


                y = (double)S*log((double)ix/S);
                counter++;
                printf("%d\t%d\t%d\t%lf\n",counter,ix,iy,y);
                fprintf(fe,"%d %d %lf\n",ix,iy,y);

        }
        fclose(fe);
}
```

Fig. 3-17. iscale3.c computes exp(x) of small s.

PARAEXAM

Paraexam is a software package that operates similar to MS-DOS Debug. It allows the user to load code to a node, peek and poke at the memory addresses in the nodes and to modify code or data in the nodes. In short it is a parallel debugger. Any node in the virtual-tree can be examined and modified with Paraexam. Paraexam also has useful commands to allow the user to examine the attention request vector and the held/released vector. These vectors can, of course, be easily modified with Paraexam. One of the more useful commands is

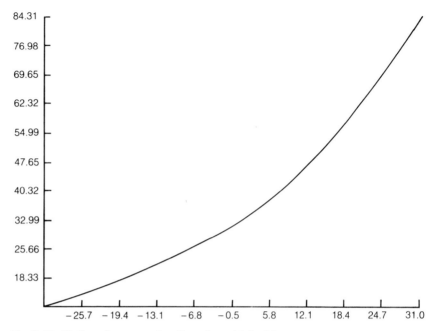

Fig. 3-18. Sixth order approximation of exp(x) S = 32.

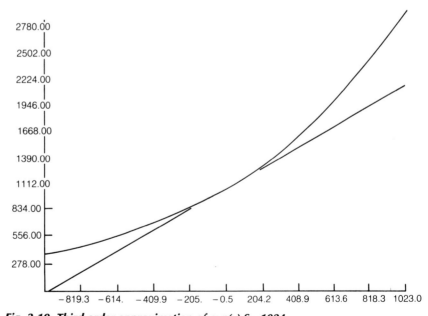

Fig. 3-19. Third order approximation of exp(x) S = 1024.

that which allows the user to clear all the memory and reset the system with a single keystroke.

POS

Iain Bason, at Human Devices, designed the Parallon Operating System (POS). This is an example of the type of software development that can be done with the Parallon 2. Recall that the chief advantage of this board is that it allows the user to experiment with and develop new parallel languages. This cannot be done with any other parallel processing card for PCs. The POS language/operating system is well described by Bogoch and Bason (1988), and I will not belabor the subject. I have simply reproduced, with permission of Human Devices, two programs written in C that call the POS level functions. The programs nodecho.c and echo.c, shown in Fig. 3-20 and Fig. 3-21 are examples of excellent program design for parallel processing. In fact, this structure and program design is similar to portable parallel program development at Argonne National Laboratory. The Parallon 2 was such a versatile design it could have been used to develop code for a diverse number of parallel processing computers.

```
/*
 * echo.c, Copyright (C) 1988, Human Devices, Inc.
 * A simple program to echo what's typed at the keyboard.
 * Each node gets its input and passes it along to the next
 * node.  The first node gets its input from the host, and the
 * last sends its output to the host.
 */

#include <dos.h>
#include <stdio.h>
#include <msghdr.h>
#include <uiodefs.h>


char far * (far * far *entry)();

main(argc, argv)
int argc;
char *argv[];
{
        msg far *m;
        struct intab far *it;
        struct outtab far *ot, far *top;
        struct ix_outtab out_tab[7];
        unsigned far *u, in_type[7];
        int c;
        char far *p;

        if(argc != 3){
                printf("Incorrect # of args\n");
                exit(1);
        }
        FP_OFF(entry) = atoi(argv[1]);
```

Fig. 3-20. echo.c

Fig. 3-20. Continued.

```
        FP_SEG(entry) = atoi(argv[2]);
        m = (*entry[P_INP])();              /* initialization message for host */
        p = u = (unsigned far *)(m + 1);
        ot = (struct outtab far *)(p + *u++);
        top = (struct outtab far *)(p + *u++);
        it = (struct inttab far *)u;

                /* We've set up the pointers, now we read the tables */

        while(it < ot){
                if(p[it->nm_off] == 'i'){        /* this is "in" */
                        in_type[0] = it->type;
                }
                it++;

                /* Do other inputs similarly */
        }

        while(ot < top){
                if(p[ot->nm_off] == 'o'){        /* this is "out" */
                        out_tab[0].type = ot->type;
                        out_tab[0].to = ot->to;
                }
                ot++;
        }

        (*entry[P_DISCARD])(0);                  /* get rid of init msg */

                /* Now we're ready to roll */

        while(1){
                c = getchar();
                (*entry[P_OUTP])(out_tab[0].type, out_tab[0].to,
                        (char far *)&c, 1);
                m = (*entry[P_INP])();
                if(m->type != in_type[0]) die(m, m->type);
                p = m + 1;
                printf("%c",*p);
                (*entry[P_DISCARD])(0);
        }
}

die(m)
msg far *m;
{
        printf("Ugggghhhhh! -- %x %x %x %x\n",m->type,m->from,m->to,m->length);
        exit(-15000);
}
```

PORTABLE PROGRAMS FOR PARALLEL PROCESSING

Portable programs for various parallel processing machines, including the Encore Multimax, Sequent Balance 21000, Alliant FX/8, Intel iPSC, Cray-2, and DEC VAX have been described by Boyle, et al (1987), from Argonne National Laboratory. There is a fair amount of similarity between this parallel language and the POS for the Parallon 2. This is an example of the principle that similar problems have similar solutions.

```
/*
 * nodecho.c, Copyright (C) 1988, Human Devices, Inc.
 * This is a simple program to echo what is typed at the keyboard.
 * Each node gets its input and passes it along to the next
 * node.  The first node gets its input from the host, and the
 * last sends its output to the host.
 */

#include <dos.h>
#include <msghdr.h>

main()
{
        msg far *m;
        struct intab far *it;
        struct outtab far *ot, far *top;
        struct ix_outtab out_tab[7];
        unsigned far *u, in_type[7];
        char far *p;              /* base address for calculations */

        m = inpt();               /* initialization message for node */
        p = u = (unsigned far *)(m + 1);
        ot = (struct outtab far *)(p + *u++);
        top = (struct outtab far *)(p + *u++);
        it = (struct inttab far *)u;

/*
```

```
        --------------------------
        |  message type          |              <- m points here
        |  from whom             |
        |  to us                 |
        |  length of message     _
        |  offset of outtab      l              <- p points here
        |  offset of strings     e
        |  intab                 n              <- u and it point here
        |       .                g
        |       .                t
        |  outtab                h              <- ot points here
        |       .
        |       .                b
        |  strings               y              <- top points here
        |       .                t
        |       .                e
        |       .                s
        --------------------------
```

```
*/

                /* We've set up the pointers, now we read the tables */

        while(it < ot){
                if(p[it->nm_off] == 'i')          /* this is "in" */
                        in_type[0] = it->type;
                it++;

                /* Do other inputs similarly */
        }

        while(ot < top){
                if(p[ot->nm_off] == 'o'){         /* this is "out" */
                        out_tab[0].type = ot->type;
                        out_tab[0].to = ot->to;
                }
                ot++;
```

Fig. 3-21. nodecho.c

Fig. 3-21. Continued.

```
        }

        discard (0);                              /* get rid of init msg */

                /* Now we're ready to roll */

        while(1){
                m = inpt();              /* real message */
                if(m->type != in_type[0]) die();
                p = (char far *)(m + 1);
                outpt(out_tab[0].type, out_tab[0].to, p, 1);
                wait(0);
                discard(0);
        }
}

die()
{
        while(1);
}
```

Each program starts with a structure declaring message types, senders and receivers. The messages themselves contain a message header with type and length. The program must set the appropriate message flags. This is an unbuffered message passing just like the POS. If you want node 1 to communicate a message to node 2 the appropriate setup for a "channel" or "pipe" is done and the actual operation then becomes almost transparent to the user. Memory Buffers can be allocated and buffered communication can also take place.

LINDA

An increasingly popular portable parallel processing language is Linda. The Linda language has been described by Gelernter (1988), Carriero and Gelernter (1988) and by Williams (1988) and was developed at Yale University. Human Devices markets a Linda package with their Macintosh-Transputer products.

Linda can be used to uncouple parallel processes from their time and space dependencies by what is known as *tuple space*. Tuple space can be thought of as a big universe of tuples. Tuples are ordered sets or sequences of typed fields. For example ("file.exe", 27, 13.09) is a three-tuple, with a string, an integer and a real number. Tuples are picked out of the tuple space by associative memory. They are not accessed by pointers or addresses. To find the appropriate tuple you search any of the fields for a match.

Tuples reduce all the software communication problems with nodes. If task R has some data for task S, it is placed in a tuple and dropped into tuple space. Process S can then use association to find and read the appropriate tuple. There are also tuples called *live tuples*. Live tuple's fields are not evaluated until they enter tuple space. When a live tuple enters tuple space it is evaluated independently and in parallel with the task that dropped it into tuple space. This means that to create 100 processes you drop 100 live tuples into tuple space.

There are several basic tuple-space operations. Out (t) adds the tuple t to the tuple space. In (s) causes a tuple to match the templet s and withdraw it from the tuple space. Rd(s) is the same as in(s) except the tuple is simply read and not withdrawn from tuple space. Finally eval(t) is just about the same as cut(t) except that it causes t to be evaluated after, rather than before, it enters tuple space.

Linda is such a simple parallel programming paradigm that it will surely become more popular.

4

The Transputer: LEGO for Fifth-Generation Computers

In this chapter I discuss the INMOS transputer and transputer plug-in boards for PCs. There are several members of the transputer family, all are high-performance microprocessors or VLSI chips designed to act as parallel processing building blocks for massively parallel computer systems. In the first section of this chapter I discuss the members of the transputer family and the OCCAM programming language. In the next section of the chapter I discuss the programming of a transputer board for a PC clone programmed in parallel-C. In the final section of the chapter I discuss the companies selling transputer boards for PCs, and some research that is being done with transputers.

TRANSPUTER FAMILY CHIPS

The best source of information on the transputer is the *Transputer Reference Manual* by INMOS. The members of the transputer family all contain processing, memory and communication links in a single VLSI package. The first member of the family, the IMS-T414, was introduced in 1985. The bottom of the line chip the T212 was introduced as a low-cost 16-bit version. The top of the line version, the T800, was introduced in 1988. Because each of the transputers contain processing, memory and communication links in a single package, a concurrent system can be built from a collection of transputers. All the members of the family are fully compatible with each other and can be mixed in almost any configuration and topology. Figure 4-1 suggests a grid topology. This figure is just to act as a reminder

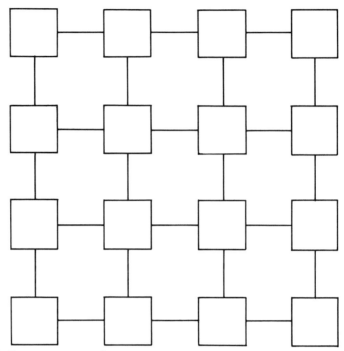

Fig. 4-1. Transputer network.

that transputers can be assembled as building blocks for parallel systems.

The flexibility of the transputer arises primarily because the architecture has been designed with concurrency in mind. The language OCCAM was designed simultaneously with the transputer and supports concurrent processes with three primitive constructs:

SEQuential—components executed one after another.
PARallel—components executed together.
ALTernative—component first ready is executed.

Each of these constructs can be considered as a process and may be used as a component of another construct. Later in this chapter I discuss OCCAM in a little more detail.

The architecture of the T414 is sketched in Fig. 4-2. It, like the T800 and T212, is a RISC architecture. In this figure the links to the outside world are shown as one block and the 32-bit bus is shown as arrows. There are, in fact, four links. The transputer uses two-wire, high-speed, point-to-point serial communication links for direct connection to other transputers. This gives a minimal amount of wiring and alleviates the bus-loading problems common with other concur-

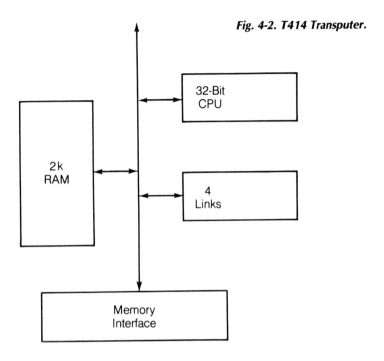

Fig. 4-2. T414 Transputer.

rent systems. The transputer also contains a microcoded scheduler for support of concurrency. This allows any number of current processes to be executed together. A software kernel is not needed for concurrent processing because the OCCAM compiler performs all the allocation of space and transputer scheduling. The microcoded process scheduler allows the user to develop and debug programs on one transputer, and then port the same program to a machine with many transputers, with little or no change in the program code.

The communication links are two-wire channels, one wire in each direction. Of course the channels can be virtual channels between processes in the OCCAM model. The communication is point-to-point, synchronized and unbuffered. The sending process expects to receive an acknowledgment from the receiving process. The acknowledgment can be transmitted as soon as the first data byte is received. Therefore transmission can be continuous and without delays.

The T800 transputer contains an on-chip floating point coprocessor as sketched on the block diagram of Fig. 4-3. This is a 32-bit CPU and a 34-bit FPU that is microcoded to do 64-bit operations. It can run at up to 30 MHz and 15 MIPS.

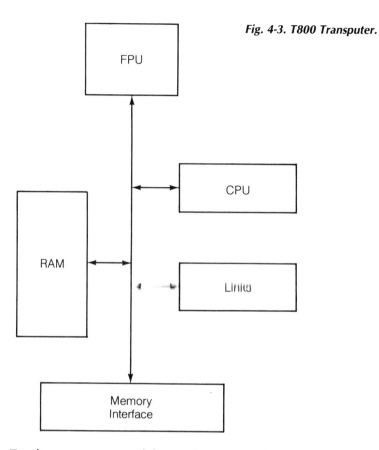

Fig. 4-3. T800 Transputer.

To show you some of the performance of transputers compared with a VAX, I have reproduced a table from the *Transputer Reference Manual*:

Processor	Whetstones
VAX 11/780	1083K
T414-20	663K
T800-20	4000K
T800-30	6000K

The whetstone benchmark can be thought of as a typical scientific program. It contains a good mix of floating point operations, procedure calls and transcendental functions. As can be seen, the T414 transputer running at 20 MHz is better than half the speed of a VAX 11/780 and the T800 at 30 MHz is almost six times faster than a VAX! Now everyone can have a super minicomputer on their desk top.

The transputers are, of course, one of the main members of the family. Other members do exist. The M212 (not to be confused with the 16-bit T212 transputer) is a general-purpose peripheral processor, which can be used to control hard disk drives, floppy drives, printers, etc. A block diagram of the device is shown in Fig. 4-4. Note that the chip contains 8-bit peripheral ports.

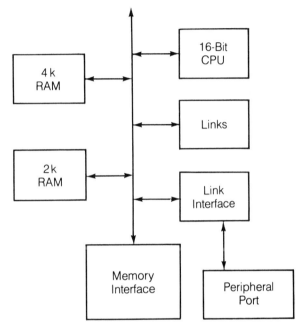

Fig. 4-4. M212 Interface.

The M212 can be used in the design of a transputer network with disk processing as shown in Fig. 4-5.

Another INMOS transputer-compatible chip is a high-speed (20 Mbits) communication link. It converts the serial link data from a transputer to parallel data streams. This chip serves as a link between a conventional microcomputer and a transputer system. Figure 4-6 is a sketch of how it could be used in a transputer network.

The last member of the transputer family that I will discuss is the C004. This is a full 32-point crossbar switch. It can run at 10 or 20 Mbits/sec and is programmed by a configuration link, serial input. Fully connected networks and butterfly networks like those discussed in Chapter 2 can easily be implemented with these crossbar switches.

OCCAM

The programming model for transputers is the OCCAM language. Hoare (1985) wrote a book on communicating sequential processes. The OCCAM language is similar to these. Processes are treated as a

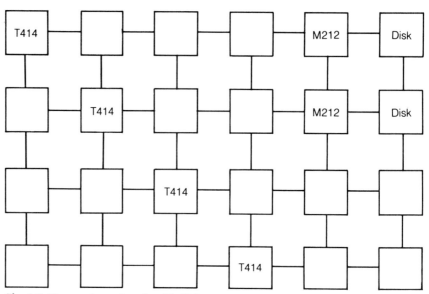

Fig. 4-5. Transputer network with disk processors.

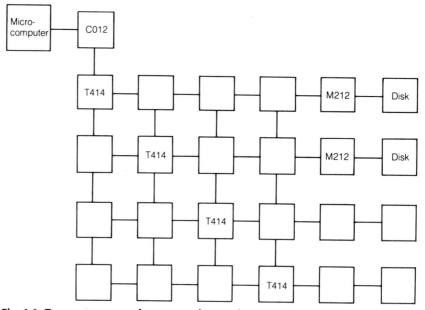

Fig. 4-6. Transputer network connected to a microcomputer.

black box and they communicate over non-buffered channels with each other. There are several good references on OCCAM. Jones (1987) and Pountain and May (1986) have written very good introductory level books on the OCCAM language. INMOS (1986,1988) has written two OCCAM reference manuals that give complete definition of the language.

All Processes in OCCAM are constructed from three primitive actions: assignment, input and output. Processes communicate using one-way channels connecting two processes. The communication is point-to-point, synchronized, and unbuffered just as it is with inter-transputer communication. You can write and test a program using channels without worrying about exactly where different processes will be executed. The same program will run as well on a single transputer as on a network of transputers. Both the transputer and OCCAM were designed together.

As I pointed out there are three actions a process can take. The assignment action is indicated by the symbolic statement:

v : = e.

This sets the value of v to the expression e.

The input statement:

c ? x

inputs a value from channel c and assigns it to a variable x.

The last action for a process is an output. The expression:

c ! e

indicates that the value of the expression e is output on channel c.

Processes are assembled into programs with three constructs. The most common construct is sequential and represented by:

```
SEQ
    p1
    p2
    p3
    .
    .
    .
```

The processes p1, p2, p3, . . . are executed sequentially. Another construct is the parallel construct represented by:

```
PAR
    p1
```

```
    p2
    p3
    . . .
```

The processes p1, p2, p3, . . . are executed in parallel. These parallel processes communicate only by using channels. Later in this chapter I give examples of communicating processes in a parallel-C language.

Another software construct developed for the transputer is the alternative construct represented by:

```
ALT
    input 1
        p1
    input 2
        p2
    input 3
        p3
```

This construct waits until one of the inputs is ready, then the appropriate process is executed. Whichever input is ready first is used to determine which process to execute.

OCCAM supports other, more common, constructs such as if.... then, while, for....next, and functions. INMOS sells an OCCAM development kit for the transputer. This includes an OCCAM compiler. In the next section I discuss a parallel-C compiler modeled after the OCCAM language.

PARALLEL-C

There are several parallel-C compilers. You could use any ASCII editor to create a C program and then cross-compile with one of these parallel-C compilers for down-loading code to a transputer for execution. Penguine Software and Logical Systems have a parallel-C cross-compiler. Another company, 3L, produces a compiler for the transputer. Because I have only had experience with the cross-compiler from Logical Systems, I will not discuss the other two compilers.

The Logical Systems C cross-compiler is available from Computer System Architects in Provo, UT. In the remainder of this section I discuss an example program supplied with the C compiler. Then in the following section I discuss several programs I have written to run on a transputer.

The program, par.c, is reproduced in Fig. 4-7 with permission from Computer System Architects. Rather than discuss each line, I will discuss only the constructs that make this a parallel program. The

```
#include "\lsc\include\conc.h"

#define WSPACE 1024

producer(p,init,end,wait,out)
Process *p;
char init,end;
Channel *out;
{
      char ch;

      for (ch = init; ch <= end; ch++) {
          ProcWait(wait);
          ChanOutChar(out,ch);
      }
      ChanOutChar(out,0);
}

consumer(p,run,in1,in2)
Process *p;
Channel *in1,*in2;
{
      char ch;

      do {
          switch (ProcAlt(in1,in2,0)) {
          case 0: ch = ChanInChar(in1); break;
          case 1: ch = ChanInChar(in2); break;
          }
          if (ch == 0) run--;
          else printf("%c",ch);
      } while (run);
      printf("\n");
}

main()
{
      Channel *c1,*c2;
      Process *prod1,*prod2,*cons;

      c1 = ChanAlloc();
      c2 = ChanAlloc();
      prod1 = ProcAlloc(producer,WSPACE,4,'a','z',10000,c1);
      prod2 = ProcAlloc(producer,WSPACE,4,'A','Z',6000,c2);
      cons = ProcAlloc(consumer,WSPACE,3,2,c1,c2);

      printf("begin par\n");
      ProcPar(prod1,prod2,cons,0);
      printf("end per\n");
}
```

Fig. 4-7. par.c, an example C program.

program starts by declaring channel and process pointers. The two channels, c1 and c2, are then initialized with statements of the type:

$$c1 = ChanAlloc(\ );$$

and the two processes, prod1 and prod2, are allocated in the statement of the type:

prod1 = ProcAlloc(producer,WSPACE,4,'a','Z',10000,c1);

A third process called the *consumer* (cons) is also allocated. There are a number of arguments in the process allocation. The first argument is the name of the function (producer or consumer in this example). The second argument is the amount of memory space allocated, and the third argument is the number of parameters to be passed. The last group of arguments is the parameter list.

The next line is the parallel function. ProcPar( ) is used to execute the processes concurrently. The argument list is terminated by a null character. When the processes end, a message is printed to the screen and the program ends.

Now look at the two processes, producer and consumer, in more detail. All processes must declare a process pointer, Process *p, and input or output channels, Channel *out, *in1, *in2. In the process producer there is the function ProcWait( ), which causes a process to wait for a specified amount of time. The process ChanOutChar (out,ch) outputs the character ch on channel out. The meaning and use of ChanInChar( ), in the process consumer, should be obvious. The function ProcAlt( ) waits until one of the channels in the argument list is ready for input.

There are many library functions, similar to the above, which make writing parallel-C code for the transputer almost as easy as using OCCAM. The cross-compiler takes care of all the details of making sure the code can run on a transputer. In the following section I discuss several programs to demonstrate certain features of the transputer.

PARALLEL-C: EXAMPLES

The first program, partest1.c in Fig. 4-8, is a simple extension of par.c. Instead of using channels to send characters, the program uses them to send integers. The main change in the program is the use of ChanInInt( ) and ChanOutInt( ). The next program, partest4.c in Fig. 4-9, is a further extension in which there are three producer processes and one consumer. These three processes send integers out their channels after performing a little arithmetic on some integers. The answers are received in the consumer and are printed to the display. The last program, which is just a simple modification, is partest5.c, shown in Fig. 4-10. In this program I made changes to the switch statement in order to format the printing of some integers sent on the channels.

```
#include "\lsc\include\conc.h"

#define WSPACE 1024

producer(p,value1,value2,wait,outchan)
Process *p;
int value1,value2;
Channel *outchan;
{
        int i;
        int result;

        for (i = value1; i <= value2; i++)
        {
                ProcWait(wait);
                result = i + 1;
                ChanOutInt(outchan, result );
        }
        ChanOutInt(outchan,0);
}

consumer(p,run,inchan1,inchan2)
Process *p;
Channel *inchan1, *inchan2;
{
        int i;

        do
        {
                switch (ProcAlt(inchan1,inchan2,0))
                {
                        case 0: i = ChanInInt(inchan1);
                                break;
                        case 1: i = ChanInInt(inchan2);
                                break;
                }
                if (i == 0)
                {
                        run--;
                }
                else
                {
                        printf("%d ",i);
                }

        }
        while (run);
        printf("\n");
}

main()
{
        Channel *c1,*c2;
        Process *prod1,*prod2,*cons;

        c1 = ChanAlloc();
        c2 = ChanAlloc();
        prod1 = ProcAlloc(producer,WSPACE,4,1,10,200,c1);
        prod2 = ProcAlloc(producer,WSPACE,4,1,10,200,c2);
        cons = ProcAlloc(consumer,WSPACE,3,2,c1,c2);
        printf("begin par\n");
        ProcPar(prod1,prod2,cons,0);
        printf("end par\n");
```

Fig. 4-8. partest1.c uses channels to send integers.

```
#include "\lsc\include\conc.h"

#define WSPACE 1024

proces1(p,value1,value2,wait,outchan)
Process *p;
int value1,value2;
Channel *outchan;
{
        int i;
        int result;

        for (i = value1; i <= value2; i++)
        {
                ProcWait(wait);
                result = i;
                ChanOutInt(outchan, result );
        }
        ChanOutInt(outchan,0);
}

proces2(p,value1,value2,wait,outchan)
Process *p;
int value1,value2;
Channel *outchan;
{
        int i;
        int result;

        for(i = value1; i <= value2; i++)
        {
                ProcWait(wait);
                result = i*18;
                ChanOutInt(outchan,result);
        }
        ChanOutInt(outchan,0);
}

proces3(p,value1,value2,wait,outchan)
Process *p;
int value1,value2;
Channel *outchan;
{
        int i;
        int result;

        for(i = value1; i <= value2; i++)
        {
                ProcWait(wait);
                result = i*100;
                ChanOutInt(outchan,result);
        }
        ChanOutInt(outchan,0);
}


consumer(p,run,inchan1,inchan2,inchan3)
Process *p;
Channel *inchan1, *inchan2, *inchan3;
{
        int i;
```

Fig. 4-9. partest4.c has three producer and one consumer process.

Fig. 4-9. Continued.

```
do
{
        switch (ProcAlt(inchan1,inchan2,inchan3,0))
        {
                case 0: i = ChanInInt(inchan1);
                        break;
                case 1: i = ChanInInt(inchan2);
                        break;
                case 2: i = ChanInInt(inchan3);
                        break;
        }
        if (i == 0)
        {
                run--;
        }
        else
        {
                printf("%d ",i);
        }
}
while (run);
printf("\n");
}

main()
{
        Channel *c1,*c2,*c3;
        Process *prod1,*prod2,*prod3,*cons;

        c1 = ChanAlloc();
        c2 = ChanAlloc();
        c3 = ChanAlloc();

        prod1 = ProcAlloc(proces1,WSPACE,4,1,10,300,c1);
        prod2 = ProcAlloc(proces2,WSPACE,4,1,10,300,c2);
        prod3 = ProcAlloc(proces3,WSPACE,4,1,10,300,c3);

        cons = ProcAlloc(consumer,WSPACE,4,3,c1,c2,c3);

        printf("begin par\n");
        ProcPar(prod1,prod2,prod3,cons,0);
        printf("end par\n");

}
```

My transputer is a T414-20 and does not contain a floating point processor. I therefore wrote short programs to perform advanced math functions. Taking the exponent and logarithm of a number is useful in itself, but can also be used to build other mathematical functions. I have included both exp( ) and log( ) functions in the programs exptest.c (Fig. 4-11) and logtest.c (Fig. 4-12). Both of these programs use a series expansion solution. A third useful math function is the ability to generate pseudorandom numbers. The Logical Systems C compiler for the transputer contains a rand( ) function. Because the

```
#include "\lsc\include\conc.h"

#define WSPACE 1024

producer(p,value1,value2,wait,outchan)
Process *p;
int value1,value2;
Channel *outchan;
{
        int i;
        int result;

        for (i = value1; i <= value2; i++)
        {
                ProcWait(wait);
                result = i + 1;
                ChanOutInt(outchan, result );
        }
        ChanOutInt(outchan,0);
}

consumer(p,run,inchan1,inchan2)
Process *p;
Channel *inchan1, *inchan2;
{
        int i,z1,z2;

        do
        {
                switch (ProcAlt(inchan1,inchan2,0))
                {
                        case 0:
                                i = ChanInInt(inchan1);
                                z1 = i;
                                if(i > 0)
                                {
                                        printf("z1 %d ",z1);
                                }
                        break;
                        case 1:
                                i = ChanInInt(inchan2);
                                z2 = i;
                                if(i > 0)
                                {
                                        printf("z2 %d \n",z2);
                                }
                        break;
                }
                if (i == 0)
                {
                        run--;
                }

        }
        while (run);
        printf("\n");
}

void main()
{
        Channel *c1,*c2;
        Process *prod1,*prod2,*cons;
```

Fig. 4-10. partest5.c is a modification of partest4.c which formats the printing of the integers.

Fig. 4-10. Continued.

```
        c1 = ChanAlloc();
        c2 = ChanAlloc();
        prod1 = ProcAlloc(producer,WSPACE,4,1,10,600,c1);
        prod2 = ProcAlloc(producer,WSPACE,4,1,10,600,c2);
        cons = ProcAlloc(consumer,WSPACE,3,2,c1,c2);

        printf("begin par\n");
        ProcPar(prod1,prod2,cons,0);

        printf("end par\n");

}
```

```
#include    "c:\lsc\include\stdio.h"
#include    "c:\lsc\include\math.h"
#include    "c:\lsc\include\float.h"


void main()
{
        double expt();
        float netinput = 2.0;
        float temperature = 1.0;

        printf("result %lf\n",expt(netinput,temperature));


}



/* claculate an exponent */
double expt(net,tem)
float net;
float tem;
{
        double answer;
        float x;

        x=-1*net/tem;

        answer = 1+x+x*x/2;
        answer = answer + x*x*x/6;
        answer = answer + x*x*x*x/24;
        answer = answer + x*x*x*x*x/120;
        answer = answer + x*x*x*x*x*x/720;
        answer = answer + x*x*x*x*x*x*x/5040;
        answer = answer + x*x*x*x*x*x*x*x/40320;
        answer = answer + x*x*x*x*x*x*x*x*x/362880;
        answer = answer + x*x*x*x*x*x*x*x*x*x/3628800;

        return (answer);
}
```

Fig. 4-11. exptest.c uses a series expansion solution.

```
#include   "c:\lsc\include\stdio.h"
#include   "c:\lsc\include\math.h"
#include   "c:\lsc\include\float.h"

void main()
{
        double loge();
        double temperature = 1.2;

        printf("result %lf\n",loge(temperature));

}



/* calculate log base e */
double loge(temp)
double temp;
{
        int ct, lt;
        double t,y,sqrt();

        ct = 1;
        lt = 1;

        if(temp < 1)
        {
                temp = 1/temp;
                lt = -1;
        }

        while(temp > 2)
        {
                temp = sqrt(temp);
                ct *= 2;
        }

        t = (temp-1)/(temp+1);
        y = 0.868591718 * t;
        y = y + 0.289335524 * (t*t*t);
        y = y + 0.177522071 * (t*t*t*t*t);
        y = y + 0.094376476 * (t*t*t*t*t*t*t);
        y = y + 0.179337714 * (t*t*t*t*t*t*t*t*t);

        return(y/0.43429466*ct*lt);

}
```

Fig. 4-12. logtest.c also uses a series expansion solution.

transputer is a 32-bit CPU, the rand( ) function will return integers between 0 and 2147483642. My program, rndtest.c in Fig. 4-13, will return a random integer in this range. In addition it will return a random floating-point number between 0 and 1.0 and a random integer between 0 and 22 (22 is an arbitrarily selected number).

In Chapter 6 I include a discussion of the Boltzmann Machine. This is a simulated neural network machine. I have included a Boltz-

```
#include    "c:\lsc\include\stdio.h"
#include    "c:\lsc\include\math.h"
#include    "c:\lsc\include\float.h"

#define RNDMAX   2147483647.0    /* use 32767 2147483647 with transputer 32-bit */
#define DILUTIONFACTOR 0.5


void main()
{
        /* declarations */
        int i,nn = 22;
        int seed;

        int rnd();
        int random();

        printf("enter seed \n");
        scanf("%d",&seed);
        srand(seed);

        for (i=0;i<6;i++)
        {
                printf("random number %d\n",rand());
                printf("rnd func %d\n",rnd());
                printf("random func %d\n\n",random(nn));

        }

}


/* return a random 0 or 1 for use in the vector generation */
int rnd()
{
        int   result;
        result=rand();
        if(result<DILUTIONFACTOR*(double)(RNDMAX))
                result=1;
        else
                result=0;
        return((int)(result));
}

/* return a random integer between 0 and number of neurons
        for use in random update of the network */
 int random(n)
 int n;
{
        int result;
        float tmp;

        tmp = rand()/RNDMAX;
        result = (int)(n * tmp);
        printf("tmp %f\n",tmp);
        return(result);
}
```

Fig. 4-13. rndtest.c returns random integers.

mann machine program here. The program tboltz9.c in Fig. 4-14 is designed to run on the transputer. It is a sequential program and makes no use of the parallel constructs available. The program simply uses the transputer as a fast CPU. The program is downloaded from the host for execution. The program can, of course, be run on the host without downloading to a transputer. Another sequential program example, to take advantage of the speed of the transputer, is tjulia.c (shown in Fig. 4-15). This is a program to generate data files of Julia sets.

```
/* program to simulate a boltzman update of
        a hopfield neural network
        Transputer    T414 version   11/88     */

#include   "c:\lsc\include\stdio.h"
#include   "c:\lsc\include\math.h"
#include   "c:\lsc\include\float.h"

#define RNDMAX 2147483647.0
#define DILUTIONFACTOR 0.2

static float weight[100][100];
static long int ivector[100],activation[100],oldvalue[100];
static long int tvector[100],ttvector[100];

void main()
{
        /* declarations */
        long int i,j,k,memories,updateno,ielement = 0;
        int noneurons, nomemories;
        float hightemp,lowtemp;
        float temperature;
        double logistic;
        float netinput;
        float randomnumber;
        double t,energy;
        float threshold;
        int seed;

        int rnd();
        int random();
        double expt(); /* compute exp base e */
        double loge(); /* compute log base e */

        /* user input */
        printf("input the number of neurons \n");
        scanf("%d",&noneurons);
        printf("input and threshold\n");
        scanf("%f",&threshold);
        printf("input seed \n");
        scanf("%d",&seed);

        /* number of memory states */
        nomemories= (int)(0.1*noneurons);

        /* calculate the weight matrix form the
                product of the memory vectors with their transpose */
```

Fig. 4-14. tboltz9.c runs on the Boltzmann machine.

Fig. 4-14. Continued.

```
srand(seed);

for(memories=0;memories<=nomemories-1;++memories)
{
        for(k=0;k<=noneurons-1;++k)
        {
                tvector[k]=(int)(rnd());   /* the memory state */
                printf("%d ",tvector[k]);
                ttvector[k]=tvector[k];    /* the transpose state */
        }
        printf("\n\n");
        for(i=0;i<=noneurons-1;++i)        /* sum the matrices */
                for(j=0;j<=noneurons-1;++j)
                {
                        weight[i][j]=weight[i][j]+tvector[i]*ttvector[j]
                        if(i==j)
                                weight[i][j]=0;
                        else
                        weight[i][j]=weight[i][j];
                }
}

/* print out the final weight matrix */
for(i=0;i<=noneurons-1;++i)
{
        for(j=0;j<=noneurons-1;++j)
        {
                printf("%d ",(int)(weight[i][j]));
        }
        /* printf("\n"); */
}
printf("\n\n");

/* clip the matrix here -- if needed */

/* input a vector to use as test vector */
for(k=0;k<=noneurons-1;++k)
{
        printf("enter the input vector element %d\n",k);
        scanf("%ld",&ielement);
        ivector[k] = ielement;
        activation[k] = ivector[k];
}



/* find a random vector to use as input to test the network
        ivector                                             */
/*    for(k=0;k<=noneurons-1;++k)
      {
              ivector[k]=(int)(rnd());
              activation[k]=ivector[k];
              printf("%d ",ivector[k]);
      }
      printf("\n\n");

*/

/* begin calculation loops form high temperature to low temp.
        ovector                                             */
temperature=10.0;
for(t = 2; t <= 50; t = t + 2 )
{
```

Fig. 4-14. Continued.

```
/* save old value for use later in energy calculation */
for(j=0; j<=noneurons-1;++j)
{
        oldvalue[j] = activation[j];
}
temperature = temperature/loge(1+t);
for(updateno = 0; updateno <= t*100.0*noneurons; updateno++)
{
        /* code here for basic calculation */
        i=(long int)(random(noneurons));
        /* netinput for single neuron */
        netinput=0;
        for(j=0;j<=noneurons-1;++j)
        {
                netinput += activation[j]*weight[i][j];
        }
        netinput = netinput - threshold;
        /*printf("%f ",netinput);*/
        /* end basic code here */

        /* update algorithm here */
        logistic=(double)(1.0/(1.0+expt(netinput,temperature)));
        randomnumber=(double)(rand()/(double)(RNDMAX));
        if (randomnumber > logistic)
                {
                activation[i]=1;
                }
        else
                {
                activation[i]=0;
                }
        if(temperature < 0.05)
        {
                if(netinput == 0.0)
                        activation[i] = 0;
                if(netinput == 1.0)
                        activation[i] = 1;
        }


}
/* energy calculation */
energy=0;
for(j=0;j<=noneurons-1;j++)
{
        energy = energy + (oldvalue[j]*activation[j]);
}
energy = -energy;
printf("\n");
for(i=0;i<=noneurons-1;i++)
{
printf("%d ",(int)(activation[i]));
}
printf("\n%lf  %lf\n\n ",temperature,energy);
}

}


/* return a random 0 or 1 for use in the vector generation */
int rnd()
{
```

Fig. 4-14. Continued.

```
  int result;
  result=rand();
  if(result<DILUTIONFACTOR*(double)(RNDMAX))
              result=1;
      else
              result=0;
      return(result);
}

/* return a random integer between 0 and number of neurons
        for use in random update of the network */
int random(n)
int n;
{
        int result;
        float tmp;

        tmp = rand()/RNDMAX;
        result = (int)(n * tmp);

        return(result);
}

/* claculate an exponent */
double expt(net,tem)
float net;
float tem;
{
        double answer;
        float x;

        x=-1*net/tem;

        answer = 1+x+x*x/2;
        answer = answer + x*x*x/6;
        answer = answer + x*x*x*x/24;
        answer = answer + x*x*x*x*x/120;
        answer = answer + x*x*x*x*x*x/720;
        answer = answer + x*x*x*x*x*x*x/5040;
        answer = answer + x*x*x*x*x*x*x*x/40320;
        answer = answer + x*x*x*x*x*x*x*x*x/362880;
        answer = answer + x*x*x*x*x*x*x*x*x*x/3628800;

        return (answer);
}

/* calculate log base e */
double loge(temp)
double temp;
{
        int ct, lt;
        double t,y,sqrt();

        ct = 1;
        lt = 1;

        if(temp < 1)
        {
                temp = 1/temp;
                lt = -1;
        }

        while(temp > 2)
        {
```

Fig. 4-14. Continued.

```
                temp = sqrt(temp);
                ct *= 2;
        }

        t = (temp-1)/(temp+1);
        y = 0.868591718 * t;
        y = y + 0.289335524 * (t*t*t);
        y = y + 0.177522071 * (t*t*t*t*t);
        y = y + 0.094376476 * (t*t*t*t*t*t*t);
        y = y + 0.179337714 * (t*t*t*t*t*t*t*t*t);

        return(y/0.43429466*ct*lt);


}
```

```
/* julia set program for transputer */
/*          01/01/89                  */

#include "\lsc\include\stdio.h"
#include "\lsc\include\math.h"
#include "\lsc\include\float.h"

void main()
{
        FILE *fe;
        char datafile[80];
        float xmax = 1.5;
        float xmin = -1.5;
        float ymax = 0.0;
        float ymin = -1.5;
        float deltax = 0.05;
        float deltay = 0.05;
        float maxrow,maxcol;
        float modulus;
        float xlast,ylast;
        float xcur,ycur;
        float p,q;
        float col,row;
        int kount = 0;
        int co;

        maxrow = (xmax-xmin)/deltax;
        maxcol = (ymax-ymin)/deltay;

        printf("input file name\n");
        scanf("%s",datafile);
        p = -0.123;
        q = 0.565;

        if((fe=fopen(datafile,"w"))==NULL)
        {
                printf("\007ERROR! can't open file\n");
                exit(0);
        }

        for(col=0;col<maxrow-1;col++)
        {
                for(row=0;row<maxcol-1;row++)
                {
                        modulus = 0.0;
```

Fig. 4-15. tjulia.c generates data files of Julia sets.

Fig. 4-15. Continued.

```
                        co = 0;
                        xlast = xmin + col*deltax;
                        ylast = ymin + row*deltay;
                        while((modulus < 4) && (co < 100))
                        {
                                xcur = (xlast * xlast) - (ylast * ylast) + p;
                                ycur = (2 * xlast * ylast) + q;
                                co++;
                                xlast = xcur;
                                ylast = ycur;
                                modulus = (xcur * xcur) + (ycur * ycur);
                        }
                        if(co == 100)
                        {
                                /* printf("%f\t%f\n",col,row); */
                                fprintf(fe,"%f   %f\t",col,row);
                                kount++;
                        }
                }
        }
        fclose(fe);
        printf("kounter = %d\n",kount);
}
```

JULIA SETS

In an earlier book (Rietman, 1989) I discussed Julia sets and fractals in detail. Much of the following is from that book. In this section I discuss iteration in the complex plain to study the Julia sets and the Mandelbrot set. Mandelbrot (1977), coined the term *fractal* for the geometric objects generated by iteration of the equation:

$$Z_{n+1} = Z_n^2 + c$$

In the complex plain you have

$$Z = X + iY$$

where X and Y are the real and imaginary parts of the complex number Z.

The primary thrust of this section is devoted to a discussion of Julia Sets. The complex number:

$$Z = X + iY$$

can be plotted on a complex plain where the X coordinate is the real axis and the Y coordinate is the imaginary axis. Using the iteration relation:

$$Z_{n+1} = Z_n^2$$

there are only two attracting points. For an initial Z less than one the attractor point is zero, and for an initial Z greater than one the attractor point is infinity. If a complex constant is added at each iteration such that:

$$Z_{n+1} = Z_n^2 + c$$

then the attracting points map out Julia sets and fractals. When the iterated points are plotted in Z-space, and the parameter c is held fixed, the function maps out Julia sets. When the iterated points are started at $Z_o = 0$ and iterated for various values of the parameter c and plotted in c-space, the function maps out the Mandelbrot set. This can be elucidated with some algebra.

The basic equation is:

$$Z_{n+1} = Z_n^2 + c$$

where Z and c are complex numbers given as follows:

$$Z = X + iY$$
$$c = P + iQ$$

The function is then

$$X_n + 1 = X_n^2 + Y_n^2 + p$$
$$Y_{n+1} = 2X_nY_n + q$$

For Julia sets you hold P and Q constant for the entire region of space, select an initial point (X_o, Y_o) and iterate this to an attractor point. The number of iterations required to reach the attractor point is recorded and assigned to a color. The point (X_o, Y_o) is then assigned this color and plotted. The Julia set then is a map of the number of iterations to reach an attractor point. Many points do not reach an attractor point other than infinity. In order to prevent this, the modulus of the complex number must be calculated. Peitgen, et al (1984) and Peitgen and Richter (1986) have shown that if the modulus is greater than two, the iterates will escape to infinity. The modulus is calculated by the following relation:

$$\text{mod}(Z) = |\text{sqr}(X^2 + Y^2)|$$

or

$$X^2 + Y^2 = 4$$

The Julia sets are an infinite number of mappings for a whole range of constant values for P and Q.

The Mandelbrot set is only one set, but the set is very large. Peitgen and Richter (1986) have shown many regions of the Mandelbrot set and Julia sets. The Mandelbrot set is found by selecting a value for the parameters P and Q and holding these fixed while $Z_0 = 0$ is iterated. The number of iterates needed to reach an attractor point or escape to infinity is assigned a color. The (P,Q) point is then plotted in c-space with the color attached to that (P,Q) point. Then another (P,Q) point is selected and $Z_0 = 0$ is iterated again and the process repeated. So, I want to reiterate that Julia sets are maps of Z-space and the Mandelbrot set is a map of c-space. In the next section I describe a computer program for Julia sets. I don't cover the Mandelbrot set because it, in addition to fractals, has been covered in the secondary literature quite well. I suggest Dewdney (1988), and Fogg (1988) for more details on the Mandelbrot set.

The program tjulia.c is a simple sequential program to prepare data files of Julia set data. The program ptjulia.c, shown in Fig. 4-16, is a parallel version of the same program. The space is partitioned into two halves, as shown in Fig. 4-17. The upper half is assigned to process 1 and the lower half is assigned to process 2. Each process does the computation for one-half of the space. There is no communication needed between the computing processes—but each process must send its results over a channel for a consumer process that prints the results to a disk file. This program is an example of using the transputer to act as a task farm where each process carries out a different task on different data. This could be thought of as virtual MIMD processing. Each process is in fact carrying out a different task because the processes are not synchronous. Figure 4-18 is a plot of a data file of Julia data prepared from the program ptjulia.c. The file was read and plotted with a MicroSoft-C version of plot1 (shown in Fig. 4-19) discussed in Chapter 1.

```
/* parallel transputer julia program */

#include "\lsc\include\conc.h"
#include "\lsc\include\math.h"
#include "\lsc\include\float.h"
#include "\lsc\include\stdio.h"
```

Fig. 4-16. ptjulia.c is a parallel program to generate data files of Julia sets.

Fig. 4-16. Continued.

```
#define WSPACE 8192

int kount = 0;
FILE *fe;

producer(p,value,wait,outchan)
Process *p;
int value;
Channel *outchan;
{
        int result;
        int col,row;
        float modulus,xlast,ylast,xcur,ycur;
        int maxrow,maxcol;
        int co;
        float deltax = 0.05;
        float deltay = 0.05;

        float pp = -0.123;    /* paramaters for julia set */
        float qq = 0.565;

        float xmax,ymax,xmin,ymin;

        int value1,value2;

        if(value == 1)
        {
                xmax = 1.5;
                xmin = -1.5;
                ymax = 1.5;
                ymin = 0.0;
        }
        if(value == 2)
        {
                xmax = 1.5;
                xmin = -1.5;
                ymax = 0.0;
                ymin = -1.5;
        }
        maxrow = (int)((xmax-xmin)/deltax);
        maxcol = (int)((ymax-ymin)/deltay);

        for (col = 1; col <= maxrow; col = col + 1)
        {
                for ( row = 1; row <= maxcol; row = row + 1)
                {
                        modulus = 0.0;
                        co = 0;

                        xlast = xmin + col*deltax;
                        ylast = ymin + row*deltay;

                        while((modulus < 4) && (co < 100))
                        {
                                xcur = (xlast * xlast) - (ylast * ylast) + pp;
                                ycur = ( 2 * xlast * ylast) + qq;
                                co++;
                                xlast = xcur;
                                ylast = ycur;
                                modulus = (xcur * xcur) + (ycur * ycur);
                        }
                        if(co == 100)
                        {
```

Fig. 4-16. Continued.

```
                                  ProcWait(wait);
                                  result = col;
                                  ChanOutInt(outchan,result);
                                  if(value == 1)
                                  {
                                          result = row+30;
                                  }
                                  else
                                  {
                                          result = row;
                                  }
                                  ChanOutInt(outchan,result);
                          }
                  }
          }
          ChanOutInt(outchan,0);
}

consumer(p,run,inchan1,inchan2)
Process *p;
Channel *inchan1, *inchan2;
{
          int i,j,z1,z2;

          do
          {
                  switch (ProcAlt(inchan1,inchan2,0))
                  {
                          case 0:
                                  i = ChanInInt(inchan1);
                                  z1 = i;
                                  if(i == 0)break;
                                  i = ChanInInt(inchan1);
                                  z2 = i;
                                  if(i == 0)break;
                                  printf("%d %d ",z1,z2);
                                  fprintf(fe,"%d  %d  ",z1,z2);
                                  kount++;
                          break;
                          case 1:
                                  i = ChanInInt(inchan2);
                                  z1 = i;
                                  if(i == 0)break;
                                  i = ChanInInt(inchan2);
                                  z2 = i;
                                  if(i == 0)break;
                                  printf("%d  %d  ",z1,z2);
                                  fprintf(fe,"%d  %d  ",z1,z2);
                                  kount++;
                          break;
                  }
                  if (i == 0)
                  {
                          run--;
                  }

          }
          while (run);
          printf("\n");
}

void main()
{
          Channel *c1,*c2;
```

Fig. 4-16. Continued.

```
Process *prod1,*prod2,*cons;

char datafile[80];

printf("input file name\n");
scanf("%s",datafile);
if((fe=fopen(datafile,"w"))==NULL)
{
        printf("\007ERROR! can't open file\n");
        exit(0);
}

c1 = ChanAlloc();
c2 = ChanAlloc();
prod1 = ProcAlloc(producer,WSPACE,3,1,600,c1);
prod2 = ProcAlloc(producer,WSPACE,3,2,600,c2);
cons = ProcAlloc(consumer,WSPACE,3,2,c1,c2);

printf("begin par\n");
ProcPar(prod1,prod2,cons,0);
fclose(fe);
printf("end par\n");
printf("kounter = %d\n",kount);
}
```

APPLICATIONS AND TRANSPUTERS FOR PCs

In all the above example programs I have used the transputer for virtual MIMD processing, or as an accelerator card for integer processing. The transputer is very probably the most economical way to get involved in MIMD processing. One transputer with a good cross-compiler is all that is needed. In this section I will briefly list, with a few comments, the major sources of transputers for PC users. First, however, I would like to mention a few references in which transpu-

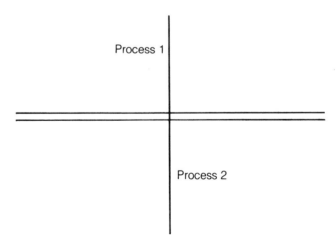

Fig. 4-17. Partitioning of space.

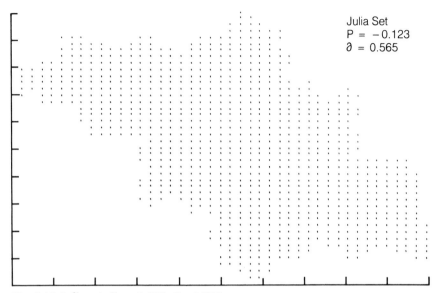

Fig. 4-18. Julia set. P = – 0.123, Q = 0.565

```
/* file reading and plotting program
        062388                                */

#include "\c\quick\include\stdio.h"
#include "\c\quick\include\graph.h"
#include "\c\quick\include\math.h"
#include "\c\quick\include\conio.h"
#include "\c\quick\include\float.h"

struct videoconfig vc;
char error_message[] = "this video mode is not suported";
float xdata[5000],ydata[5000];


main()
{

        /* declarations */
        FILE *fe;
        float t,x,y;
        char datafile[80];
        int n,kount;
        int i,j;
        float x0,y0;
        double xmax,ymax,xmin,ymin;
        char junk;
        int xmaxscreen=280,ymaxscreen=160;
        int ymaxtext=30;
        float xcoord,ycoord;
        float text[80];

        /* user input section */
        printf("input file name\n");
        scanf("%s",datafile);
        printf("input number of data pairs to be read\n");
```

Fig. 4-19. plot1.c plotted the Julia set in Fig. 4-18.

Fig. 4-19. Continued.

```
        scanf("%i",&n);


        /* set mode of screen */
        if (_setvideomode(_MRESNOCOLOR) == 0)
        {
                printf("%s\n",error_message);
                exit(0);
        }
        _getvideoconfig(&vc);
        _setcolor(1);
        _clearscreen(_GCLEARSCREEN);


        /* open file */
        if((fe=fopen(datafile,"r"))==NULL)
                {
                printf("\007ERROR! can't open file\n");
                exit();
                }

        /* file reading section & dump to array */
        for(kount=0;kount<=n;++kount)
                {
        fscanf(fe,"%f %f ",&x,&y);
        xdata[kount]=x;
        ydata[kount]=y;
        }
fclose(fe);


/* find min and max of x and y
    (tdata is set as xdata)       */
xmax= -1e+20;
xmin= -xmax;
ymax= -1e20;
ymin= -ymax;
for(i=0;i<=n;++i)
{
        if(ymin > ydata[i])
                ymin=ydata[i];
        if(ymax < ydata[i])
                ymax=ydata[i];
        if(xmax < xdata[i])
                xmax=xdata[i];
        if(xmin > xdata[i])
                xmin=xdata[i];
}

/* printf("xmin, xmax, ymin, ymax:%lf %lf %lf %lf\n",xmin,xmax,ymin,ymax)


/* draw axes */
_setviewport(20,20,300,180);
_moveto(0,0);
_lineto(0,ymaxscreen);
_moveto(0,ymaxscreen);
_lineto(xmaxscreen,ymaxscreen);
for(i=0;i<=ymaxscreen; i=i+ymaxscreen/10)
{
        _moveto(0,i);
        _lineto(5,i);
}
/* tic marks */
```

Fig. 4-19. Continued.

```
for(i=0;i<=xmaxscreen; i=i+xmaxscreen/10)
{
        _moveto(i,ymaxscreen-5);
        _lineto(i,ymaxscreen);
}
/* lables on axes */
for(i=0;i<=ymaxtext;i= i+ymaxtext/10)
{
        _settextwindow(0,0,14,20);
        _wrapon(_GWRAPOFF);
        _settextposition(i,1);
        sprintf(text,"%3.2f\n",((ymax-ymin)*i/ymaxtext));
        _outtext(text);
}


/* plot data */
for(i=0;i<=n;++i)
{
        xcoord=((xdata[i]-xmin)/(xmax-xmin))*xmaxscreen;
        ycoord=ymaxscreen-((ydata[i]-ymin)/(ymax-ymin))*ymaxscreen;
        _setpixel(xcoord,ycoord);
}


/* clear screen & return control hit enter */
while(!kbhit());
_clearscreen(_GCLEARSCREEN);
_setvideomode(_DEFAULTMODE);
```

ters were used as the primary computational machine in some areas of scientific computing.

The transputer has been discussed in a simple general paper by Walker (1985). Vaughan, et al (1987) have used a PC transputer plug-in board with one T414 transputer in the study of speech recognition. The system was programmed in OCCAM and recognized one word. It is speculated that building a massively parallel system in which each node is used for recognition of one word would be an efficient system.

The transputer point-to-point link has been discussed at length by Taylor (1986). Jesshope (1988) has discussed using transputers and switches as objects in OCCAM. Crookes, et al (1988) has discussed array processing with massive transputer networks. In addition they develop and discuss an array processing language. In Chapter 3 I discuss using a MIMD machine for Monte Carlo integration. This is an excellent application for MIMD, asynchronous processing. Askew, et al (1988) discuss using T414 transputers in a Monte Carlo simulation of physics problems. Forrest, et al (1987) discuss the use of transputer arrays to implement neural network models. These ideas will be further developed in Chapter 6.

The November 1988 issue of *BYTE* focused on parallel processing. Much of that issue has discussions about transputers. There are a fair number of distributors of transputer boards for PCs.

INMOS, in Colorado Springs, Colorado is manufacturing the transputer. They also make and sell transputer boards that plug into PCs. Their boards are compatible with IBM clones and other computers such as the S 100 bus and DEC computers.

Paracom, in West Chicago, Illinois sells transputer boards for PC/AT clones, PS2 and Mac-II computers.

Levco, in San Diego, California sells transputer cards for the Mac-II and Mac-SE. They also have neural network accelerator cards for the Mac.

Deficion Systems in Newbury Park, California has available transputer boards for the IBM clones.

Microway, in Kingstone, Massachusetts is well known for 80×87 coprocessors and accelerator boards for PCs. In addition they distribute transputer boards for PCs.

Computer System Architects in Provo, Utah, builds and sells transputer boards for IBM clones. This company offers the most cost-effective transputer boards and the most cost-effective way to begin studying MIMD parallel processing. I purchased the PART.2 system, which contains the T414-20 and includes a C cross-compiler from Logical Systems. All the programs in this chapter were written for this board.

In summary, I would like to reiterate that a transputer board is very cost-effective for parallel processing. With only one transputer on the card doing virtual parallel processing, Wilson (1988) has shown that the penalty for adding more processes is small and is even smaller for large tasks. This confirms the performance analysis I gave in Chapter 2, where I stated that it is possible to achieve almost linear speedup with massively parallel, fine-grained processing.

5

Cellular Automata as Parallel Processors

Cellular automata are discrete space-time models that can be used to model any system in the universe and they are a universe unto themselves. Cellular automata have been used to model biological systems from the level of cell activity, clusters of cells, and populations of organisms. In chemistry cellular automata have been used to model kinetics of molecular systems and crystal growth. In physics they have been used to study dynamical systems as diverse as interaction of particles and the clustering of galaxies. In computer science cellular automata have been used to model parallel processing and von Neumann machines or self-reproducing machines. A cellular automata machine could be called a universe synthesizer.

Cellular automata were invented in the late 1940s by J. von Neumann. Burks (1966) gives an excellent overview of the work by von Neumann. In cellular automata space is discretized into small units called cells or sites. The sites take on a value, typically binary, of 0 or 1. At time t, all the cells will have a specific binary value. Rules local to a specific cell determine what the binary value of that cell will be at time $t+1$. Like space, time takes on discrete values. For the last several hundred years scientists have modeled the world with differential equations. Margolus (1984), Vichniac (1984) and Toffoli (1984) have shown that cellular automata are good alternatives to differential equations.

In this chapter I discuss cellular automata as dynamical systems. By taking this approach you will see that cellular automata are parallel computers. Examples of local cellular automata rules will be given with actual computer programs to simulate them. The final, and largest, section of this chapter will discuss cellular automata machines and set the stage for Chapter 6 on artificial neural networks, which are specialized cellular automata. Much of this section is from an earlier book I wrote on dynamical systems (Rietman 1989).

ATTRACTORS AND LIMIT CYCLES

In order to discuss the dynamics of cellular automata I will introduce a program called LIFE (shown in Fig. 5-1). This program will be the framework I will use to discuss attractors, limit cycles and chaos. The game of LIFE was first introduced by John Conway who has written about it at length in a book he coauthored with Berlekanp, et al (1982). Poundstone (1985) has also discussed LIFE at length. While describing the program line-by-line, I will diverge to discuss various concepts and then return to the program description.

```
10 DEF SEG =&HB800
20 DEFINT A-Y
30 SCREEN 0,0,0
40 RANDOMIZE TIMER
50 CLS
60 DIM A(25,80),D(25,80),E(25,80),HAMMING(30)
70 REM 219 IS ASCII FOR WHITE PIXEL
80 REM 255 IS ASCII FOR BLACK PIXEL
90 FOR I%=0 TO 24
100 FOR J%=0 TO 79
110 Z=RND(1)
120 IF Z<.1   THEN POKE I%*160+J%*2,219 ELSE POKE I%*160+J%*2,255
130 NEXT J%
140 NEXT I%
150 WHILE CYCLE < 30
160 CYCLE=CYCLE+1
170 FOR I%=0 TO 24
180 FOR J%=0 TO 79
190 B=PEEK(I%*160+J%*2)
200 IF B=219 THEN A(I%,J%)=219 ELSE A(I%,J%)=0
210 D(I%,J%)=A(I%,J%)
220 NEXT J%
230 NEXT I%
240 'INSERT CODE HERE FOR CELLULAR AUTOMATA RULES
250 FOR I%=1 TO 23
260 FOR J%=1 TO 78
270    C=A(I%-1,J%-1)+A(I%,J%-1)+A(I%+1,J%-1)
280    C=C+A(I%-1,J%)+A(I%+1,J%)
290    C=C+A(I%-1,J%+1)+A(I%,J%+1)+A(I%+1,J%+1)
300  IF C<=219*1 THEN    POKE I%*160+J%*2,255 : E(I%,J%)=0
310  IF C=219*3 THEN    POKE I%*160+J%*2,219 : E(I%,J%)=219
320  IF C>=219*4 THEN    POKE I%*160+J%*2,255 : E(I%,J%)=0
330 IF E(I%,J%)<>D(I%,J%) THEN 340 ELSE 350
340 HAMMING(CYCLE)=HAMMING(CYCLE)+1
350 NEXT J%
360 NEXT I%
370 LPRINT CYCLE;HAMMING(CYCLE)
380 WEND
390 END
```

Fig. 5-1. LIFE demonstrates the dynamics of cellular automata.

Line 10 sets the current segment of memory to screen buffer address for an IBM XT clone. Line 20 defines integers, line 30 sets up the screen, line 40 randomizes the time, and line 50 clears the screen. After a DIM in line 60, the program begins with two nested loops starting in line 90. The screen is set up to be a grid 25×80. ASCII values are POKEd into random places in this matrix. The density of "1's" can be adjusted by the parameter Z in line 120. If Z is less than 0.1 then the density is 0.1. Before I discuss the WHILE loop in line 150 I'd like to discuss the fundamental characteristics of cellular automata. The first property is the geometry of the cell. In this program the cell is rectangular. Because the grid is 25×80 there are 2000 cells total. A two-dimensional hexagonal array is possible or even a one-dimensional array or three-dimensional array of cubic cells. Within a given array it is necessary to specify the neighborhood that each cell examines in calculating its next state as it evolves in time from t to time $t+1$. When the state of neighbors at time t determines the state of a cell at time $t+1$ it is said to be local rules. The two most common neighborhoods are the von Neumann and Moore, shown in Fig. 5-2.

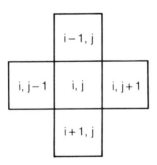

Von Neumann Neighborhood   Moore Neighborhood

Fig. 5-2. The primary neighborhoods for cellular automata.

In the von Neumann neighborhood the cell (i,j) determines its state at time $t+1$ based on the state of the four nearest neighbors. The Moore neighborhood uses the four diagonal neighbors also. The number of states per cell can be high. von Neumann found a self-replicating pattern with cells of 29 states. Codd (1968) and Langton (1984) have discussed self-reproducing automata with only seven states per cell. If k is the number of states per cell and n is the number of cells in the neighborhood then there are k^{k^n} possible rules. For a binary automata in a Moore neighborhood, where $n=8$ there are 10^{77} possible rules. The game of LIFE uses the Moore neighborhood. With 10^{77} possible rules it can model the universe.

Continuing with the program description; in line 150 a WHILE loop starts for 30 cycles. These cycles are the time steps. All the cells change in parallel, with respect to a single time step, before the next time step. These time steps, or iterations, are called *cycles* in the program. Line 160 increments the cycle by one. The FOR-NEXT loops begin in lines 170 and 180 to PEEK into the screen address and write a value to the two-dimensional arrays A and D. The loops end in line 220 and 230. The updating of each cell begins in lines 250 and 260. The actual rules are in lines 270 to 320. A variable, C, is assigned to the sum of the pixel values PEEKed and stored in the array A, as shown in Fig. 5-3.

```
270    C=A(I%-1,J%-1)+A(I%,J%-1)+A(I%+1,J%-1)
280    C=C+A(I%-1,J%)+A(I%+1,J%)
290    C=C+A(I%-1,J%+1)+A(I%,J%+1)+A(I%+1,J%+1)
300 IF C<=219*1 THEN    POKE I%*160+J%*2,255 : E(I%,J%)=0
310 IF C=219*3 THEN     POKE I%*160+J%*2,219 : E(I%,J%)=219
320 IF C>=219*4 THEN    POKE I%*160+J%*2,255 : E(I%,J%)=0
```

Fig. 5-3. The LIFE algorithm in BASIC.

This code results in summing the site value for the elements of the Moore neighborhood. For the LIFE automata game, this sum is then checked with three threshold values. If the sum is less than or equal to one, then the cell (i,j) will take a zero state at time t+1. That is, the cell will die from exposure. If the sum is equal to three then this means that the (i,j) cell has three neighbors, each with a state value of one. The cell (i,j) will then take on the value of one. In the LIFE game this is said to be a birth. Three cells generate the birth of a fourth cell. If the cell (i,j) already has a state value of one then this value is maintained. If the sum is greater than or equal to four then the cell (i,j) will take on a state value of zero at a time t+1. The cell is said to die from overcrowding. In the Moore neighborhood the maximum value the sum can obtain is eight because the cell (i,j) has eight neighbors and you are concerned only with binary states. In the von Neumann neighborhood the maximum sum value is four because there are only four neighbors. After these threshold decisions take place, an element in a small array called HAMMING(cycle) is incremented if a cell change has taken place. The element HAMMING requires some explanation.

If you are given two binary vectors of equal length:

A = (1 0 0 1 1 0)
B = (1 1 0 1 0 0)

these two vectors can be compared on a bit-by-bit basis. The number of differing bits is called the Hamming distance. For this example, the two vectors differ by two bits. So the Hamming distance is said to be two. As you would expect when the cellular automata begins its processing, or updating, at $t=1$ there are a greater number of changes than at $t=30$. Plots of the iteration time, or number of cycle updates, versus Hamming distance can show the activity of the cellular automata network. This activity relation can be thought of as a entropy. At high entropy there is a higher Hamming distance. At low entropy there is a low Hamming distance. Figure 5-4 shows a run of the program. This figure includes two limit cycles, two attractor points and three regions of high entropy. By the terminology of LIFE the two attractor points are known as *beehives* and the two limit cycles, both of period two, are known as *blinkers*. Because I wished to keep the program short and simple to discuss cellular automata, I did not consider edge effects. This causes stagnation at the edges. Some programs do a wrap around to make the screen a torus. Figures 5-5 through 5-7 show runs for three different density values. After 20 iterations, Fig. 5-5 shows three attractor points and two limit cycles. The corresponding Hamming plot for this system is shown in Fig. 5-8. Notice that after about nine iterations the Hamming distance has settled down to a constant. Figure 5-6 shows a system after 50 iterations, starting with an initial density of $Z=0.15$. There is a high degree of entropy as can be seen in the Hamming plot of Fig. 5-9. Also from Fig. 5-6 you can see some attractor points and limit cycles. Figures 5-7 and 5-10 are a system configuration after 50 iterations, and a Hamming plot for an

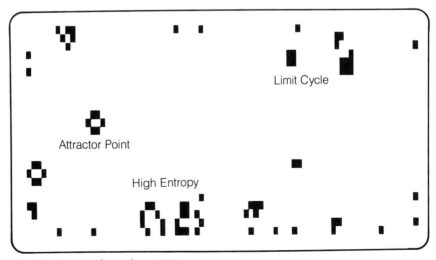

Fig. 5-4. Screen dump from LIFE.

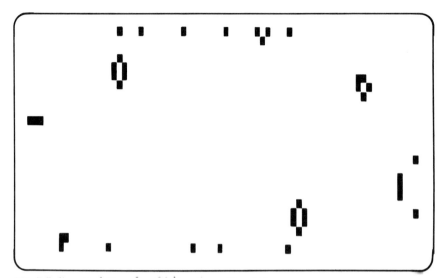

Fig. 5-5. Screen dump after 20 iterations. Z = 0.1.

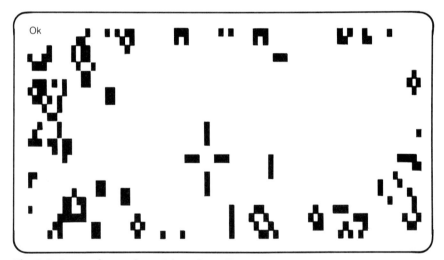

Fig. 5-6. Screen dump after 50 iterations. Z = 0.15.

initial density of $Z = 0.20$. The high entropy region can be considered to be chaos at this time in evolution, but as the system evolves the chaos gives limit cycles and attractor points.

Before closing this section and moving on to a discussion of entropy and Liapounov exponents, I would like to give a mathemati-

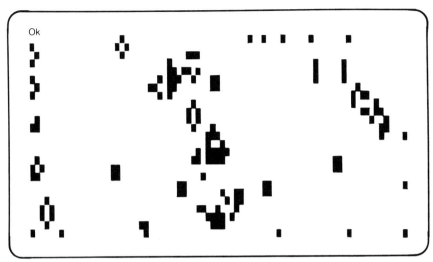

Fig. 5-7. Screen dump after 50 iterations. Z = 0.20.

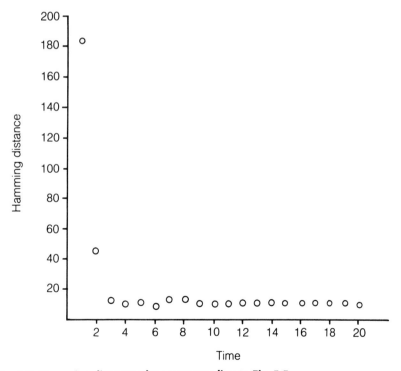

Fig. 5-8. Hamming distance plot corresponding to Fig. 5-5.

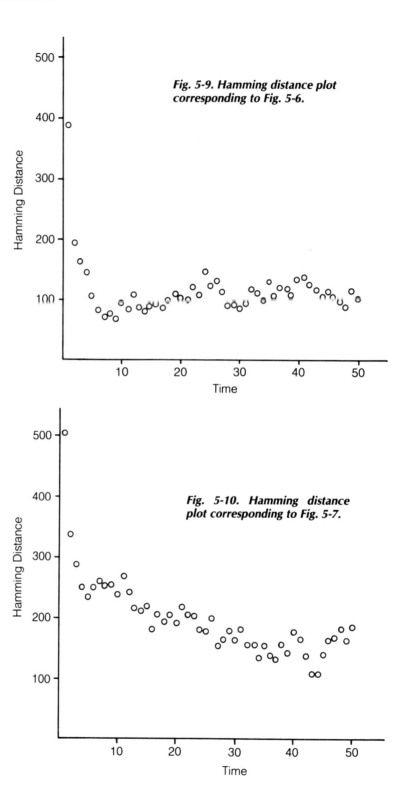

Fig. 5-9. Hamming distance plot corresponding to Fig. 5-6.

Fig. 5-10. Hamming distance plot corresponding to Fig. 5-7.

cal summary of the LIFE algorithm. The LIFE algorithm can be generalized as follows:

$$\delta(a_0, a_1, ..., a_8) = \begin{cases} 1 \text{ if} \begin{cases} a_0 = 1 \text{ and } 2 \leq \sum_{i=1}^{8} a_i < 3 \\ \text{or} \\ a_0 = 0 \text{ and } \sum_{i=1}^{8} a_i = 3 \end{cases} \\ 0 \text{ otherwise} \end{cases}$$

From this algorithm you can see how to construct other rules. Furthermore this type of algorithm and notation will be used to describe the behavior of artificial neural networks in Chapter 6. It might be interesting to change the threshold rule in this program to a random integer between one and eight to produce a stochastic rule. Another interesting experiment would be to allow different sites to follow different update rules, thus creating an inhomogenous cellular automata.

ENTROPY AND LIAPOUNOV FUNCTIONS

Cellular automata, like LIFE, show self-organization out of chaos. Fixed attractor points and limit cycles are the end result of many iterations. These self-organizing systems appear to violate the Second Law of thermodynamics. They actually circumvent this law the same way other dynamical systems such as strange attractors do, by shrinking in time the volume element of the phase space. The dynamics are irreversible in time. Any given configuration can have a large number of paths that lead to this one configuration. Symmetric structures often arise as a result of irreversibility, and symmetric structures can have symmetric and asymmetric parents.

A negative Liapounov exponent is a measure of the rate of convergence of different initial conditions toward a common attractor or fixed point. You can measure the amount of merging in a binary system by:

$$S^{(N)}(t) = -\sum_{x=0}^{2^{n-1}} P^{(N)}(X,t) \log P^{(N)}(X,x)$$

In this expression $p^{(N)}(X,t)$ is the probability that a configuration $X = (x_1, x_2, ..., x_N)$ is reached at time t and N is the number of sites. This relation is also the definition of entropy. The synchronous parallel updating makes this a decreasing function in time:

$$S^{(N)}(t+1) \leq S^{(N)}(t)$$

In order to discuss the Liapounov exponent in more detail I will first introduce the classes of cellular automata. Wolfram (1983, 1985) has done extensive analysis of one-dimensional cellular automata and has discovered four classes of cellular automata. All four classifications are based on the limiting configuration after many iterations. In the first class all sites ultimately attain the same value. In the second class, simple stable or periodic separated structures are formed. The LIFE rules are an example of this class. In the third class chaotic patterns are formed, such as strange attractors. In the fourth class complex localized structures are formed.

The sensitive dependence on initial conditions can easily be observed. Start with a randomly chosen initial configuration and let the system evolve for a large number of iterations, say M iterations, and observe the resulting configurations. Now go back to the same random initial configuration and change one cell and let the system evolve for M iterations again. Class I automata will show no effect. Class II automata might show very small effect confined to a small region near the site of the change. Class III automata will show a large effect, just as you would expect for a strange attractor. Class IV automata are so rare and unpredictable that the best way to predict the outcome is to allow the cellular automata to compute the final state.

All of Wolfram's analysis was based on one-dimensional cellular automata. His rules for one-dimensional cellular automata are as follows: Each binary cell assumes one of two values at each iteration. The output state is a binary digit, which is determined by previous states of three binary digits. The rule might be thought of as a three-input binary logic gate. Because there are eight possible input combinations, there are $2^8 = 256$ possible iteration rules. Each rule might be expressed as an eight-digit binary number. From these 256 rules Wolfram deduced 32 legal rules. A legal rule is one which is reflection-symmetric and under which the state containing all zeros is stable. This eliminates many systems. These 32 legal rules he has studied intensively for $k = 2$ and $r = 1,2,3$ where K is the number of states per site—in other words, binary cells with the range r, as the number of nearest neighbors. Wolfram's results are summarized in Table 5-1, which shows the fraction of legal cellular automata in each of the four basic classes. You can clearly see that class four is very rare.

Strange attractors have a positive Liapounov exponent, and limit

Table 5-1.

Class of Automata	k=2 r=1	k=2 r=2	k=2 r=3	k=3 r=1
I	0.50	0.25	0.09	0.12
II	0.25	0.16	0.11	0.19
III	0.25	0.53	0.73	0.60
IV	0.00	0.06	0.06	0.07

cycles have a zero exponent. Packard (1985) has calculated the Liapounov exponents for most of the legal rules of Wolfram's one-dimensional cellular automata. Packard has found that all class I and II cellular automata have a zero Liapounov exponent. Class III automata have a positive Liapounov exponent, as you would expect for strange attractors. Some of the class III cellular automata Liapounov exponents are given in Table 5-2.

All class III cellular automata have a positive Liapounov exponent for all initial conditions.

Table 5-2.	**Class III Rule**	**Liapounov Exponent**
	90	1.0
	18	0.99
	193	0.5
	86	0.98
	22	0.82

REVERSIBLE CELLULAR AUTOMATA

A reversible cellular automata can be followed in reverse, after M time steps, to its initial configuration. Margolus (1984) has studied reversible cellular automata and Fredkin and Toffoli (1982) have studied reversible logic. Any cellular automata can be described by the relation:

$$S_{i,t+1} = f(S_{i,t})$$

where $S_{i,t+1}$ is the state of cell i at time $t+1$ and $f(S_{i,t})$ is a function of the cells in the neighborhood of i at time t. Given the relation:

$$S_{t+1} = f(S_t) + S_{t-1}$$

The function will be reversible when:

$$S_{t-1} = f(S_t) - S_{t+1}$$

any function, f that follows this relation will be reversible.

Now look at a program that follows Fredkin logic. The program FREDKIN, shown in Fig. 5-11, is a modification of the program LIFE. Only the cellular automata rules have been changed. In the Fredkin cellular automata, a cell will be on in the next iteration if and only if one or three of its four von Neumann neighbors are presently on. If zero or two of its neighbors are on, the cell will be off in the next generation. This logical rule gives rise to self-reproducing cellular automata. When you run the program FREDKIN you will see the center cell has a state value of one. This cell will continue to reproduce as shown in Fig. 5-12.

Notice that at even times the cells in state one are not touching at their corners whereas at odd times they are. This even/odd time result is a result of the even/odd rules for the state of the cellular automata.

Another related cellular automata program is CELL 1, shown in Fig. 5-13. This program uses bit graphics rather than POKE and PEEK graphics, and is therefore much faster. The cellular automata rules for this program are random at each iteration. The program starts with the

```
10 DEF SEG =&HB800
15 DEFINT A-Y
20 SCREEN 0,0,0
30 CLS
40 DIM A(25,80),B(25,80)
50 REM 219 IS ASCII FOR WHITE PIXEL
60 REM 255 IS ASCII FOR BLACK PIXEL
70 FOR I%=0 TO 24
80 FOR J%=0 TO 79
100 IF I%=12 AND J%=40 THEN POKE I%*160+J%*2,219 ELSE POKE I%*160+J%*2,255
120   POKE  I%*160+J%*2+1,10
140 NEXT J%
150 NEXT I%
160 FOR I%=0 TO 24
170 FOR J%=0 TO 79
180 B=PEEK(I%*160+J%*2)
190 IF B=219 THEN A(I%,J%)=219 ELSE A(I%,J%)=0
210 NEXT J%
211 NEXT I%
215 'INSERT CODE HERE FOR CELLULAR AUTOMATA RULES
220 FOR I%=1 TO 23
230 FOR J%=1 TO 78
260    C=A(I%,J%-1)
270    C=C+A(I%-1,J%)+A(I%+1,J%)
280    C=C+A(I%,J%+1)
292  IF C=219 OR C=219*3 THEN POKE I%*160+J%*2,219 ELSE POKE I%*160+J%*2,255
300 POKE I%*160+J%*2+1,10
400 NEXT J%
401 NEXT I%
402 CYCLE = CYCLE + 1
450 GOTO 160
1000 END
```

Fig. 5-11. FREDKIN is a modification of LIFE from Fig. 5-1.

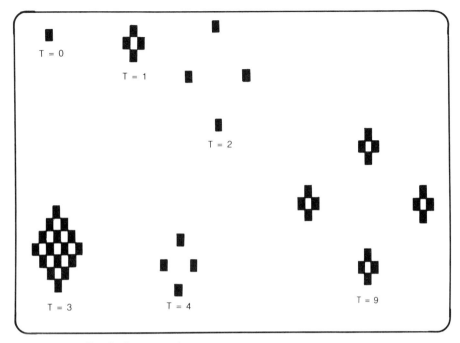

Fig. 5-12. Fredkin logic screen dumps.

Fig. 5-13. CELL1 uses poke and peek graphics.

```
10 KEY OFF
20 CLS
30 CLEAR
40 DEFINT A-Z
50 SCREEN 1
60 P=8000
70 DIM A(P)
80 PSET(1,1)
90 GET (1,1)-(318,198),A
100 XI=SGN(RND-.5)
110 YI=SGN(RND-.5)
120 PUT(1+XI,1+YI),A
130 GOTO 90
```

upper-left corner cell active. The cellular automata rules, even though they are random, give rise to a reasonable degree of self-generation as can be seen in Fig. 5-14. This figure, after scores of iterations, shows self-reproduction on the advancing front. In the next section I will discuss the fractal nature of cellular automata.

LATTICE ANIMALS AND FRACTALS

In this section I discuss what is known as stochastic models of cluster growth. With cellular automata rules that are appropriate, clusters and aggregates evolve after many iterations. These cluster models have applications in modeling the formation of microparticles such as

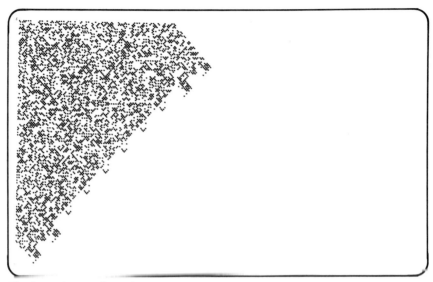

Fig. 5-14. Screen dump from program CELL1.

metallic aggregates, soot and smoke. They also can be used in model-ing two-phase flow or *percolation* and electric discharge in solids. Vannimenus et al (1985), have shown that many clusters formed from very small particles do not behave like ordinary matter. In these micro clusters the density goes to zero as the size increases. The only way for this to happen is if cluster growth is fractal. The number N of the constituent particles and the size of the clusters R is given by the scal-ing law:

$$N \approx AR^D$$

where D is the fractal dimension. If D is less than the space dimen-sion, then the average density goes to zero for large N. This particle growth can be modeled with cellular automata and the fractal dimen-sion can be deduced.

There are several types of aggregation models. One class, called *lattice animals*, consists of all types of connected graphs. Growing animals, or Eden models, are a second class. These are called growing animals because new particles are added at random on the boundary sites. If particles are allowed to diffuse randomly before sticking to the growing cluster or leaving to infinity, the model is called *diffusion-limited-aggregation* (DLA). Another type of cluster is clustering of clusters, like the formation of galactic superclusters. Vannimenus, et al (1985) have calculated the fractal dimension for these four models of cluster growth. Their results are summarized in Table 5-3.

Table 5-3.

d	Lattice Animals	Eden Model	Diffusion	Superclusters
2	1.56	2	1.7	1.4
3	2	3	2.4	
4	2.4		3.3	

The results in Table 5-3 show that the effects of kinetic growth significantly modify the fractal dimension.

Another interesting class of cluster growth is directed clusters, or directed aggregation. The program DIRECT, shown in Fig. 5-15, was written from a simple modification of the program LIFE. This program has the simple cellular automata rule that if one of the upper or lower nearest neighbors to cell i has a state value of one at time t then cell i will have a state value of one at time $t+1$. Figure 5-16 shows a run of this program after 28 iterations. The simulation started with a random initial configuration. The self-organization behavior of this cellular automata is very evident. This could be called a directed lat-

```
10 DEF SEG =&HB800
20 DEFINT A-Y
30 SCREEN 0,0,0
40 RANDOMIZE TIMER
50 CLS
60 DIM A(25,80),D(25,80),E(25,80),HAMMING(30)
70 REM 219 IS ASCII FOR WHITE PIXEL
80 REM 255 IS ASCII FOR BLACK PIXEL
90 FOR I%=0 TO 24
100 FOR J%=0 TO 79
110 Z=RND(1)
120 IF Z<.1   THEN POKE I%*160+J%*2,219 ELSE POKE I%*160+J%*2,255
130 NEXT J%
140 NEXT I%
150 WHILE CYCLE < 1000
160 CYCLE=CYCLE+1
170 FOR I%=0 TO 24
180 FOR J%=0 TO 79
190 B=PEEK(I%*160+J%*2)
200 IF B=219 THEN A(I%,J%)=219 ELSE A(I%,J%)=0
210 D(I%,J%)=A(I%,J%)
220 NEXT J%
230 NEXT I%
240 'INSERT CODE HERE FOR CELLULAR AUTOMATA RULES
250 FOR I%=1 TO 23
260 FOR J%=1 TO 78
270 IF A(I%-1,J%)=219 OR A(I%+1,J%)=219 THEN 280 ELSE 290
280 POKE I%*160+J%*2,219
285 GOTO 350
290 POKE I%*160+J%*2,255
350 NEXT J%
360 NEXT I%
380 WEND
390 END
```

Fig. 5-15. DIRECT is another simple modification of LIFE.

Fig. 5-16. Screen dump from the program DIRECT.

tice animal cellular automata. Although the program LIFE does not consider boundary effects and it is slow, its major advantage is that is is easy to modify, as the previous examples show, to study other cellular automata rules.

OTHER CELLULAR AUTOMATA PROGRAMS (*.c)

The following section discusses programs written in C and includes special graphics for IBM clones. The first program, poke.c, shown in Fig. 5-17, is a simple program to explore peek and poke type graphics on the PC using C. A far pointer at address 0XB8000000 is declared for the graphics address. Nested for( ) loops are then implemented to poke a value in the far addresses. This program was used to develop life4.c, shown in Fig. 5-18, which is a straightforward C version of life.bas. It produces very low resolution graphics and does not consider edge effects.

The next program, life4hr4.c, shown in Fig. 5-19, uses high-resolution graphics and includes edge effects. On a 10MHz XT-clone with

```
#include <stdio.h>
#include <stdlib.h>

void main()
{
        unsigned char far *a;
        int i,j,counter=0;
        int address;
        a = (char far *) 0xb8000000;
        for(;;)
        {
                counter = 0;
                for(i=1;i<24;i++)
                {
                        for(j=2;j<159;j++)
                        {


                                address = counter;
                                *(a + address) = 88;
                                counter++;
                        }
                }
                if(kbhit())
                {
                        printf("%d ",address);
                        exit(0);
                }
        }
}
```

Fig. 5-17. poke.c merely explores peek and poke graphics.

```
/* life simulation */

#include "\c\quick\include\stdio.h"
#include "\c\quick\include\stdlib.h"

static unsigned short int am[25][160];

FILE *fe;

void main()
{
        /* declarations */
        unsigned char far *a;
        unsigned short int b;
        int i,j,x,y,counter,sigma,address;
                        /* counter is used in address decoding */
        int cycle = 0;
        int seed;

        a = (unsigned char far *) 0xb8000000;

        /* user input */
        printf("input random seed \n");
        scanf("%d",&seed);

        /* clear graphics memory */
        counter = 0;
        for(x=0;x<25;x++)
```

Fig. 5-18. life4.c is a straightforward version of LIFE.BAS from Fig. 5-1.

Fig. 5-18. Continued.

```
{
        for(y=0;y<160;y++)
        {
                *(a + counter) = 0;
                counter ++;
        }
}


/* poke (random) */
counter = 0;
for(x=0;x<25;x++)
{
        for(y=0;y<160;y++)
        {
                if(rand()/32767.0 < 0.5)
                {
                        *(a + counter) = 255;
                }
                counter ++;
        }
}

/* begin life iterations */
for(;;)
{
        if(kbhit())
        {
                exit(0);
        }
/* peek to fill matrix */
counter = 0;
for(i=1;i<24;i++)
{
        for(j=2;j<159;j++)
        {
                address = i*160 + j;
                b = *(a + address);
                am[i][j] = b;
                counter = counter + 1;
        }
}

/* cellular automata rules for life */
counter = 0;
for(i=1;i<24;i++)
{
        for(j=2;j<159;j++)
        {
                sigma = am[i-1][j-1]+am[i][j-1]+am[i+1][j-1];
                sigma = sigma + am[i-1][j] + am[i+1][j];
                sigma = sigma + am[i-1][j+1] + am[i][j+1] + am[i
                counter = counter + 1;
                address = i*160 + j;
                if(sigma<=255*1)
                {
                        *(a + address) = 0;
                }
                if(sigma==255*3)
                {
                        *(a + address) = 255;
                }
                if(sigma>=255*4)
                {
```

Fig. 5-18. Continued.

```
                                                        *(a + address) = 0;
                                          }
                                }
                        }
                }
        }
}
```

```
#include <float.h>
#include <stdio.h>
#include <graph.h>
#include <math.h>

unsigned short int huge am[320][200];
unsigned short int huge newam[320][200];

struct videoconfig vc;
char error_message[] = "this video mode is not suported";

void main()
{
        /* declarations */
        int i,j,k;
        int sigma;
        int xmaxscreen=320,ymaxscreen=200;
        int xcoord,ycoord;
        double rnd;


        /* set mode of screen */
        if (_setvideomode(_MRESNOCOLOR) == 0)
        {
                printf("%s\n",error_message);
                exit(0);
        }
        _getvideoconfig(&vc);
        _clearscreen(_GCLEARSCREEN);


        _setviewport(0,0,320,200);


        /* load array */
        for(j=0;j<200;++j)
        {
                for(i=0;i<320;i++)
                {
                        rnd = rand()/32767.0;
                        if(rnd<0.4)
                        {
                                am[i][j] = 1;
                                _setcolor(1);
                        }
                        else
                        {
                                am[i][j] = 0;
                                _setcolor(0);
                        }
                        _setpixel(i,j);
                }
```

Fig. 5-19. life4hr4.c uses high-resolution graphics.

Fig. 5-19. Continued.

```
        }

        /* cellular automata rules */
        for(k=0;k<99;k++)
        {
                /* read array */
        for(j=0;j<200;j++)
        {
                for(i=0;i<320;i++)
                {
                        sigma = am[(i%320)-1][(j%200)-1]+
                                am[i%320][(j%200)-1]+
                                am[(i%320)+1][(j%200)-1];
                        sigma = sigma + am[(i%320)-1][j%200]+
                                am[(i%320)+1][j%200];
                        sigma = sigma + am[(i%320)-1][(j%200)+1]+
                                am[i%320][(j%200)+1]+
                                am[(i%320)+1][(j%200)+1];
                        if(sigma<=1)
                        {
                                newam[i%320][j%200] = 0;
                        }
                        if(sigma==3)
                        {
                                newam[i%320][j%200] = 1;
                        }
                        if(sigma>=4)
                        {
                                newam[i%320][j%200] = 0;
                        }
                }
        }

        /* set new values */
        for(j=0;j<200;j++)
        {
                for(i=0;i<320;i++)
                {
                        if(newam[i%320][j%200]==1)
                        {
                                am[i%320][j%200] = 1;
                                _setcolor(1);
                        }
                        if(newam[i%320][j%200]==0)
                        {
                                am[i%320][j%200] = 0;
                                _setcolor(0);
                        }
                        _setpixel(i,j);
                }
        }

        }

        /* clear screen & return control hit enter */
        while(!kbhit());
        _clearscreen(_GCLEARSCREEN);
        _setvideomode(_DEFAULTMODE);


}
```

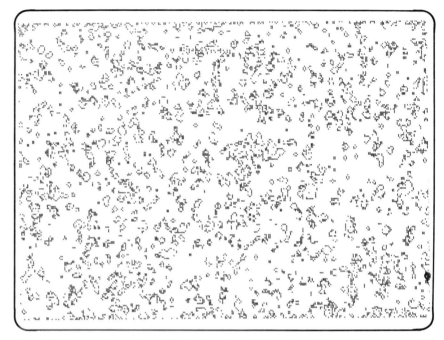

Fig. 5-20. Screen dump from life4hr4.c after 30 iterations. Edge effects not considered.

a pipelined V30 processor, each iteration in this program takes about 38 seconds. On a 10MHz 286 each iteration takes about 12 seconds. The program is quite straightforward and heavily commented. After declarations and setup of the screen graphics, then the initial screen is drawn with 40% of the screen filled with 1's and 60% with 0's. The cellular automata rules for the life simulation then begin and the new values are set. Figure 5-20 is a screen dump of a life simulation in which edge effects were not considered. This figure should be compared with Fig. 5-21. In this case the same number of iterations and same seed were used, but edge effects were considered. (The mod operator, %, in C allows you to wrap the arrays around for edge effect elimination.) Figure 5-22 is a screen dump of the life4hr4.c program after 100 iterations. Typical attractors and limit cycles can be seen in this figure.

The next program, fractal.c, shown in Fig. 5-23, creates fractal flakes resembling the growth of salt crystals (also similar to the Sierpinski carpet). The program was built up from life4hr4.c with appropriate changes to the cellular automata rules. In words, the rule for this is that a cell turns on only if it sees exactly one live cell among its eight neighbors, and will remain unchanged otherwise. Figure 5-24 is a screen dump of a run of this program with 0.1% of the cells ON for

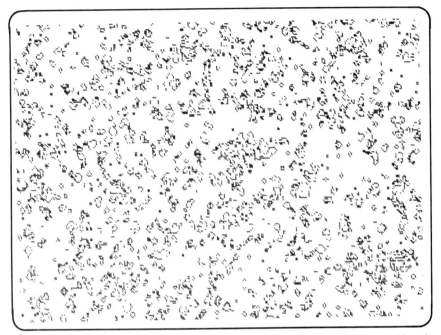

Fig. 5-21. Screen dump from life4hr4.c after 30 iterations. Edge effects considered.

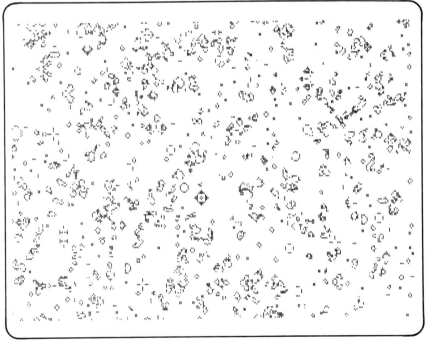

Fig. 5-22. LIFE after 100 iterations.

```
#include <float.h>
#include <stdio.h>
#include <graph.h>
#include <math.h>

unsigned short int huge am[320][200];
unsigned short int huge newam[320][200];

struct videoconfig vc;
char error_message[] = "this video mode is not suported";

void main()
{

        /* declarations */
        int i,j,k;
        int sigma;
        int xmaxscreen=320,ymaxscreen=200;
        int xcoord,ycoord;
        double rnd;


        /* set mode of screen */
        if (_setvideomode(_MRESNOCOLOR) == 0)
        {
                printf("%s\n",error_message);
                exit(0);
        }
        _getvideoconfig(&vc);
        _clearscreen(_GCLEARSCREEN);


        _setviewport(0,0,320,200);


        /* load array */
        for(j=0;j<200;++j)
        {
                for(i=0;i<320;i++)
                {
                        rnd = rand()/32767.0;
                        if(rnd<0.001)
                        {
                                am[i][j] = 1;
                                _setcolor(1);
                        }
                        else
                        {
                                am[i][j] = 0;
                                _setcolor(0);
                        }
                        _setpixel(i,j);
                }
        }

        /* cellular automata rules */
        for(k=0;k<10;k++)
        {
                /* read array */
        for(j=0;j<200;j++)
        {
                for(i=0;i<320;i++)
                {
```

Fig. 5-23. fractal.c creates fractal flakes.

Fig. 5-23. Continued.

```
                              sigma = am[(i%320)-1][(j%200)-1]+
                                      am[i%320][(j%200)-1]+
                                      am[(i%320)+1][(j%200)-1];
                              sigma = sigma + am[(i%320)-1][j%200]+
                                      am[(i%320)+1][j%200];
                              sigma = sigma + am[(i%320)-1][(j%200)+1]+
                                      am[i%320][(j%200)+1]+
                                      am[(i%320)+1][(j%200)+1];
                              if(sigma==1)
                              {
                                      newam[i%320][j%200] = 1;
                              }
                              else
                              {
                                      newam[i%320][j%200] = am[i%320][j%200];
                              }
                      }
              }

              /* set new values */
              for(j=0;j<200;j++)
              {
                      for(i=0;i<320;i++)
                      {
                              if(newam[i%320][j%200]==1)
                              {
                                      am[i%320][j%200] = 1;
                                      _setcolor(1);
                              }
                              else
                              {
                                      am[i%320][j%200] = newam[i%320][j%200];
                                      _setcolor(am[i%320][j%200]);
                              }
                              _setpixel(i,j);
                      }
              }

      }

      /* clear screen & return control hit enter */
      while(!kbhit());
      _clearscreen(_GCLEARSCREEN);
      _setvideomode(_DEFAULTMODE);



}
```

the initial condition. After 10 iterations these beautiful fractal flakes form on the screen. The program, fractal1.c, shown in Fig. 5-25, starts with a single seed in the center of the screen and then grows one big fractal. Figure 5-26 is a screen dump after 50 iterations.

The last C program is banks2.c, shown in Fig. 5-27. This program models the cellular automata developed by Banks and discussed by Toffoli and Margolus (1987). Banks was attempting to develop models of robots performing a computational task. The resulting cel-

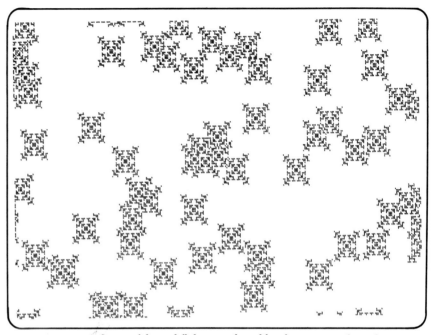

Fig. 5-24. Screen dump of fractal flakes produced by the program fractal1.c.

```
#include <float.h>
#include <stdio.h>
#include <graph.h>
#include <math.h>

unsigned short int huge am[320][200];
unsigned short int huge newam[320][200];

struct videoconfig vc;
char error_message[] = "this video mode is not suported";

void main()
{

        /* declarations */
        int i,j,k;
        int sigma;
        int xmaxscreen=320,ymaxscreen=200;
        int xcoord,ycoord;
        double rnd;


        /* set mode of screen */
        if (_setvideomode(_MRESNOCOLOR) == 0)
        {
                printf("%s\n",error_message);
                exit(0);
        }
        _getvideoconfig(&vc);
        _clearscreen(_GCLEARSCREEN);
```

Fig. 5-25. fractal1.c starts with a simple seed in the center of the screen.

Fig. 5-25. Continued.

```
_setviewport(0,0,320,200);


/* load array */
for(j=0;j<200;++j)
{
        for(i=0;i<320;i++)
        {
                if((i==160) && (j==100))
                {
                        am[i][j] = 1;
                        _setcolor(1);
                }
                else
                {
                        am[i][j] = 0;
                        _setcolor(0);
                }
                _setpixel(i,j);
        }
}

/* cellular automata rules */
for(k=0;k<50;k++)
{
        /* read array */
        for(j=1;j<199;j++)
{
        for(i=1;i<319;i++)
        {
                sigma = am[i-1][j-1]+
                        am[i][j-1]+
                        am[i+1][j-1];
                sigma = sigma + am[i-1][j]+
                        am[i+1][j];
                sigma = sigma + am[i-1][j+1]+
                        am[i][j+1]+
                        am[i+1][j+1];
                if(sigma==1)
                {
                        newam[i][j] = 1;
                }
                else
                {
                        newam[i][j] = am[i][j];
                }
        }
}

/* set new values */
for(j=1;j<199;j++)
{
        for(i=1;i<319;i++)
        {
                if(newam[i][j]==1)
                {
                        am[i][j] = 1;
                        _setcolor(1);
                }
                else
                {
                        am[i][j] = newam[i][j];
                        _setcolor(am[i][j]);
                }
        }
```

Fig. 5-25. Continued.

```
                            _setpixel(i,j);
                            }
                    }

            }

        /* clear screen & return control hit enter */
        while(!kbhit());
        _clearscreen(_GCLEARSCREEN);
        _setvideomode(_DEFAULTMODE);



    }
```

---

lular automata universe is rich enough to construct universal computers. Furthermore, by starting from a random initial condition small computational systems will self-organize. This cellular automata universe provides materials and devices for computer construction. The program banks2.c is a straightforward adaptation of life4hr4.c. The rules have been changed as follows. The cellular automata involves the von Neumann neighborhood. If a cell is ON and has two neighbors ON, it will be OFF in the next iteration. If a cell is OFF and has three or four neighbors ON it will be ON in the next iteration. All other conditions will result in no change in the cell. Starting with a random configuration of 55% ON, after 40 iterations the system will almost be settled down to only limit cycles. These limit cycles have periods of up to 16 and can generate small pulses that travel down wires in the cellular automata universe. Figure 5-28 is a screen dump

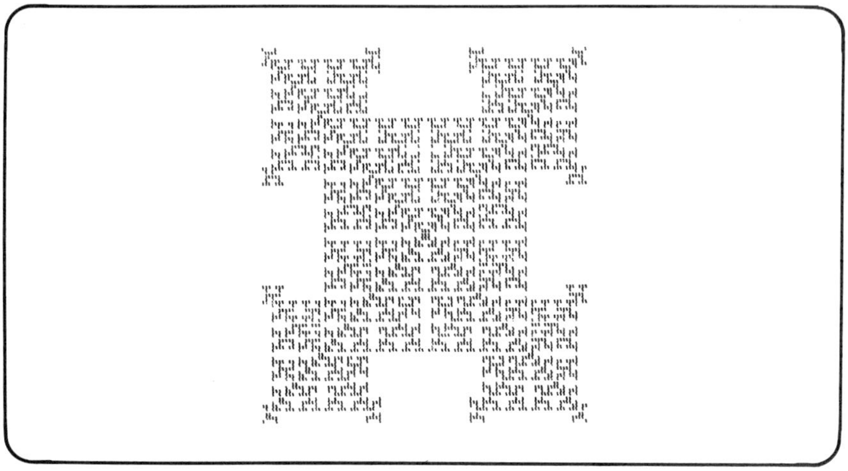

Fig. 5-26. Large fractal produced by fractal1.c.

```
#include <float.h>
#include <stdio.h>
#include <graph.h>
#include <math.h>

unsigned short int huge am[320][200];
unsigned short int huge newam[320][200];

struct videoconfig vc;
char error_message[] = "this video mode is not suported";

void main()
{
        /* declarations */
        int i,j,k;
        int sigma;
        int xmaxscreen=320,ymaxscreen=200;
        int xcoord,ycoord;
        double rnd;


        /* set mode of screen */
        if (_setvideomode(_MRESNOCOLOR) == 0)
        {
                printf("%s\n",error_message);
                exit(0);
        }
        _getvideoconfig(&vc);
        _clearscreen(_GCLEARSCREEN);


        _setviewport(0,0,320,200);


        /* load array */
        for(j=0;j<200;++j)
        {
                for(i=0;i<320;i++)
                {
                        rnd = rand()/32767.0;
                        if(rnd<0.55)
                        {
                                am[i][j] = 1;
                                _setcolor(1);
                        }
                        else
                        {
                                am[i][j] = 0;
                                _setcolor(0);
                        }
                        _setpixel(i,j);
                }
        }

        /* cellular automata rules */
        for(k=0;k<50;k++)
        {
                /* read array */
        for(j=0;j<200;j++)
        {
                for(i=0;i<320;i++)
                {
```

Fig.5-27. banks2.c models Banks' cellular automata.

Fig. 5-27. Continued.

```
sigma = am[i%320][(j%200)-1];
sigma = sigma + am[(i%320)-1][j%200]+
        am[(i%320)+1][j%200];
sigma = sigma + am[i%320][(j%200)+1];
        /* the following line takes care
                    of all the cases not covered
                    bellow */
newam[i%320][j%200] = am[i%320][j%200];

if((sigma==2)&(am[i%320][j%320]==1))
{
        newam[i%320][j%200] = 0;
}
if((sigma==3)&(am[i%320][j%200]==0))
{
        newam[i%320][j%200] = 1;
}
if((sigma==4)&(am[i%320][j%200]==0))
{
        newam[i%320][j%200] = 1;
}
        }
    }

    /* set new values */
    for(j=0;j<200;j++)
    {
            for(i=0;i<320;i++)
            {
                    am[i][j] = newam[i][j];
                    _setcolor(am[i][j]);
                    _setpixel(i,j);
            }
    }

 }
/* clear screen & return control hit enter */
while(!kbhit());
_clearscreen(_GCLEARSCREEN);
_setvideomode(_DEFAULTMODE);



}
```

of this condition. The traveling pulses can best be seen in a high-speed cellular automata machine similar to that discussed in the next section.

CELLULAR AUTOMATA COMPUTERS AND MACHINES

In the above sections I have gone into some detail on complex dynamics of systems—in particular cellular automata. Computers are almost always used for information processing. Dynamical systems are excellent information processing systems, and cellular automata are an excellent way of modeling complex systems. Furthermore, in

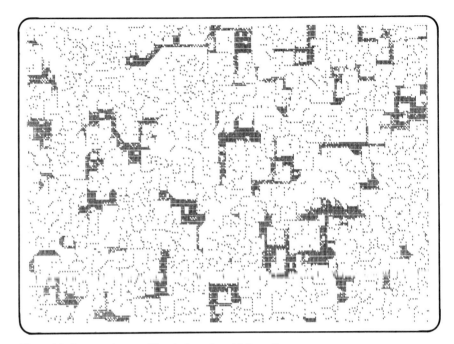

Fig. 5-28. Screen dump of banks2.c after 40 iterations.

order to make use of cellular automata for information processing, it is necessary to understand the dynamics of complex systems.

As I stated earlier, a cellular automata is essentially a parallel processing computing unit. The initial condition is the data input, the cellular automata rules are the program, and the final configuration is the computed result. Each iteration is a clock cycle. The parallel processing can be synchronous or asynchronous depending on the updating procedure during each iteration. However, this is a rather abstract computer. The more conventional computer made from AND, OR, and NOT gates can also be simulated with a cellular automata such as the program banks2.c. Berlekaup, et al (1982), Poundstone (1985) and Dewdney (1985) have given excellent descriptions of how to construct a computer with the LIFE algorithm. Poundstone (1985) has given great detail on the construction starting from simple logic gates and building up to a computer that can reproduce itself. These self-reproducing computers are called von Neumann machines.

Several other cellular automata computers have been described in the literature. Margolus (1984) has described a billiard ball model based on reversible cellular automata, and Carter (1984) has described molecular-scale computers built on the principles of molecular engineering and cellular automata.

Toffoli (1984) was tired of watching slow cellular automata evolve on a computer screen, and decided to build a special-purpose cellular automata machine. The entire unit consists of a black box with some logic boards interfaced to a VIC-20 computer and a color monitor. Later Toffoli and Margolus (1987) described extensive research they have conducted with a cellular automata machine that plugs into an IBM-PC clone. The rest of this chapter is a discussion of that PC board.

The cellular automata board, hereinafter called the CAM-6, is available from AUTOMATRIX (Box 196, Rexford, NY 12148) and from SYSTEM CONCEPTS in San Francisco; and I recommend this board for the serious cellular automata hacker. With this board, however, I had many problems. First the board is PC compatible. However, my computer is not a true XT clone. There are some changes in the bus structure, and the indigenous monitor is not PC compatible at all. I attempted to disable the PAL chip on the monitor drive board and install a STB EGA card. In addition, I installed a bus correction board from W. ALLEN ASSOCIATES in Cupertino CA. and tested the system out with a new NEC multisync monitor. The CAM-6 was still not compatible. I then tried the board in every type of AT&T (80×86) computer. After consultation with one of the codevelopers of the CAM-6 and engineers, I realized I would need a different computer. The board is not compatible with my computer, AT&T Olivetti or Xerox computers. The board is not compatible with Samsung 386 systems, but is compatible with Wise 286 and cheap noname brand clones. I purchased a mail order cheap noname brand clone but it only lasted two weeks and the power supply smoked (caveat emptor). I settled on a Tandy 3000 which is a 286 system. Tandy offers a complete line of computers and they have never orphaned a system. The Model I and Model III are still supported by Tandy. Furthermore the systems are built very rugged so experimenters can get inside and attach other boards to use the system for experimentation. All this effort was worth it, however. The CAM-6 allows one to do cellular automata simulations much faster than a Cray computer. If you have many simulations to run and each takes several hours, the time adds up quickly. Now, I'll get into the board discussion and the language for communication.

The language for communication with the CAM-6 is FORTH. A FORTH interpreter is included with the system, and a FORTH tutorial is in the Appendix of the book by Toffoli and Margolus (1987). An excellent introduction to FORTH is given by Brodie (1987), but the tutorial by Toffoli and Margolus is quite adequate and you should not have to resort to other FORTH books.

Now examine two FORTH programs designed for operation on the CAM-6. The first program FOO.EXP, shown in Fig. 5-29, will reproduce the fractal experiments from the programs fractal.c and fractal1.c. This will draw a screen-size fractal in about 2 seconds. The 286 machine will do the same in about 1 hour. The first line of the program is a comment, then the line NEW-EXPERIMENT is used to initialize the hardware. N/MOORE indicates that the Moore neighborhood will be used. The program then continues with a routine called 8SUM. This is used to sum the neighbors of the cell under consideration. The next section of the program is FOO which is the equivalent of the cellular automata rules section of the C program. The last section of the program MAKE-TABLE FOO essentially compiles the program and sends it to the look-up tables for the CAM-6 hardware.

```
1 LIST
Scr # 1              C:FOO.EXP
  0 \ FOO (fractal expt)                              10oct89cam
  1
  2 NEW-EXPERIMENT
  3
  4 N/MOORE
  5
  6 N.WEST NORTH N.EAST
  7 WEST              EAST
  8 S.WEST SOUTH S.EAST
  9       + + + + + +       ;
 10                         : FOO
 11 8SUM 1 = IF
 12       1 ELSE
 13 CENTER THEN
 14        >PLNO            ;
 15
 ok
2 LIST
Scr # 2             C:FOO.EXP
  0                         : ECHO
  1 CENTER >PLN1    ;
  2 MAKE-TABLE ECHO
  3 MAKE-TABLE FOO
  4
  5
  6
  7
  8
  9
 10
 11
 12
 13
 14
 15
 ok
```

Fig. 5-29. FOO.EXP reproduces the fractal experiments from fractal.c and fractal1.c on the CAM-6.

A second program, the equivalent of banks.c, is FOO1.EXP, shown in Fig. 5-30. This program allows you to see the signals and pulses in the self-organized logic systems.

```
1 LIST
Scr # 1              C:FOO1.EXP
  0 \ FOO1 (bank's experiment)                           11Oct89cam
  1 NEW-EXPERIMENT
  2 N/VONN
  3                                      : U
  4                         CENTER ;
  5                                      : CORNER?
  6 NORTH SOUTH = IF U ELSE 0 THEN ;
  7                                      : BANKS
  8     NORTH SOUTH WEST EAST + + +
  9      ( U U CORNER? 1 1 ) >PLNO;
 10
 11
 12 MAKE-TABLE BANKS
 13
 14
 15
ok
```

Fig. 5-30. FOO1.EXP is the FORTH equivalent of banks.c for the CAM-6.

The real beauty of this board is its speed (pipelined architecture and look-up hardware tables). You can easily simulate a different cellular automata universe every few seconds with 100 or more iterations in each universe. For the von Neumann neighborhood there are five neighbors; each can have one of two states. That means that there are over four billion rules or possible cellular automata universes that can be visited. For the Moore neighborhood there are over 2^{512} worlds to visit.

I spent about one hour visiting several hundred von Neumann worlds and discovered several very interesting ones. The cellular automata rules for a von Neumann world can be represented as a 32-bit number. Figure 5-31 is a table, similar to that in Toffoli and Margolus's book, showing the allowed states for the neighbors.

State	C_{New}	State	C_{New}	State	C_{New}	State	C_{New}
00000		01000		10000		11000	
00001		01001		10001		11001	
00010		01010		10010		11010	
00011		01011		10011		11011	
00100		01100		10100		11100	
00101		01101		10101		11101	
00110		01110		10110		11110	
00111		01111		10111		11111	

Fig. 5-31. State table for von Neumann neighborhood.

The blanks are the new states for the center cell. Each of these boxes can take only one bit—a zero or a one. There are four boxes per row in the table and if you represent this as a hexadecimal number then you have an eight-digit hexadecimal number for the code to represent the cellular automata rules. I discovered four interesting worlds represented by the rules:

2A64F988—This resulted in drifting objects for random initial conditions with <72% filled cells.

22D07513—This resulted in drifting objects and attractors with periods of 16.

2F08FA6C—This resulted in self-organizing systems that underwent catastrophies. The initial conditions must be >2% and <97% of the cells filled.

A120CFED—At a minimum of 3% fractal trees start to grow. At the ends of the branches there are limit cycles of period 16.

CONCLUSIONS

Cellular automata are large arrays of finite state machines. Each cell or finite state machine is limited in its ability as a computing device. However, massive arrays of these cells or automata can be used for computation. The collective behavior of these parallel machines can result in useful computation.

I haven't spent nearly as much time discussing the CAM-6 as I have the other boards in this book because it is a more special-purpose board. Furthermore, the documentation that comes with the board is very well-written. I recommend the board for serious cellular automata hackers.

The cellular automata machine (CAM) can be purchased from:

Automatrix
Department C
P.O. Box 196
Rexford, NY 12148-0196

6

Neural Network Processing: Massively Parallel Sixth-Generation Computers

In this chapter I discuss neural network processing and massively parallel sixth-generation computers. Neural network processing is significantly different from binary information processing in that it is a non-token processing paradigm. Token processing is information processing by manipulation of little objects known as bits. This gives rise to digital processing. Neural networks are massively parallel analog processors. In this chapter I will discuss the fundamentals of neural network processing and I will review several neural network software packages commercially available. These allow you to simulate neural networks on the PC. For a review on how to build neural network hardware from analog processors I recommend my earlier book: *Experiments in Artificial Neural Networks*.

THRESHOLD LOGIC AND NON-LINEAR SYSTEMS

The human brain is a massive parallel personal computer based on organic threshold logic devices. These logic devices are known as *neurons*. A neuron is sketched in Fig. 6-1.

The cell body has an output line called the *axon*. The input lines are called *dendrites*. There are about 1000 dendrite connections to an average neuron in the human brain. The neurons are interconnected by a *synapse*. A neuron can have both excitatory and inhibitory connections. An *excitatory* connection tells the neuron to fire and an *inhibitory* connection tells a neuron to not fire. The input signals are summed in the neuron. At a certain threshold level the neuron will fire and below this level not fire. This is diagrammed in Fig. 6-2.

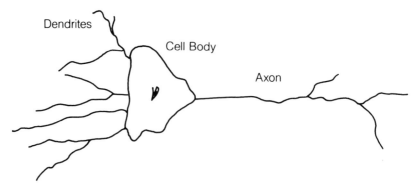

Fig. 6-1. Schematic of a biological neuron.

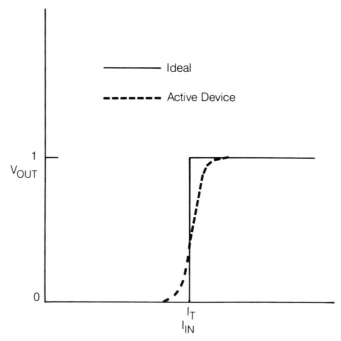

Fig. 6-2. Threshold logic device transfer curve. Solid curve is ideal device and dotted curve is active, real device.

If the sum of the input signal I_{in} is less than I_t, threshold, then V_{out} goes low, logic 0. If the sum of input signal I_{in} is above threshold I_t, then V_{out} goes high, logic 1. This idea can be represented algebraically as follows:

$$V_{out} = \begin{cases} 1 \\ 0 \end{cases} \text{if } I_{in} \begin{matrix} > \\ < \end{matrix} \begin{matrix} I_t \\ I_t \end{matrix}$$

Software implementation of this idea is presented later in this chapter.

This model is a little naive, because the synapse connections to the inputs of the threshold logic device have not been considered. In hardware implementation of threshold logic circuits, the synapse is a resistive interconnection between logic devices. A less naive model in algebraic terms is given below.

$$V_{out} = \begin{cases} 1 & \text{if } \sum_{j \neq i} W_{ij}V_j \begin{array}{c} > I_t \\ < I_t \end{array} \\ 0 \end{cases}$$

In this relation the V_j is the input signal to neuron j and W_j is the conductance of the connection between the ith and j^{th} neuron. Each threshold logic unit randomly and asynchronously computes whether it is above or below threshold and readjusts accordingly. Therefore a network of these threshold logic units is a parallel computer, but it is not a token processor.

This parallel computer can be used in optimization problems, and content addressable memories. The content addressable memory implementation of these parallel computation circuits is discussed at length in this chapter. Later I discuss how to teach a neural network and explore other learning paradigms.

The information storage algorithm for content addressable memories, discussed in this chapter, is called the Hebb learning rule. A memory state is given as a binary vector. In a binary vector all the elements are either 1 or 0. The outer product of this memory vector with its transpose gives a storage matrix. Taking an example: The ASCII code for the letter A is given by the standard binary representation (0 1 0 0 0 0 0 1). The outer product of this eight-dimensional binary vector with its transpose is given below.

$$\begin{bmatrix} 0 \\ 1 \\ 0 \\ 0 \\ 0 \\ 0 \\ 0 \\ 1 \end{bmatrix} [0\ 1\ 0\ 0\ 0\ 0\ 0\ 1] = \begin{bmatrix} 0 & 0 & 0 & 0 & 0 & 0 & 0 & 0 \\ 0 & 1 & 0 & 0 & 0 & 0 & 0 & 1 \\ 0 & 0 & 0 & 0 & 0 & 0 & 0 & 0 \\ 0 & 0 & 0 & 0 & 0 & 0 & 0 & 0 \\ 0 & 0 & 0 & 0 & 0 & 0 & 0 & 0 \\ 0 & 0 & 0 & 0 & 0 & 0 & 0 & 0 \\ 0 & 0 & 0 & 0 & 0 & 0 & 0 & 0 \\ 0 & 1 & 0 & 0 & 0 & 0 & 0 & 1 \end{bmatrix}$$

This storage algorithm can be represented in algebraic terms as

$$W = m^t m \qquad (W = 0 \text{ if } W < 0)$$

W is the information storage matrix, m is the memory vector and m^t is the transpose of vector m.

This model does not consider an important point. The elements W_{ii} should be set to zero. Hopfield (1982, 1984) and McEliece, et al (1985), have shown that if W_{ii} is not zero then the hardware implementation of the model can result in chaotic oscillations. The correct algebraic relation is

$$W = m^t\, m - I_n$$

Where I_n is the n × n identity matrix. So the storage algorithm consists of the outer product of the memory vector with itself, except that 0's are placed on the diagonal. Below is an example using the ASCII code for the letter Z:

$$
\begin{bmatrix} 0 \\ 1 \\ 0 \\ 1 \\ 1 \\ 0 \\ 1 \\ 0 \end{bmatrix}
[0\ 1\ 0\ 1\ 1\ 0\ 1\ 0] =
\begin{bmatrix}
0 & 0 & 0 & 0 & 0 & 0 & 0 & 0 \\
0 & 0 & 0 & 1 & 1 & 0 & 1 & 0 \\
0 & 0 & 0 & 0 & 0 & 0 & 0 & 0 \\
0 & 1 & 0 & 0 & 1 & 0 & 1 & 0 \\
0 & 1 & 0 & 1 & 0 & 0 & 1 & 0 \\
0 & 0 & 0 & 0 & 0 & 0 & 0 & 0 \\
0 & 1 & 0 & 1 & 1 & 0 & 0 & 0 \\
0 & 0 & 0 & 0 & 0 & 0 & 0 & 0
\end{bmatrix}
$$

Hopfield (1982, 1984) has shown that the storage matrix must be symmetric, $W_{ij} = W_{ji}$, that $W_{ii} = 0$ and the matrix must be dilute. That is, there must be a smaller number of 1's than 0's in the matrix. Notice the lines drawn in the matrix. This shows at a glance the symmetric nature of the matrix.

To show how this storage matrix can produce the correct memory state, an eight-dimensional binary vector with bit errors—when multiplied by this storage matrix to give the inner product—will generate the correct memory state. The number of bit errors cannot be too great, but a partial memory will certainly work to give the complete memory state. (The correct memory state is known as an *eigenvector*.) For example:

$$
\begin{bmatrix}
0 & 0 & 0 & 0 & 0 & 0 & 0 & 0 \\
0 & 0 & 0 & 1 & 1 & 0 & 1 & 0 \\
0 & 0 & 0 & 0 & 0 & 0 & 0 & 0 \\
0 & 1 & 0 & 0 & 1 & 0 & 1 & 0 \\
0 & 1 & 0 & 1 & 0 & 0 & 1 & 0 \\
0 & 0 & 0 & 0 & 0 & 0 & 0 & 0 \\
0 & 1 & 0 & 1 & 1 & 0 & 0 & 0 \\
0 & 0 & 0 & 0 & 0 & 0 & 0 & 0
\end{bmatrix}
\begin{bmatrix} 0 \\ 1 \\ 0 \\ 0 \\ 1 \\ 0 \\ 0 \\ 1 \end{bmatrix}
=
\begin{bmatrix} 0 \\ 1 \\ 0 \\ 1 \\ 1 \\ 0 \\ 1 \\ 0 \end{bmatrix}
$$

The number of bit errors is called the *Hamming* distance. Given the two vectors

v = (0 1 0 0 1 0 0 1)
u = (0 1 0 1 1 0 1 0)

the Hamming distance in this example is, 3. Only vectors of equal dimensionality can be compared.

Hopfield (1982, 1984) has shown that if the matrix is symmetric and dilute with $W_{ii} = 0$, and if you define the dimension of the matrix as n then m memories can be stored—where m = 0.15n. Table 6-1 is a list of the number of memories for a given matrix size.

Table 6-1.

Memories	Neurons (matrix size)
1	8
2	16
3	24
4	32
6	40

Notice in the table the actual number of memories has been rounded down to the nearest whole number. It doesn't make sense to store a fraction of a memory state.

All of this can be expressed more formally to assist in writing code for a digital computer simulation.

The Hebb rule is used to determine the values of the W matrix. This is a vector outer product rule.

$$W_{ij} = \begin{cases} 1 & \text{if } \sum_{\text{bits}} V^s{}_i U^s{}_j > 0 \\ 0 & \text{otherwise} \end{cases}$$

This states that the element W_{ij} is found by summing the outer product of the input vector element j and output vector element i. It is a simple outerproduct of these vectors. The W_{ij} element is then found by summing the W_i matrices. In other words the outer product of the input vector U_s and the output vector v^s results in a matrix W^s. The elements of the final W matrix are found by summing the W^s matrices.

$$W = \sum_{S=1}^{\text{all states}} W^s$$

The sum is over all memory states. Each memory produces one matrix. The total memory matrix is the sum of these matrices. Hopfield (1982, 1984), has shown that if:

$$W_{ii} = 0 \quad \text{and} \quad W_{ij} = W_{ji}$$

then stable states will exist and the network will not oscillate chaotically.

Given the W matrix, then the matrix vector product—the inner product of this W with u^s, the input vector state—will result in the output vector v^s.

$$v^s = W\, u^s \qquad \text{state} \quad s$$

The elements of this vector v^s are given by:

$$v^s_i = \sum_{j=1}^{N} W_{ij} u_j^s$$

What this says is that the output vector element v_i is given by the sum of the products of elements $W_{ij}u_j$ summed over all j. For example:

$$W = \begin{bmatrix} W_{11} & W_{12} & W_{13} \\ W_{21} & W_{22} & W_{23} \\ W_{31} & W_{32} & W_{33} \end{bmatrix}$$

$$u_s = [u_1^s u_2^s u_3^s]$$

then

$$v_s = \begin{bmatrix} W_{11} & W_{12} & W_{13} \\ W_{21} & W_{22} & W_{23} \\ W_{31} & W_{32} & W_{33} \end{bmatrix} \begin{bmatrix} u_1^s \\ u_2^s \\ u_3^s \end{bmatrix} = \begin{bmatrix} v_1^s \\ v_2^s \\ v_3^s \end{bmatrix}$$

$$v_1^s = W_{11}u_1^s + W_{12}u_2^s + W_{13}u_3^s$$

$$v_2^s = W_{21}u_1^s + W_{22}u_2^s + W_{23}u_3^s$$

$$v_3^s = W_{31}u_1^s + W_{32}u_2^s + W_{33}u_3^s$$

This output vector should include a term for the information input, bias and noise. If these terms are added together to give one term I_i, then you get:

$$v_i = \sum_j W_{ij} u_j + I_i$$

The actual vector is given by

$$v_i = \begin{cases} 1 & \text{if} \quad \sum_j W_{ij}\, u_j + I_i < I_t \\ 0 & \text{otherwise} \end{cases}$$

where I_t is threshold (see Fig. 6-2) and W_{ij} is the conductance of the connection between threshold logic units i and j. In other words, W_{ij} is the synaptic strength.

The energy corresponding to the stable states, as given by Hopfield (1982, 1984), is:

$$E = -\frac{1}{2} \sum_{i=1}^{N} \sum_{j=1}^{N} W_{ij}\, v_i\, v_j$$

where $W_{ij} = W_{ji}$ and $W_{ii} = 0$.

Goles and Vichniac (1986) write this equation in a form which clearly shows how to calculate the energy function.

$$E = -\frac{1}{2} \sum_{i=1}^{N} v_i^{t+1} \sum_{j=1}^{N} W_{ij} v_j^{t}$$

CONTENT-ADDRESSABLE MEMORIES AND ENERGY CALCULATIONS——

When the inner product between a vector and a matrix is found, a vector is generated. If the starting vector doesn't differ too much from the stored memory state in the matrix, then the resulting vector is the correct memory state. This has obvious applications as a content-addressable memory.

Some examples might make this more clear. Figure 6-3a shows a partial memory state for the complete memory state of Fig. 6-3b. If the partial memory state is digitized and operated on by an appropriate memory matrix, then the correct memory is generated or recalled.

Taking another example: Fig. 6-4a shows a partial spectral pattern. In this partial memory state no fine structure is observed, but

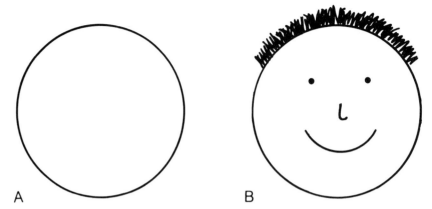

Fig. 6-3. Partial memory state; Complete memory state.

when this spectrum is digitized and operated on by the appropriate storage matrix then the spectrum of Fig. 6-4b is recalled or generated.

This memory recall often happens to people, also. You see a person in the distance with lime-green socks but other details are not clear. Then you recall your friend had lime-green socks. This produces in your mind the entire picture of your friend. Further examples of content-addressable memory are easy to conceive. Looking in a tool box you might see only five percent of a wrench handle because the rest of the wrench is hidden by the other tools, but this is enough of a pattern for you to recognize it as the wrench you need.

The first step in an algorithm for content-addressing is to find the inner product of a vector and a matrix.

$$v^s = Tu^s$$

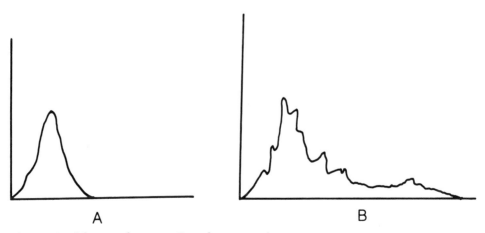

Fig. 6-4. Partial spectral pattern; Complete spectral pattern.

The connection strength matrix T is given by:

$$T = \begin{bmatrix} T_{11}\ T_{12} \dots T_{1N} \\ T_{21}\ T_{22} \dots T_{2N} \\ \cdot \\ \cdot \\ \cdot \\ T_{i1}\ T_{i2} \dots T_{NN} \end{bmatrix}$$

It was shown earlier that the elements of the resulting vector from the inner product of T with vector u is:

$$v_i^s = \sum_{j=1}^{N} T_{ij} u_j^s$$

It was further shown that the diagonal elements of the T matrix must be zero, and the matrix should be symmetric and dilute.

The program NEURON4P, shown in Fig. 6-5, implements these ideas and calculates the inner product of a vector with a matrix. This simple program is not too useful by itself; but it will be used to build other programs. A simplified flow diagram of the program logic is shown in Fig. 6-6.

```
10 CLS
20 INPUT "INPUT RANDOM SEED ";SEED
30 RANDOMIZE SEED
40 INPUT "ENTER THE NUMBER OF NEURONS (100 MAXIMUM) ";N
50 INPUT "INPUT THE THRESHOLD VALUE (0 TO 2 ARE REASONABLE VALUES) ";IO
60 INPUT "ENTER THE VALUE OF THE INFORMATION (0 TO 1 IS A GOOD VALUE)";INFO
70 INPUT "DO YOU WANT TO ENTER THE INPUT VECTOR YOURSELF (1/YES 0/NO)? ";VECTOR
80 INPUT "DO YOU WANT TO INPUT THE T MATRIX (1/Y 0/NO) ";MATRIX
90 DIM T(100,100),V(100),U(100)
100 REM FILL T(I,J) MATRIX
110 IF MATRIX=0 THEN 190
120 FOR I=1 TO N
130 FOR J=1 TO N
140 PRINT "T(";I;",";J;") "
150 INPUT T(I,J)
160 NEXT J
170 NEXT I
180 GOTO 360 : 'FILL INPUT VECTOR
190 FOR I=1 TO N
200 FOR J=I TO N
210 R=RND(1)
220 IF R<.75 THEN R=0 ELSE R=+1: REM DILUTE MATRIX
230 T(I,J)=R
240 NEXT J
250 LPRINT
```

Fig. 6-5. NEURON4P calculates the inner product of a vector with a matrix.

Fig. 6-5. Continued.

```
260 NEXT I
270 FOR I=1 TO N
280 FOR J=1 TO N
290 IF I=J THEN T(I,J)=0
300 T(J,I)=T(I,J)
310 LPRINT T(I,J);
320 NEXT J
330 LPRINT
340 NEXT I
350 LPRINT:LPRINT:LPRINT
360 REM FILL INPUT VECTOR U
370 IF VECTOR=0 THEN 430
380 FOR I=1 TO N
390 PRINT "INPUT U(";I;")"
400 INPUT U(I)
410 NEXT I
420 GOTO 470 : 'BEGIN CALCULATIONS OF OUTPUT VECTOR
430 FOR I=1 TO N
440 GOSUB 670
450 U(I)=R
460 NEXT I
470 REM BEGIN CALCULATION
480 FOR I=1 TO N
490 FOR J=1 TO N
500 SIGMA=T(I,J)*U(J)+SIGMA
510 NEXT J
520 SIGMA=SIGMA+INFO
530 IF SIGMA > IO THEN SIGMA=1 ELSE SIGMA=0
540 V(I)=SIGMA
550 SIGMA=0
560 NEXT I
570 FOR I=1 TO N
580 LPRINT U(I);
590 NEXT I
600 LPRINT:LPRINT
610 FOR I=1 TO N
620 LPRINT V(I);
630 NEXT I
640 LPRINT:LPRINT
650 LPRINT:LPRINT
660 GOTO 360
670 R=RND(1)
680 IF R<.5 THEN R=0 ELSE R=+1
690 RETURN
```

This brief flow chart shows that after the T matrix is filled then the input vector, u, is filled then the inner product is found between the T matrix and vector u. After vector v is computed, vector u and v are printed to the line printer. Then a new u vector is selected and the process starts over again.

Now examine this BASIC program in more detail. In lines 10-20 a randomized seed is entered. In most digital computers the random number generator needs a seed. Often the seed number can be generated by the timer. If the operator has control of the seed then the same random number sequence is always generated. This is convenient for testing and developing programs. In line 40 the number of neurons,

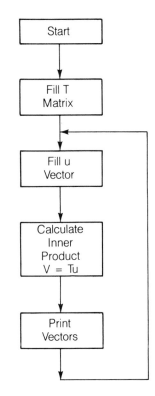

Fig. 6-6. General flow chart for program NEURONXP.BAS.

N, is entered. A maximum has been set at 100 in the DIM statement of line 90. This can be changed as desired by the user.

Continuing with the theory: Recall Fig. 6-2 defines the threshold value, I_t from the equation:

$$V_i = \begin{cases} 1 & \text{if } \sum_j T_{ij}u_j + I_{info} > I_T \\ 0 & \text{otherwise} \end{cases}$$

The output of the ith neuron is logic 1 if the sum of the products of the elements $T_{ij}u_j$ and I_{info} is greater than threshold. Otherwise the output is logic 0.

The threshold is input in line 50 as variable IO. For small networks it is sufficient to choose 0 or 1 for the threshold. This is equivalent to shifting the curve of Fig. 6-2 to the left or right. The information input to the neuron is entered in line 60. This information to the neuron can be thought of as a bias from another signal source or noise. It is simply called INFO in the program. By experimenting with the INFO and IO variable the user can get very different results.

Lines 70 and 80 ask if the user would like to enter the input vector and synapse matrix from the keyboard or else the program will select a random binary vector for input and also select a random, dilute, symmetric matrix with $T_{ii} = 0$.

Line 110 is a decision point for operator-entered T matrix or machine-generated matrix. Lines 120-170 allow the user to enter the matrix from the keyboard. Lines 190-350 are for a machine-generated matrix. A random variable R, between 0 and 1 is selected in line 210. Lines 220 dilutes the selection. If $R < 0.75$ then $R = 0$ else $R = +1$. The T_{ij} element being addressed is set equal to this R value in line 230. At the completion of line 260 the matrix is now filled and dilute. Line 270 begins a routine to diagonalize the matrix and in line 290, T_{ii} is set to zero. Line 300 symmetrizes the matrix with $T_{ij} = T_{ji}$. Finally in line 310 the matrix is printed out to the line printer.

In line 360 the process to fill the input vector, u, is started. If the operator chooses to enter the vector from the keyboard then lines 380-410 are executed; otherwise the machine selects a random binary vector in lines 430-460. This routine calls a subroutine, lines 670-690, to select a random number and decide if the vector element should be a 0 or 1.

In line 470 the calculation of the inner product of the input vector and the T matrix is started. In line 500 the variable named SIGMA is assigned to the result of this calculation. To this SIGMA value is added the INFO value in line 520. Finally in line 530, SIGMA is compared with the threshold value IO and set equal to 0 or 1, depending on results. This final result becomes output vector element v_i. After the v vector is filled by calculation, the u vector and v vector are sent to the line printer in lines 580 and 620. In line 660 the process continues by selecting a new input vector u. The program will end only by a Break.

Now that this program has been discussed in detail you can move on to other programs. Table 6-2 summarizes the programs and their differences. These will be explained in a little more detail below.

The next program to be examined is NEURON5P, shown in Fig. 6-7. With this program you can see the effects of a a random dilute matrix. In line 210 the random element is chosen, and in line 220 the matrix is diluted. In this program the matrix will be more dilute than in NEURON4P. In this program if $R < 0.85$ then $R = 0$ else R is set equal to $+1$. This results in less than 15% of the elements being set to 1. In NEURON4P the dilution was 25%. The rest of this program is similar to NEURON4P.

A run of NEURON5P will produce some stable states, but it also

Table 6-2.

BASIC Program	Comments
NEURON4P	Basic program to find inner product of a vector and a matrix. $T_{ij} = T_{ji}$ and $T_{ii} = 0$
NEURON5P	Same as NEURON4P but matrix is random and a little more dilute. $T_{ij} \# T_{ji}$
NEURON6P	Iterated version of NEURON5P. Eight iterations then prints resulting vector.
NEURON8P	Includes energy calculations between each iteration.
HEBB2P	One memory vector
HEBB3P	m memory vectors

```
10 CLS
20 INPUT "INPUT RANDOM SEED ";SEED
30 RANDOMIZE SEED
40 INPUT "ENTER THE NUMBER OF NEURONS (100 MAXIMUM) ";N
50 INPUT "INPUT THE THRESHOLD VALUE (0 TO 2 ARE REASONABLE VALUES) ";IO
60 INPUT "ENTER THE VALUE OF THE INFORMATION (0 TO 1 IS A GOOD VALUE ) ";INFO
70 INPUT "DO YOU WANT TO ENTER THE INPUT VECTOR YOURSELF (1/YES 0/NO)? ";VECTOR
80 INPUT "DO YOU WANT TO INPUT THE T MATRIX (1/Y 0/NO) ";MATRIX
90 DIM T(100,100),V(100),U(100)
100 REM FILL T(I,J) MATRIX
110 IF MATRIX=0 THEN 190
120 FOR I=1 TO N
130 FOR J=1 TO N
140 PRINT "T(";I;",";J;") "
150 INPUT T(I,J)
160 NEXT J
170 NEXT I
180 GOTO 360 : 'FILL INPUT VECTOR
190 FOR I=1 TO N
200 FOR J=1 TO N
210 R=RND(1)
220 IF R<.85 THEN R=0 ELSE R=+1: REM DILUTE MATRIX
230 T(I,J)=R
240 NEXT J
250 LPRINT
260 NEXT I
270 FOR I=1 TO N
280 FOR J=1 TO N
290 IF I=J THEN T(I,J)=0
300 REM    T(J,I)=T(I,J)
310 LPRINT T(I,J);
320 NEXT J
330 LPRINT
```

Fig. 6-7. NEURON5P shows the effects of a random dilute matrix.

Fig. 6-7. Continued.

```
340 NEXT I
350 LPRINT:LPRINT:LPRINT
360 REM FILL INPUT VECTOR U
370 IF VECTOR=0 THEN 430
380 FOR I=1 TO N
390 PRINT "INPUT U(";I;")"
400 INPUT U(I)
410 NEXT I
420 GOTO 470 : 'BEGIN CALCULATIONS OF OUTPUT VECTOR
430 FOR I=1 TO N
440 GOSUB 670
450 U(I)=R
460 NEXT I
470 REM BEGIN CALCULATION
480 FOR I=1 TO N
490 FOR J=1 TO N
500 SIGMA=T(I,J)*U(J)+SIGMA
510 NEXT J
520 SIGMA=SIGMA+INFO
530 IF SIGMA > IO THEN SIGMA=1 ELSE SIGMA=0
540 V(I)=SIGMA
550 SIGMA=0
560 NEXT I
570 FOR I=1 TO N
580 LPRINT U(I);
590 NEXT I
600 LPRINT:LPRINT
610 FOR I=1 TO N
620 LPRINT V(I);
630 NEXT I
640 LPRINT:LPRINT
650 LPRINT:LPRINT
660 GOTO 360
670 R=RND(1)
680 IF R<.5 THEN R=0 ELSE R=+1
690 RETURN
```

---

produces many superfluous states. Stable states can be thought of as low points on an energy hyperplane in an n-dimensional hypercube. This will be explained more clearly later in this chapter. It is interesting to note that a run of program NEURON5P results in some spurious states. There are two problems. One is that the matrix is nonsymmetric. The second is that an iterative dynamics has not been implemented in this program. By *iterative dynamics* I mean that the results from one vector-matrix product should be sent back into the network and operated on again by the same matrix. Only by iterative operation can these massively parallel networks compute stable states. As pointed out earlier in this chapter the neurons or threshold logic processors are connected to each other through a synapse or conductance matrix. The output of a processor may be connected to the input of several other processors. Each threshold logic device sums the inputs it receives. So the signal travels around this feedback loop, but not to itself, many times in a second before the stable state is reached. Iterative dynamics has been introduced in the next program.

In NEURON6P a new variable, ITERATE, has been introduced (see Fig. 6-8). This variable is a counter in a loop that starts in line 480. The output vector forms the inner product of the input vector and the matrix is set equal to a new input vector in line 640. The inner product of this vector and the matrix is then found and the process repeated eight times. Later you will see that eight times is a few too many. Only from three to four times is needed. This program prints the matrix. Then it prints the initial input vector followed by the eighth iterated resulting vector as the output. A new initial vector is then selected and the process started over again. A run of this program is shown in Fig. 6-9. Notice you still appear to have more than one stable state. From Table 6-1 you know that for an eight-neuron circuit you can have only one stable state. This can be explained from an energy consideration. By the iterative dynamics the algorithm computes the minimal states in an n-dimensional hyperspace. By definition there will be more than one minimum on this hypersurface. In fact, all the corners of the hypercube are stable states. These do not all have the same degree of stability and might only be metastable states.

```
10 CLS
20 INPUT "INPUT RANDOM SEED ";SEED
30 RANDOMIZE SEED
40 INPUT "ENTER THE NUMBER OF NEURONS (100 MAXIMUM) ";N
50 INPUT "INPUT THE THRESHOLD VALUE (0 TO 2 ARE REASONABLE VALUES) ";IO
60 INPUT "ENTER THE VALUE OF THE INFORMATION (0 TO 1 IS A GOOD VALUE ) ";INFO
70 INPUT "DO YOU WANT TO ENTER THE INPUT VECTOR YOURSELF (1/YES 0/NO)? ";VECTOR
80 INPUT "DO YOU WANT TO INPUT THE T MATRIX (1/Y 0/NO) ";MATRIX
90 DIM T(100,100),V(100),U(100)
100 REM FILL T(I,J) MATRIX
110 IF MATRIX=0 THEN 190
120 FOR I=1 TO N
130 FOR J=1 TO N
140 PRINT "T(";I;",";J;") "
150 INPUT T(I,J)
160 NEXT J
170 NEXT I
180 GOTO 360 : 'FILL INPUT VECTOR
190 FOR I=1 TO N
200 FOR J=1 TO N
210 R=RND(1)
220 IF R<.8 THEN R=0 ELSE R=+1: REM DILUTE MATRIX
230 T(I,J)=R
240 NEXT J
250 LPRINT
260 NEXT I
270 FOR I=1 TO N
280 FOR J=1 TO N
290 IF I=J THEN T(I,J)=0
300          T(J,I)=T(I,J)
310 LPRINT T(I,J);
320 NEXT J
330 LPRINT
```

Fig. 6-8. NEURON6P introduces a new variable: ITERATE.

Fig. 6-8. Continued.

```
340 NEXT I
350 LPRINT:LPRINT:LPRINT
360 REM FILL INPUT VECTOR U
370 IF VECTOR=0 THEN 430
380 FOR I=1 TO N
390 PRINT "INPUT U(";I;")"
400 INPUT U(I)
410 NEXT I
420 GOTO 470 : 'BEGIN CALCULATIONS OF OUTPUT VECTOR
430 FOR I=1 TO N
440 GOSUB 720
450 U(I)=R
460 NEXT I
470 REM BEGIN CALCULATION
480 FOR ITERATE=1 TO 8: REM THIS ALLOWS THE OUTPUT VECTOR TO BE FEED BACK
490 FOR I=1 TO N
500 FOR J=1 TO N
510 SIGMA=T(I,J)*U(J)+SIGMA
520 NEXT J
530 SIGMA=SIGMA+INFO
540 IF SIGMA > IO THEN SIGMA=1 ELSE SIGMA=0
550 V(I)=SIGMA
560 SIGMA=0
570 NEXT I
580 IF ITERATE=1 THEN 590 ELSE 630
590 FOR I=1 TO N
600 LPRINT U(I);
610 NEXT I
620 LPRINT
630 FOR I=1 TO N
640 U(I)=V(I): REM FOR FEEDBACK
650 NEXT I
660 NEXT ITERATE
670 FOR I=1 TO N
680 LPRINT V(I);
690 NEXT I
700 LPRINT:LPRINT:LPRINT:LPRINT
710 GOTO 360
720 R=RND(1)
730 IF R<.5 THEN R=0 ELSE R=+1
740 RETURN
```

These minima are strange attractors, and although the Lorentz system shown in Fig. 6-10 (Abraham & Shaw, 1984) has two strange attracting points, they are not energy surface attracting points, but are examples of strange attractors. A convenient way of thinking about the energy surface is like a sheet of rubber being pulled in many directions, from many points on its surface. This results in a surface with hills, valleys and wells. If a small marble is dropped on this surface it will be attracted to the nearest lowest point. This point might not be the lowest point in the entire hypersurface; it is just a local minima or attractor. If the marble is kicked around hard enough it will jump out of this local minima and settle to the next. Repeating this process will result in the marble settling in the deepest basin of attraction. This is the most stable memory state of the network.

```
0 0 0 0 0 0 0 1          0 1 0 0 0 1 1 1
0 0 1 0 0 0 0 0          1 1 0 0 0 1 1 1
0 1 0 0 0 0 0 0
0 0 0 0 0 1 0 0          1 0 1 1 0 1 1 0
0 0 0 1 0 0 0 0          1 0 1 1 0 1 1 0
0 0 0 0 0 0 0 0
0 0 0 0 0 0 0 1          0 1 1 1 1 1 1 0
1 0 0 0 0 0 1 0          1 1 1 1 0 1 1 0

0 0 0 1 0 1 1 0          1 1 0 0 0 0 0 1
1 0 0 1 0 1 1 0          1 1 0 0 0 0 1 1

0 0 0 0 1 1 0 1          1 0 1 0 0 0 0 0
0 0 0 0 0 1 0 1          1 0 1 0 0 0 1 0

0 0 1 0 0 1 0 0          1 1 0 1 0 0 1 1
0 0 1 0 0 1 0 0          1 1 0 1 0 0 1 1

1 0 1 0 1 1 0 1          1 0 1 0 0 0 1 1
1 0 1 0 0 1 1 1          1 0 1 0 0 0 1 1

0 1 1 0 0 0 1 1          1 1 1 1 1 1 1 1
1 1 1 0 0 0 1 1          1 1 1 1 0 1 1 0

1 1 1 0 0 1 1 0          0 1 0 0 0 0 0 1
1 1 1 0 0 1 1 0          0 1 0 0 0 0 0 0

0 0 1 1 0 1 0 1          1 0 1 0 1 0 0 0
0 0 1 1 0 1 0 1          1 0 1 0 0 0 1 0

0 1 0 1 1 1 1 1          0 0 1 1 0 0 1 1
1 1 0 1 0 1 1 1          1 0 1 1 0 0 1 1

0 1 0 1 0 0 0 1          1 1 0 1 0 0 1 1
0 1 0 1 0 0 0 1          1 1 0 1 0 0 1 1

                         1 0 1 0 0 1 0 1
                         1 0 1 0 0 1 1 1
```

Fig. 6-9. Example run of program NEURON6P.BAS. Seed 72873, threshold 1, information 1.

The computed result shows several minima. Because of Johnson noise and other component noise in real neural network hardware circuits, you will see that only one stable state results for an eight-neuron circuit. This noise is the analogous effect of kicking the marble around till it settles in the deepest basin of attraction.

In the next program you calculate the energy after each iteration. Goles and Vichniac (1986) give the energy calculation for a Hopfield (1982, 1984) model as:

$$E\,(t) \;=\; -\frac{1}{2}\sum_{i=1}^{N} v_i^{t+1} \sum_{j=1}^{N} T_{ij} v_j^t$$

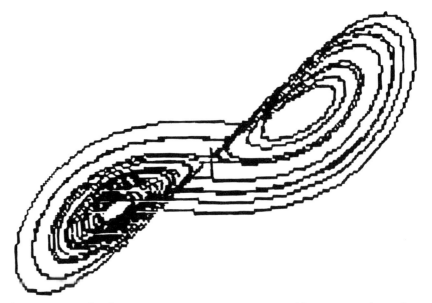

Fig. 6-10. Example of strange attractor. Lorentz curves with two attracting points.

What this algorithm says is that the inner product of vector v at time t with connection strength matrix T is multiplied with the vector v at time $t+1$. Let time t count the number of sweeps through the network and $t+1$ is the next sweep. This second multiplication is an inner product of two vectors and results in a scalar. This scalar value is proportional to the energy. From this dynamical equation it is clear that the energy reaches a minimum when:

$$v^{t+1} = v^t$$

This is clearly seen in a computer simulation. After a few iterations, usually four or less, the energy settles to a stable point. Now examine the program NEURON8P in Fig. 6-11.

The program NEURON8P introduces the new variable ENERGY. The energy calculation takes place within the ITERATE loop. The energy is set equal to zero in line 660 and calculations take place in a loop starting at 670 and ending at 690. The final energy is printed out in line 700. In line 750 the energy is set equal to zero again and the next iteration begins. Figure 6-12 shows a run of this program. After the matrix is printed the random binary vector is printed, then the resulting inner product vector and energy is printed. The program then begins the next iteration by feeding the resulting vector back into the matrix calculation.

```
10 CLS
20 INPUT "INPUT RANDOM SEED ";SEED
30 RANDOMIZE SEED
40 INPUT "ENTER THE NUMBER OF NEURONS (100 MAXIMUM) ";N
50 INPUT "INPUT THRESHOLD VALUE (0 TO 2 ARE REASONABLE VALUES) ";IO
60 INPUT "ENTER THE VALUE OF THE INFORMATION (0 TO 1 IS A GOOD VALUE ) ";INFO
70 INPUT "DO YOU WANT TO ENTER THE INPUT VECTOR YOURSELF (1/YES 0/NO)? ";VECTOR
80 INPUT "DO YOU WANT TO INPUT THE T MATRIX (1/Y 0/NO) ";MATRIX
90 DIM T(100,100),V(100),U(100)
100 REM FILL T(I,J) MATRIX
110 IF MATRIX=0 THEN 190
120 FOR I=1 TO N
130 FOR J=1 TO N
140 PRINT "T(";I;",";J;") "
150 INPUT T(I,J)
160 NEXT J
170 NEXT I
180 GOTO 360 : 'FILL INPUT VECTOR
190 FOR I=1 TO N
200 FOR J=1 TO N
210 R=RND(1)
220 IF R<.8 THEN R=0 ELSE R=+1: REM DILUTE MATRIX
230 T(I,J)=R
240 NEXT J
250 LPRINT
260 NEXT I
270 FOR I=1 TO N
280 FOR J=1 TO N
290 IF I=J THEN T(I,J)=0
300         T(J,I)=T(I,J)
310 LPRINT T(I,J);
320 NEXT J
330 LPRINT
340 NEXT I
350 LPRINT:LPRINT:LPRINT
360 REM FILL INPUT VECTOR U
370 IF VECTOR=0 THEN 430
380 FOR I=1 TO N
390 PRINT "INPUT U(";I;")"
400 INPUT U(I)
410 NEXT I
420 GOTO 470 : 'BEGIN CALCULATIONS OF OUTPUT VECTOR
430 FOR I=1 TO N
440 GOSUB 790
450 U(I)=R
460 NEXT I
470 REM BEGIN CALCULATION
480 FOR ITERATE=1 TO 8:REM THIS ALLOWS THE OUTPUT VECTOR TO BE FEED BACK
490 FOR I=1 TO N
500 FOR J=1 TO N
510 SIGMA=T(I,J)*U(J)+SIGMA
520 NEXT J
530 SIGMA=SIGMA+INFO
540 IF SIGMA > IO THEN SIGMA=1 ELSE SIGMA=0
550 V(I)=SIGMA
560 SIGMA=0
570 NEXT I
580 FOR I=1 TO N
590 LPRINT U(I);
600 NEXT I
610 LPRINT
620 FOR I=1 TO N
630 LPRINT V(I);
```

Fig. 6-11. NEURON8P introduces an energy calculation.

Fig. 6-11. Continued.

```
640 NEXT I
650 LPRINT
660 ENERGY=0
670 FOR I=1 TO N : REM ENERGY CALCULATION
680 ENERGY=ENERGY+(U(I)*V(I))
690 NEXT I
700 ENERGY=-.5*ENERGY
710 LPRINT "    ENERGY ";ENERGY:PRINT
720 FOR I=1 TO N
730 U(I)=V(I): REM FOR FEEDBACK
740 NEXT I
750 ENERGY=0
760 NEXT ITERATE
770 LPRINT:LPRINT:LPRINT:LPRINT
780 GOTO 360
790 R=RND(1)
800 IF R<.5 THEN R=0 ELSE R=+1
810 RETURN
```

Looking at Fig. 6-12 you see that, in the case of the first random binary vector, the energy has a value of −4 after the first iteration and −5.5 after the second iteration, finally settling to a stable state at −6.5 energy units. In the next two programs you will examine associative learning using the Hebb learning rule.

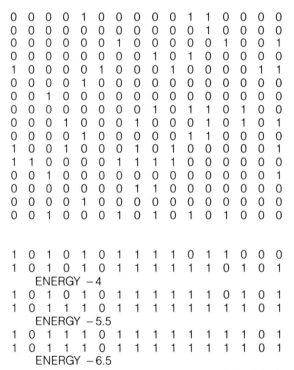

Fig. 6-12. Example run of the program NEURON8P.BAS. Seed 0, threshold 1, information 0.

Fig. 6-12. Continued.

```
1 0 1 1 1 0 1 1 1 1 1 1 1 0 1
1 0 1 1 1 0 1 1 1 1 1 1 1 0 1
    ENERGY −6.5
1 0 1 1 1 0 1 1 1 1 1 1 1 0 1
1 0 1 1 1 0 1 1 1 1 1 1 1 0 1
    ENERGY −6.5
1 0 1 1 1 0 1 1 1 1 1 1 1 0 1
1 0 1 1 1 0 1 1 1 1 1 1 1 0 1
    ENERGY −6.5
1 0 1 1 1 0 1 1 1 1 1 1 1 0 1
1 0 1 1 1 0 1 1 1 1 1 1 1 0 1
    ENERGY −6.5
1 0 1 1 1 0 1 0 1 1 0 1 0 1 1 1
1 0 1 0 1 0 1 1 1 1 1 1 0 0 1
    ENERGY −4
1 0 1 0 1 0 1 1 1 1 1 1 0 0 1
1 0 1 1 1 0 1 1 1 1 1 1 1 0 1
    ENERGY −5.5
1 0 1 1 1 0 1 1 1 1 1 1 1 0 1
1 0 1 1 1 0 1 1 1 1 1 1 1 0 1
    ENERGY −6.5
1 0 1 1 1 0 1 1 1 1 1 1 1 0 1
1 0 1 1 1 0 1 1 1 1 1 1 1 0 1
    ENERGY −6.5
1 0 1 1 1 0 1 1 1 1 1 1 1 0 1
1 0 1 1 1 0 1 1 1 1 1 1 1 0 1
    ENERGY −6.5
1 0 1 1 1 0 1 1 1 1 1 1 1 0 1
1 0 1 1 1 0 1 1 1 1 1 1 1 0 1
    ENERGY −6.5
1 0 1 1 1 0 1 1 1 1 1 1 1 0 1
1 0 1 1 1 0 1 1 1 1 1 1 1 0 1
    ENERGY −6.5
1 0 1 1 1 0 1 1 1 1 1 1 1 0 1
1 0 1 1 1 0 1 1 1 1 1 1 1 0 1
    ENERGY −6.5


1 1 0 1 1 1 0 0 1 1 0 0 0 1 0 0
0 0 0 0 1 0 0 1 1 0 1 1 0 0 0 1
    ENERGY −1
0 0 0 0 1 0 0 1 1 0 1 1 0 0 0 1
1 0 0 1 0 0 0 1 1 1 1 1 0 1 0 1
    ENERGY −2.5
1 0 0 1 0 0 0 1 1 1 1 1 0 1 0 1
1 0 0 1 1 0 0 1 1 1 1 1 0 1 0 1
    ENERGY −4.5
1 0 0 1 1 0 0 1 1 1 1 1 0 1 0 1
1 0 0 1 1 0 0 1 1 1 1 1 0 1 0 1
    ENERGY −5
1 0 0 1 1 0 0 1 1 1 1 1 0 1 0 1
1 0 0 1 1 0 0 1 1 1 1 1 0 1 0 1
    ENERGY −5
```

Fig. 6-12. Continued.
```
1 0 0 1 1 0 0 1 1 1 1 1 0 1 0 1
1 0 0 1 1 0 0 1 1 1 1 1 0 1 0 1
      ENERGY − 5
1 0 0 1 1 0 0 1 1 1 1 1 0 1 0 1
1 0 0 1 1 0 0 1 1 1 1 1 0 1 0 1
      ENERGY − 5
1 0 0 1 1 0 0 1 1 1 1 1 0 1 0 1
1 0 0 1 1 0 0 1 1 1 1 1 0 1 0 1
      ENERGY − 5
```

ASSOCIATIVE LEARNING: THE HEBB LEARNING RULE

The program HEBB2P is a basic building unit for the Hebb learning rule. The original Hebb learning rule (Hebb, 1949) was not quantitative enough to build a good model. The rule in its original version stated that if neuron A and neuron B are simultaneously excited then the synaptic connection strength between them is increased. An excellent example of associative learning in humans is when you hold a red apple in front of a baby and repeatedly say red. Synaptic connection strengths will be increased when the appropriate neurons from the optic center are simultaneously activated with those from the auditory center for the sound of the word red. Another example is Pavlov's experiments in which, after repeated trials, a dog learned to associate the sound of a bell with food. Using this learning rule you could train a simple network such as that shown in Fig. 6-13. An input vector would be presented to both the auditory and optic neurons. The appropriate synaptic connections would then be strengthened.

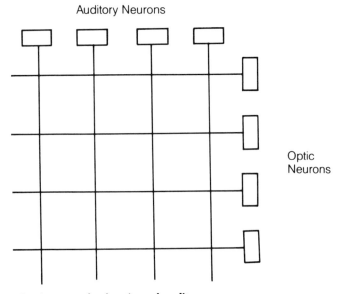

Auditory Neurons

Optic Neurons

Fig. 6-13. Simple network of optic and auditory neurons.

The appropriate synaptic connections would then be strengthened.

In digital simulations of this model, the outer product of two vectors is found to produce a synaptic connection strength matrix. This is given symbolically as:

$$W = v^t u$$

For a one-dimensional vector of length four, you would get the following matrix W.

$$u = [3\ 1\ 2\ 4]$$
$$v = [0\ 1\ 1\ 6]$$

$$W = \begin{bmatrix} 0 \\ 1 \\ 1 \\ 6 \end{bmatrix} [3\ 1\ 2\ 4] = \begin{bmatrix} 0 & 0 & 0 & 0 \\ 3 & 1 & 2 & 4 \\ 3 & 1 & 2 & 4 \\ 18 & 6 & 12 & 24 \end{bmatrix}$$

Notice I used the transpose of the vector v. Symbolically, to find an element of the matrix you write:

$$W = v_i^t u_j$$

The connection strengths are the elements of the matrix. These represent the stored memory state or states. If the storage matrix is small then only one memory state can be stored. For larger storage matrices more than one memory can be stored. In that case each memory state will generate one matrix:

$$W^s = (v^t)^s u^s \qquad \text{(state s)}$$

To store all the memories in one matrix, the matrices are added over all states:

$$W = \sum_{\text{all states}} W^s$$

Table 6-1 summarizes the number of memories versus number of neurons. In order to recover the memory state from the storage matrix, the inner product of a practical memory and the memory matrix is calculated.

Now I'll discuss the program HEBB2P, shown in Fig. 6-14. Figure 6-15 is a simplified flow diagram of the program logic. The first observation is that there is no END. In order to end, the Break key must be pressed. Another obvious fact is that only one memory state is stored in this matrix. This program will be used to develop the next program, HEBB3P, which can store m memory states for N neurons.

```
10 CLS
20 INPUT "INPUT RANDOM SEED ";SEED
30 RANDOMIZE SEED
40 INPUT "ENTER THE NUMBER OF NEURONS (100 MAXIMUM) ";N
50 INPUT "INPUT THE THRESHOLD VALUE (0 TO 2 ARE REASONABLE VALUES) ";IO
60 INPUT "ENTER THE VALUE OF THE INFORMATION (0 TO 1 IS A GOOD VALUE ) ";INFO
70 INPUT "DO YOU WANT TO ENTER THE INPUT VECTOR YOURSELF (1/YES 0/NO)? ";VECTOR
80 PRINT "BINARY MATRIX WITH Tii=0 AND Tij=Tji."
90 DIM T(100,100),V(100),U(100)
100 REM FILL T(I,J) MATRIX
110 PRINT:PRINT:PRINT
120 PRINT "INPUT THE MEMORY VECTOR FOR THE HEBB MATRIX"
130 FOR I=1 TO N
140 PRINT "V(";I;")"
150 INPUT V(I)
160 U(I)=V(I)
170 NEXT I
180 FOR I=1 TO N
190 FOR J=1 TO N
200 T(I,J)=V(I)*U(J)
210 IF I=J THEN T(I,J)=0
220 LPRINT T(I,J);
230 NEXT J
240 LPRINT
250 NEXT I
260 LPRINT:LPRINT:LPRINT
270 REM FILL INPUT VECTOR U
280 IF VECTOR=0 THEN 340
290 FOR I=1 TO N
300 PRINT "INPUT U(";I;")"
310 INPUT U(I)
320 NEXT I
330 GOTO 380 : 'BEGIN CALCULATIONS OF OUTPUT VECTOR
340 FOR I=1 TO N
350 GOSUB 630
360 U(I)=R
370 NEXT I
380 REM BEGIN CALCULATION
390 FOR ITERATE=1 TO 8: REM THIS ALLOWS THE OUTPUT VECTOR TO BE FEED BACK
400 FOR I=1 TO N
410 FOR J=1 TO N
420 SIGMA=T(I,J)*U(J)+SIGMA
430 NEXT J
440 SIGMA=SIGMA+INFO
450 IF SIGMA > IO THEN SIGMA=1 ELSE SIGMA=0
460 V(I)=SIGMA
470 SIGMA=0
480 NEXT I
490 IF ITERATE=1 THEN 500 ELSE 540
500 FOR I=1 TO N
510 LPRINT U(I);
520 NEXT I
```

Fig. 6-14. HEBB2P stores only one memory state.

Fig. 6-14. Continued.

```
530 LPRINT
540 FOR I=1 TO N
550 U(I)=V(I): REM FOR FEEDBACK
560 NEXT I
570 NEXT ITERATE
580 FOR I=1 TO N
590 LPRINT V(I);
600 NEXT I
610 LPRINT:LPRINT:LPRINT:LPRINT
620 GOTO 270
630 R=RND(1)
640 IF R<.5 THEN R=0 ELSE R=+1
650 RETURN
```

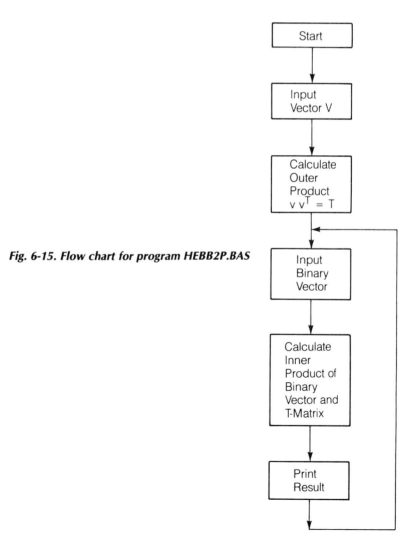

Fig. 6-15. Flow chart for program HEBB2P.BAS

Looking at the program line by line, you see that the memory state is entered in lines 130 to 170. In line 160 the transpose is found by changing the label. Beginning in line 180 the T matrix is filled by finding the outer product of the desired storage vector and its transpose. Line 210 puts 0's on the diagonal of the matrix, and line 220 prints the T matrix at the line printer. The rest of the program is exactly like earlier programs. A random binary vector is filled. Then the inner product of this vector with the T matrix is calculated. This calculation is iterated eight times, and the random vector and final product vector is printed at the line printer.

Program HEBB3P, shown in Fig. 6-16, includes a routine to allow the user to choose the number of memory states to store. This program asks the user how many neurons are to be simulated. It then asks the user how many memory states are to be stored and reminds the user that the number of memory states stored is given by:

$$m = INT(0.15N)$$

where N is the number of neurons. This equation for the number of memories is empirically derived. You can experiment with these programs and deduce more or less the same equation for number of memory states. After the user enters the first memory vector, the first T matrix is found and printed at the line printer. The next memory vector is entered and the new T matrix is printed. This new T matrix includes the sum of the T matrix for state one and state two. This continues through m memory states. Then a random binary vector is chosen or entered from the keyboard and the inner product of this vector and the summed T matrix is found and printed at the line printer along with the random vector.

```
10 CLS
20 INPUT "INPUT RANDOM SEED ";SEED
30 RANDOMIZE SEED
40 INPUT "ENTER THE NUMBER OF NEURONS (100 MAXIMUM) ";N
50 INPUT "DO YOU WANT TO ENTER THE INPUT VECTOR YOURSELF (1/YES 0/NO)? ";VECTOR
60 DIM T(100,100),V(100),U(100)
70 REM FILL T(I,J) MATRIX
80 PRINT:PRINT:PRINT
90 INPUT "INPUT THE NUMBER OF MEMORY VECTORS (M=INT(.15*N) ";M
100 FOR MEMS=1 TO M
110 PRINT "INPUT THE MEMORY VECTOR ";MEMS;"FOR THE HEBB MATRIX."
120 FOR I=1 TO N
130 PRINT "V(";I;")"
140 INPUT V(I)
150 U(I)=V(I)
160 NEXT I
170 FOR I=1 TO N
```

Fig. 6-16. HEBB3P stores any number of memory states.

Fig. 6-16. Continued.

```
180 FOR J=1 TO N
190 T(I,J)=T(I,J)+V(I)*U(J)
200 IF I=J THEN T(I,J)=0
210 IF T(I,J)>1 THEN T(I,J)=1
220 LPRINT T(I,J);
230 NEXT J
240 LPRINT
250 NEXT I
255 LPRINT:LPRINT:LPRINT:LPRINT:LPRINT
260 NEXT MEMS
270 LPRINT:LPRINT:LPRINT
280 REM FILL INPUT VECTOR U
290 IF VECTOR=0 THEN 350
300 FOR I=1 TO N
310 PRINT "INPUT U(";I;")"
320 INPUT U(I)
330 NEXT I
340 GOTO 390 : 'BEGIN CALCULATIONS OF OUTPUT VECTOR
350 FOR I=1 TO N
360 GOSUB 640
370 U(I)=R
380 NEXT I
390 REM BEGIN CALCULATION
400 FOR ITERATE=1 TO 8: REM THIS ALLOWS THE OUTPUT VECTOR TO BE FEED BACK
410 FOR I=1 TO N
420 FOR J=1 TO N
430 SIGMA=T(I,J)*U(J)+SIGMA
440 NEXT J
450 SIGMA=SIGMA
460 IF SIGMA > 0  THEN SIGMA=1 ELSE SIGMA=0
470 V(I)=SIGMA
480 SIGMA=0
490 NEXT I
500 IF ITERATE=1 THEN 510 ELSE 550
510 FOR I=1 TO N
520 LPRINT U(I);
530 NEXT I
540 LPRINT
550 FOR I=1 TO N
560 U(I)=V(I): REM FOR FEEDBACK
570 NEXT I
580 NEXT ITERATE
590 FOR I=1 TO N
600 LPRINT V(I);
610 NEXT I
620 LPRINT:LPRINT:LPRINT:LPRINT
630 GOTO 280
640 R=RND(1)
650 IF R<.5 THEN R=0 ELSE R=+1
660 RETURN
```

Figure 6-17 is a run of this program with 16 neurons and two memory states. The two states entered were:

(1 0 0 0 1 0 0 0 1 0 0 0 1 0 0 0)
(0 1 1 0 0 0 1 1 0 0 0 0 0 1 1 0)

Notice that these states did not come out from random vectors, except twice for the second vector and once for the first vector. In the other cases the Hamming distance is too great to result in a correct memory state. The end result is a stable spurious state. You can see that this same stable spurious state arises many times, indicating that it is probably a deeper energy minima than the two stored states. These spurious states can be caused by overlapping vectors in Hamming space—in other words, too many interconnections among the neurons. Some interesting programming experiments would be to include energy calculations between each iteration and see if there are in fact deeper stable states than the stored memory states. Another experiment would be a study of Hamming distance to see how far off one can be in Hamming space and still "pull in" to one of the stored states.

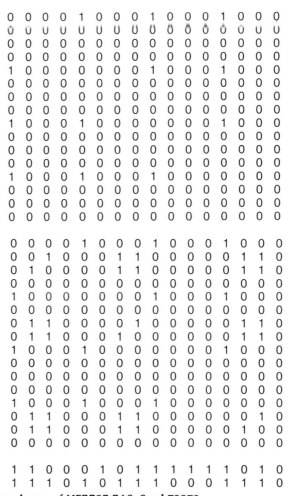

Fig. 6-17. Example run of HEBB3P.BAS. Seed 72873.

Fig. 6-17. Continued.

```
0 1 0 0 1 1 0 1 1 0 0 0 0 1 1 0
1 1 1 0 1 0 1 1 1 0 0 0 1 1 1 0

1 0 0 0 1 0 1 1 0 0 0 0 1 1 0 0
1 1 1 0 1 0 1 1 1 0 0 0 1 1 1 0

0 0 0 1 1 1 1 1 0 1 1 1 0 0 1 0
1 1 1 0 1 0 1 1 1 0 0 0 1 1 1 0

0 0 0 1 0 1 1 0 0 0 0 0 1 1 0 1
1 1 1 0 1 0 1 1 1 0 0 0 1 1 1 0

0 0 1 0 0 1 0 0 1 0 1 0 1 1 0 1
1 1 1 0 1 0 1 1 1 0 0 0 1 1 1 0

0 1 1 0 0 0 1 1 1 1 1 0 0 1 1 0
1 1 1 0 1 0 1 1 1 0 0 0 1 1 1 0

0 0 1 1 0 1 0 1 0 1 0 1 1 1 1 1
1 1 1 0 1 0 1 1 1 0 0 0 1 1 1 0

0 1 0 1 0 0 0 1 0 1 0 0 0 1 1 1
0 1 1 0 0 0 1 1 0 0 0 0 0 1 1 0

1 0 1 1 0 1 1 0 0 1 1 1 1 1 1 0
1 1 1 0 1 0 1 1 1 0 0 0 1 1 1 0

1 1 0 0 0 0 0 1 1 0 1 0 0 0 0 0
1 1 1 0 1 0 1 1 1 0 0 0 1 1 1 0

1 1 0 1 0 0 1 1 1 0 1 0 0 0 1 1
1 1 1 0 1 0 1 1 1 0 0 0 1 1 1 0

1 1 1 1 1 1 1 0 0 1 0 0 0 0 0 1
1 1 1 0 1 0 1 1 1 0 0 0 1 1 1 0

1 0 1 0 1 0 0 0 0 0 1 1 0 0 1 1
1 1 1 0 1 0 1 1 1 0 0 0 1 1 1 0

1 1 0 1 0 0 1 1 1 0 1 0 0 1 0 1
1 1 1 0 1 0 1 1 1 0 0 0 1 1 1 0

1 1 1 1 0 1 0 0 1 1 1 0 0 0 1 0
1 1 1 0 1 0 1 1 1 0 0 0 1 1 1 0

1 1 1 0 1 1 0 1 0 1 0 0 1 0 1 0
1 1 1 0 1 0 1 1 1 0 0 0 1 1 1 0

1 1 1 0 1 0 1 0 0 0 0 0 0 1 1 0
1 1 1 0 1 0 1 1 1 0 0 0 1 1 1 0

1 1 1 1 0 1 0 0 1 0 1 0 0 1 0 0
1 1 1 0 1 0 1 1 1 0 0 0 1 1 1 0
```

Fig. 6-17. Continued.

```
1 1 1 1 0 0 1 1 1 1 1 0 0 0 1 1
1 1 1 0 1 0 1 1 1 0 0 0 1 1 1 0

1 0 0 1 1 1 0 0 1 1 0 1 0 0 0 0
1 0 0 0 1 0 0 0 1 0 0 0 1 0 0 0

1 0 1 0 0 0 0 1 1 1 1 0 1 0 1 0
1 1 1 0 1 0 1 1 1 0 0 0 1 1 1 0

1 0 1 1 0 0 1 0 1 1 0 1 0 1 1 0
1 1 1 0 1 0 1 1 1 0 0 0 1 1 1 0

1 1 1 1 1 0 1 1 1 1 1 1 1 0 0 0
1 1 1 0 1 0 1 1 1 0 0 0 1 1 1 0

1 0 0 0 1 1 1 1 1 1 1 0 1 1 1 0
1 1 1 0 1 0 1 1 1 0 0 0 1 1 1 0

1 0 1 0 1 1 1 1 1 0 0 1 1 1 1 0
1 1 1 0 1 0 1 1 1 0 0 0 1 1 1 0

1 0 0 0 0 1 0 1 0 0 0 0 0 1 0 1
1 1 1 0 1 0 1 1 1 0 0 0 1 1 1 0

0 1 1 0 0 0 1 1 0 0 0 0 1 0 1 0
1 1 1 0 1 0 1 1 1 0 0 0 1 1 1 0

1 1 1 0 0 0 0 1 0 1 0 1 1 0 0 1
1 1 1 0 1 0 1 1 1 0 0 0 1 1 1 0

0 1 0 0 0 0 0 1 1 1 0 0 0 0 1 0
1 1 1 0 1 0 1 1 1 0 0 0 1 1 1 0

1 1 0 1 0 0 0 1 0 0 0 0 0 0 1 1
1 1 1 0 1 0 1 1 1 0 0 0 1 1 1 0

1 1 1 0 1 1 1 0 1 0 1 0 1 0 1 1
1 1 1 0 1 0 1 1 1 0 0 0 1 1 1 0

0 1 1 1 0 1 0 0 0 1 0 0 0 1 0 0
0 1 1 0 0 0 1 1 0 0 0 0 0 1 1 0

1 0 1 0 0 1 0 0 0 0 1 0 0 1 1 0
1 1 1 0 1 0 1 1 1 0 0 0 1 1 1 0

0 1 0 1 1 0 0 0 0 0 0 1 0 1 0 0
1 1 1 0 1 0 1 1 1 0 0 0 1 1 1 0

1 0 0 0 0 1 1 0 0 0 0 1 1 1 0 0
1 1 1 0 1 0 1 1 1 0 0 0 1 1 1 0

1 0 0 1 0 0 0 1 0 1 0 0 0 0 1 1
1 1 1 0 1 0 1 1 1 0 0 0 1 1 1 0
```

Fig. 6-17. Continued.

```
1 1 1 1 1 0 0 1 0 0 0 0 0 0 0 1
1 1 1 0 1 0 1 1 1 0 0 0 1 1 1 0

1 1 1 1 1 0 1 0 1 1 0 1 0 1 0 1
1 1 1 0 1 0 1 1 1 0 0 0 1 1 1 0

0 1 1 0 0 0 0 1 1 1 1 1 0 0 0 1
1 1 1 0 1 0 1 1 1 0 0 0 1 1 1 0

0 1 1 0 0 1 0 1 1 0 0 0 1 1 0 1
1 1 1 0 1 0 1 1 1 0 0 0 1 1 1 0

0 0 1 0 0 0 0 0 1 0 1 0 1 0 0 0
1 1 1 0 1 0 1 1 1 0 0 0 1 1 1 0

0 0 0 1 1 1 1 0 1 1 1 1 0 0 0
```

BOLTZMANN MACHINES AND STATISTICAL LEARNING————————

Boltzmann machines are neural network-like architectures with a Boltzmann statistical algorithm for updating the processing elements. Hinton and Sejnowski (1986) were early developers of the mathematical technique for Boltzmann machines. Wasserman (1989) has presented a very readable account of the method. The method is derived from Metropolis et al (1953). The Boltzmann distribution is shown in Fig. 6-18 and is given by the relation:

$$P(x) = e^{-x/kT}$$

where P(x) is the probability of change in x, k is a constant and T is an artificial temperature.

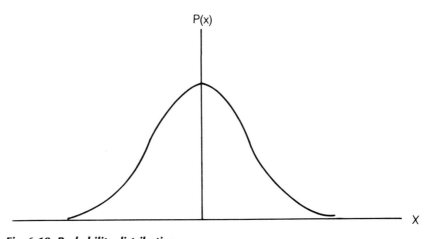

Fig. 6-18. Probability distribution.

This probability distribution is used to select the state of the neurons. In the case shown in Fig. 6-2 I wanted to approach the ideal step function for threshold logic. The Boltzmann machine output function is related to the probability. It is a function of pseudotemperature as shown in Fig. 6-19.

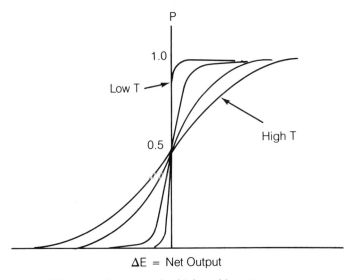

Fig. 6-19. Probability transfer curves for high and low T.

The Boltzmann updating starts a high pseudotemperature and is slowly cooled to a much lower temperature. This results in preventing the output state of the system from being confined to a local minimum in the energy space. The higher temperature acts as a noise to provide enough energy to escape from local minima. Table 6-3 is actual values for the relation

$$P(\Delta E) = \frac{1}{1 + e^{-\Delta E/T}}$$

This relation is sometimes called the *logistic* equation.

The actual plot of this data is given in Fig. 6-20. Notice that at lower temperatures the curve has a steeper slope where it crosses the P axes at P = 0.5. In actual practice a random number, r, is selected in the range:

$$0 \leq r \leq 1$$

and state selection is based on a comparison of the result of the logistic equation and the random number r. The C code in Fig. 6-21 shows how this decision is implemented in software.

Table 6-3.

T	ΔE	P
1.0	1.0	0.731
1.0	2.0	0.880
1.0	3.0	0.952
1.0	−1.0	0.269
1.0	−2.0	0.119
0.1	1.0	0.999
0.1	2.0	0.999
0.1	3.0	1.000
0.1	−1.0	4.5×10^{-5}
0.1	2.0	2.0×10^{-9}

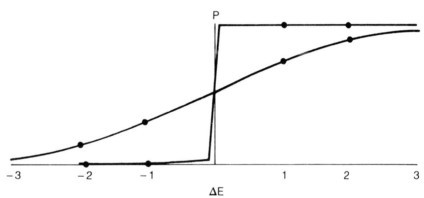

Fig. 6-20. Plot of data from Table 6-3.

```
if((r (p) && (p> 0.5))
        return(1):
else
        return(0);
```

Fig. 6-21. Random updating algorithm in C.

```
r is a random number
p = 1/(1 + exp( ΔE/T))
```

The Boltzmann machine is capable of demonstrating learning behavior. By clamping the input units to a pattern and allowing the network to go from a high temperature to a low temperature, the network can effectively learn to generate a specific output pattern for a given input pattern. For details on how to use a Boltzmann machine for learning, I recommend Wasserman (1989). To demonstrate the basic ideas of Boltzmann annealing I have written a program that is a hybrid of a Hopfield network and a Boltzmann machine.

The program tboltz9.c, shown in Fig. 6-22, is a C code program to simulate a Boltzmann updating of a Hopfield network on a T414 transputer. The code could be modified for another type of CPU. Look at each block of the code to help understand the Boltzmann method of updating a neural network.

```
/* program to simulate a boltzman update of
        a hopfield neural network
        Transputer   T414 version   11/88      */

#include   "c:\lsc\include\stdio.h"
#include   "c:\lsc\include\math.h"
#include   "c:\lsc\include\float.h"

#define RNDMAX 2147483647.0
#define DILUTIONFACTOR 0.2

static float weight[100][100];
static long int ivector[100],activation[100],oldvalue[100];
static long int tvector[100],ttvector[100];

void main()
{
        /* declarations */
        long int i,j,k,memories,updateno,ielement = 0;
        int noneurons, nomemories;
        float hightemp,lowtemp;
        float temperature;
        double logistic;
        float netinput;
        float randomnumber;
        double t,energy;
        float threshold;
        int seed;

        int rnd();
        int random();
        double expt(); /* compute exp base e */
        double loge(); /* compute log base e */

        /* user input */
        printf("input the number of neurons \n");
        scanf("%d",&noneurons);
        printf("input and threshold\n");
        scanf("%f",&threshold);
        printf("input seed \n");
        scanf("%d",&seed);

        /* number of memory states */
        nomemories= (int)(0.1*noneurons);

        /* calculate the weight matrix form the
                product of the memory vectors with their transpose */

        srand(seed);

        for(memories=0;memories<=nomemories-1;++memories)
```

Fig. 6-22. tboltz9.c simulates a Boltzmann updating of a Hopefield network.

Fig. 6-22. Continued.

```
                {
                        for(k=0;k<=noneurons-1;++k)
                        {
                                tvector[k]=(int)(rnd());   /* the memory state */
                                printf("%d ",tvector[k]);
                                ttvector[k]=tvector[k];    /* the transpose state */
                        }
                        printf("\n\n");
                        for(i=0;i<=noneurons-1;++i)      /* sum the matrices */
                        for(j=0;j<=noneurons-1;++j)
                        {
                                weight[i][j]=weight[i][j]+tvector[i]*ttvector[j]
                                if(i==j)
                                        weight[i][j]=0;
                                else
                                weight[i][j]=weight[i][j];
                        }
                }

        /* print out the final weight matrix */
        for(i=0;i<=noneurons-1;++i)
        {
                for(j=0;j<=noneurons-1;++j)
                {
                        printf("%d ",(int)(weight[i][j]));
                }
                /* printf("\n"); */
        }
        printf("\n\n");

        /* clip the matrix here -- if needed */

        /* input a vector to use as test vector */
        for(k=0;k<=noneurons-1;++k)
        {
                printf("enter the input vector element %d\n",k);
                scanf("%ld",&ielement);
                ivector[k] = ielement;
                activation[k] = ivector[k];
        }


        /* find a random vector to use as input to test the network
                ivector                                              */
/*        for(k=0;k<=noneurons-1;++k)
        {
                ivector[k]=(int)(rnd());
                activation[k]=ivector[k];
                printf("%d ",ivector[k]);
        }
        printf("\n\n");

*/

        /* begin calculation loops form high temperature to low temp.
                ovector                                              */
        temperature=10.0;
        for(t = 2; t <= 50; t = t + 2 )
        {
                /* save old value for use later in energy calculation */
                for(j=0; j<=noneurons-1;++j)
                {
                        oldvalue[j] = activation[j];
```

Fig. 6-22. Continued.

```
                              }
                              temperature = temperature/loge(1+t);
                              for(updateno = 0; updateno <= t*100.0*noneurons; updateno++)
                              {

                              /* code here for basic calculation */
                              i=(long int)(random(noneurons));
                              /* netinput for single neuron */
                              netinput=0;
                              for(j=0;j<=noneurons-1;++j)
                              {
                                      netinput += activation[j]*weight[i][j];
                              }
                              netinput = netinput - threshold;
                              /*printf("%f ",netinput);*/
                              /* end basic code here */

                              /* update algorithm here */
                              logistic=(double)(1.0/(1.0+expt(netinput,temperature)));
                              randomnumber=(double)(rand()/(double)(RNDMAX));
                              if (randomnumber > logistic)
                                      {
                                      activation[i]=1;
                                      }
                              else

                                      {
                                      activation[i]=0;
                                      }
                              if(temperature < 0.05)
                              {
                                      if(netinput == 0.0)
                                              activation[i] = 0;
                                      if(netinput == 1.0)
                                              activation[i] = 1;
                              }



                              }
                              /* energy calculation */
                              energy=0;
                              for(j=0;j<=noneurons-1;j++)
                              {
                                      energy = energy + (oldvalue[j]*activation[j]);
                              }
                              energy = -energy;
                              printf("\n");
                              for(i=0;i<=noneurons-1;i++)
                              {
                              printf("%d ",(int)(activation[i]));
                              }
                              printf("\n%lf  %lf\n\n ",temperature,energy);
                              }

}


/* return a random 0 or 1 for use in the vector generation */
int rnd()
{
        int result;
        result=rand();
        if(result<DILUTIONFACTOR*(double)(RNDMAX))
                result=1;
```

Fig. 6-22. Continued.

```
        else
                result=0;
        return(result);
}

/* return a random integer between 0 and number of neurons
        for use in random update of the network */
int random(n)
int n;
{
        int result;
        float tmp;

        tmp = rand()/RNDMAX;
        result = (int)(n * tmp);

        return(result);
}

/* claculate an exponent */
double expt(net,tem)
float net;
float tem;
{
        double answer;
        float x;

        x=-1*net/tem;

        answer = 1+x+x*x/2;
        answer = answer + x*x*x/6;
        answer = answer + x*x*x*x/24;
        answer = answer + x*x*x*x*x/120;
        answer = answer + x*x*x*x*x*x/720;
        answer = answer + x*x*x*x*x*x*x/5040;
        answer = answer + x*x*x*x*x*x*x*x/40320;
        answer = answer + x*x*x*x*x*x*x*x*x/362880;
        answer = answer + x*x*x*x*x*x*x*x*x*x/3628800;

        return (answer);
}

/* calculate log base e */
double loge(temp)
double temp;
{
        int ct, lt;
        double t,y,sqrt();

        ct = 1;
        lt = 1;

        if(temp < 1)
        {
                temp = 1/temp;
                lt = -1;
        }

        while(temp > 2)
        {
                temp = sqrt(temp);
                ct *= 2;
        }
```

Fig. 6-22. Continued.

```
t = (temp-1)/(temp+1);
y = 0.868591718 * t;
y = y + 0.289335524 * (t*t*t);
y = y + 0.177522071 * (t*t*t*t*t);
y = y + 0.094376476 * (t*t*t*t*t*t*t);
y = y + 0.179337714 * (t*t*t*t*t*t*t*t*t);

return(y/0.43429466*ct*lt);

}
```

After some sharp includes, RNDMAX is defined as 2147483647.0. This value reflects the fact that the 32-bit transputer chip returns an integer number between 0 and 2147483647. The DILUTIONFACTOR represents the dilution of the weight matrix by 20%.

The program continues, after declarations, with user input for the number of neurons (noneurons), the threshold, and a random seed. The number of memory states is calculated by the equation.

nomemories = (int) (0.1*noneurons)

The weight matrix is then computed from random binary vectors of dilution 0.2. The vectors, or memory states and final weight matrix are printed out. A test vector is then entered by the user. (A section for random test vectors has been commented out.)

The annealing starts at 10 pseudodegrees and is decreased by the relation:

temperature = temperature/$\log_e$ (1 + t)

where t is an increasing variable.

The neuron to update is selected at random. This results in asynchronous parallel updating and the vector matrix product is found for a net input to that neuron. The output state, activation[i], of neuron i, is then selected based on the C code in Fig. 6-21. Then after energy calculations, the main loop ends.

There are several functions in the program that are well annotated. The function rnd( ) returns a 0 or 1 to use on the binary vector generation. The function random(n), returns a random integer between 0 and the total number of neurons selected by the user. This allows asynchronous updating. The function expt(net,tem) returns an exponent of a quotient. The last function loge(temp) returns the natural logrithm of the temperature for use in updating the cooling cycle.

The program is very slow. As all Boltzmann – Monte Carlo simulations are. I have not included a test run because it is similar to the Hopfield network. For more details on the Boltzmann machine I recommend the book by Aarts and Korst (1989).

LEARNING BY BACK-PROPAGATION OF ERRORS

The major learning algorithm for neural networks is the back-propagation of errors discussed by Rumelhart, et al (1986) which is a generalization of the delta rule developed by Widrow and Hoff (1960, 1962) and by LeCun (1986). The method seeks to minimize the error in the output of the network, as compared to a target, or desired response. For a network having multiple outputs, the rms error is given by:

$$E = \left[\sum_j (o_j - t_j)^2 \right]^{1/2}$$

where t_j and o_j are the target and actual output values for the jth component of the vectors. The goal of the back-propagation learning procedure is to minimize this error. If the network is time invariant, then its output will depend only on its inputs, i_i and the current value of the connection weight matrices, w_{ij}. For a given input vector, therefore, the error is determined by the values of the weighting coefficients that connect the network. The approach used in the adaptive procedure is to modify these connections by an amount proportional to the gradient of the error in weight space:

$$\Delta w_{ij} \propto - \frac{\partial E}{\partial w_{ij}}$$

This procedure generally results in reductions in the average error as the weight matrices in the network evolve. The changes in the weights after each trial are proportional to the error itself. This naturally leads to a system that settles out to a stable weight configuration as the errors become small.

The adaptive technique described above has been applied to layered feedforward networks of the type shown in Fig. 6-23 rather than the Hopfield feedback networks.

Figure 6-24 is a generic layer within a layered, feed forward network. In this representation, the output of the layer is a vector of signals o_j. Its input vector, o_i, might itself be an output from a preceding

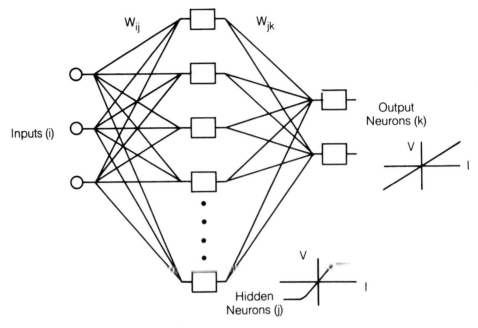

Fig. 6-23. Layered network architecture.

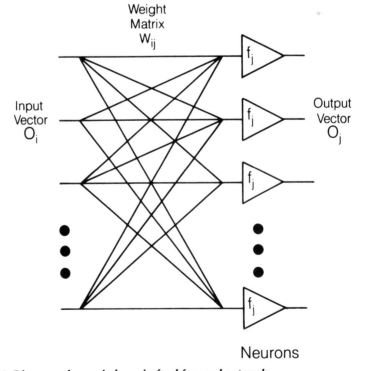

Fig. 6-24. Diagram of generic layer in feed forward network.

layer and its output vector o_j might, in turn, provide input to a subsequent layer. The neurons have an activation function f_j and are coupled to the input vector by a weight matrix w_{ij}. The net input to each neuron is given by:

$$net_j = \sum_i o_i \, w_{ij}$$

and the output vector is given by

$$o_j = f_j \, (net_j)$$

By generalized delta rule the weight changes are:

$$\Delta w_{ij} = \eta o_i \, \delta_j$$

In this relationship, η is the learning rate. If the layer in question is an output layer, then δ_j is given by:

$$\delta_j = (t_j - o_j) \, f_j' \, (net_j)$$

where t_j is the target, or desired output vector and f_j' denotes differentiation of the neuron's activation function with respect to the input signal. If the layer is hidden inside the network, it is not immediately apparent what its target response should be. In this case, δ_j is computed iteratively using:

$$\delta_j = f_j'(net_j) \sum_k \delta_k \, w_{jk}$$

where δ_k and w_{jk} refer to the layer immediately after the one in question.

Now look at a simple neural network program to demonstrate learning by back-propagation. The program back8.c, in Fig. 6-25, is a C program to simulate the back-propagation learning in a neural network. The network has three input nodes, 10 hidden nodes, and two output nodes. The objective of this simple simulation is for the neural network to learn Newton's laws of gravity and predict where a projectile will be in 10 time units. The input to the network is angle and velocity of the projectile. These are chosen at random with boundary conditions to keep the projectile confined to the given space. A third input is a constant to act as a threshold to adjust the neurons. The two outputs are the x,y coordinates of the predicted position of the projectile. The program begins with some sharp defines after the sharp includes. The first sharp define is PI 3.14159. The second, third, and fourth are the numbers of neurons in the input, hidden and output layers of the network. The next six sharp defines are concerned with graphics and the next two are maximum time or number of iterations and a variable FREQUENCY which is the frequency of updating the graphic display. There are three additional sharp defines used in a random number generation routine. The random number generator is from the book NUMERICAL RECIPES IN C, by Press et al (1988).

```
/* back propagation -- neural network simulation
                120888                                 */

#include "\c\quick\include\stdio.h"
#include "\c\quick\include\math.h"
#include "\c\quick\include\float.h"
#include "\c\quick\include\stdlib.h"
#include "\c\quick\include\graph.h"


#define PI 3.14159
#define IUNITS   3
#define HUNITS   10
#define OUNITS   2
#define XMAXSCREEN 320
#define YMAXSCREEN 200
#define YDOWN 60 /* upper limit of lower box */
#define XOVER 240 /* left limit of RH box */
#define WBORD 6 /* width of border */
#define ERMAX 100 /* maximum error on plot */
#define TRMAX (long int)(50000) /* maximum time */
#define FREQUENCY 100

#define M 714025 /* see Press, et al. 1988 */
#define IA 1366
#define IC 150889

static  double  itohweight[IUNITS][HUNITS];
static  double  htooweight[HUNITS][OUNITS];
static  double  target[OUNITS];
static  double  invector[IUNITS];
static  double  netih[HUNITS];
static  double  oout[OUNITS];
static  double  error[OUNITS];
static  double  sigma[HUNITS];
static  double  fprime[HUNITS];
static  double  hout[HUNITS];


struct videoconfig vc;
char error_message[] = "this video mode is not supported";

void main()
{
```

Fig. 6-25. back8.c demonstrates learning by back-propagation.

Fig. 6-25. Continued.

```
        /* declarations */
        int     i,j,k;
        long int     iterate = 0;
        int counter = 0;
        double  d1,d2,d;
        double  eta1 = 0.33;    /* 1/IUNITS  */
        double  eta2 = 0.1;     /* 1/HUNITS */
        double  a = 0.02;
        double  t1,t2,vel,theta;
        double  temp,delta;
        double  rnd();
        int exmin,exmax,eymin,eymax; /* error box mins and maxs */
        int nxmin,nxmax,nymin,nymax; /* neuron box */
        int sxmin,sxmax,symin,symax; /* space box */
        int u;
        double miss, percent = 0.0;
        double oldxt,oldyt,xt,yt,xo,yo; /* used in space plot */
        long dummy;

        /* rnd test stuff */
        for(i=1;i<=5;i++)
        {
                printf("%lf  ",rnd(dummy));
        }
/*        exit(0);
*/
        /* set ups */
        for(i=0;i<IUNITS;i++)
        {
                for(j=0;j<HUNITS;j++)
                {
                        itohweight[i][j] = 0.1*rnd(dummy);
                }
        }

        for(j=0;j<HUNITS;j++)
        {
                for(k=0;k<OUNITS;k++)
                {
                        htooweight[j][k] = 0.1*rnd(dummy);
                }
        }

                /* setup graphics screen */
        if(_setvideomode(_MRES4COLOR) == 0)
        {
                printf("%s\n",error_message);
                exit(0);
        }

        _setbkcolor(_BLACK);
        _selectpalette(3);
        _setviewport(0,0,320,200);
        _setcolor(1);
        _rectangle(_GFILLINTERIOR,0,0,XMAXSCREEN,YMAXSCREEN);

        _setcolor(3);
                        /* error rect */
        _rectangle(_GFILLINTERIOR,WBORD,WBORD,XOVER-WBORD,YDOWN-WBORD);
                        /* neurons rect */
        _rectangle(_GFILLINTERIOR,XOVER,WBORD,XMAXSCREEN-WBORD,
                                                        YMAXSCREEN-WBORD);
                        /* space rect */
        _rectangle(_GFILLINTERIOR,WBORD,YDOWN,XOVER-WBORD,
```

Fig. 6-25. Continued.

```
                                                      YMAXSCREEN-WBORD);
             /* set up error box axes */
   exmin = 2*WBORD;
   exmax = XOVER-2*WBORD;
   eymin = YDOWN-2*WBORD;
   eymax = 2*WBORD;

   _setcolor(0);
   _moveto(exmin,eymin);
_lineto(exmin,eymax);
_moveto(exmin,eymin);
_lineto(exmax,eymin);

for(u=1;u<11;u++)
{
        _moveto(exmin+u*(exmax-exmin)/10,eymin);
        _lineto(exmin+u*(exmax-exmin)/10,eymin+(eymax-eymin)/15);
}
for(u=1;u<6;u++)
{
        _moveto(exmin,eymin+u*(eymax-eymin)/5);
        _lineto(exmin+(exmax-exmin)/75,eymin+u*(eymax-eymin)/5);
}
             /* setup axes for neuron box */
nxmin = XOVER + WBORD;
nxmax = XMAXSCREEN - 2*WBORD;
nymin = YMAXSCREEN - 2*WBORD;
nymax = 4*WBORD;

                 /* blue boxes */
_setcolor(1);
for(u=0;u<10;u++)
{
        _rectangle(_GBORDER,nxmin,nymin+u*(nymax-nymin)/10,
                             nxmax,nymin+(u+1)*(nymax-nymin)/10);
}

                 /* line */
                 /* repeat this code after update */
_setcolor(0);
_moveto((nxmax+nxmin)/2,nymin);
_lineto((nxmax+nxmin)/2,nymax);

                 /* + and - signs */
_moveto(nxmin+0.2*(nxmax-nxmin),nymax-WBORD);
_lineto(nxmin+0.3*(nxmax-nxmin),nymax-WBORD);
_moveto(nxmin+0.7*(nxmax-nxmin),nymax-WBORD);
_lineto(nxmin+0.8*(nxmax-nxmin),nymax-WBORD);
_moveto(nxmin+0.75*(nxmax-nxmin),nymax-WBORD+0.05*(nxmax-nxmin));
_lineto(nxmin+0.75*(nxmax-nxmin),nymax-WBORD-0.05*(nxmax-nxmin));

             /* space axes */
sxmin = 2*WBORD;
sxmax = 0.75*(XOVER - 4*WBORD) + 2*WBORD;
symin = YMAXSCREEN - 2*WBORD;
symax = YDOWN + WBORD;

_setcolor(0);
_moveto(sxmin,symax);
_lineto(sxmin,symin);
_lineto(sxmax,symin);
for(u=1;u<11;u++)
{
        _moveto(sxmin+u*(sxmax-sxmin)/10,symin);
        _lineto(sxmin+u*(sxmax-sxmin)/10,symin+(symax-symin)/40);
```

Fig. 6-25. Continued.

```
}
for(u=1;u<13;u++)
{
        _moveto(sxmin,symin+u*(symax-symin)/12);

        _lineto(sxmin+(sxmax-sxmin)/60,symin+u*(symax-symin)/12);
}




/* learning loop */
for(iterate=0;iterate<TRMAX;iterate++)
{
        if(kbhit())
        {
                _setvideomode(_DEFAULTMODE);
                exit(0);
        }

        /* select random numbers */
        t1 = rnd(dummy);
        t2 = rnd(dummy);
        vel = 0.116 + (0.2 - 0.116)*t1;
        theta = (60 + 30*t2)*PI/180;

        /* compute the target vector using the model */
        target[0] = 10*vel*cos(theta);
        target[1] = 10*vel*sin(theta)-0.5*a*100;

        /* select input vector */
        invector[0] = t1;
        invector[1] = t2;
        invector[2] = 1.0;

        /* feed forward  --  input to hidden */
        for(j=0;j<HUNITS;j++)
        {
                netih[j] = 0;
                for(i=0;i<IUNITS;i++)
                {
                        netih[j] = netih[j] + itohweight[i][j]*invector[
                }
                hout[j] = tanh(netih[j]);

        }


        /* feed forward  --  hidden to output */
        for(k=0;k<OUNITS;k++)
        {
                oout[k] = 0;
                for(j=0;j<HUNITS;j++)
                {
                        oout[k] = oout[k] + htooweight[j][k]*hout[j];
                }
                error[k] = target[k] - oout[k];
        }


        /* compute the error correction for htooweight matrix elements *
        for(k=0;k<OUNITS;k++)
        {
```

Fig. 6-25. Continued.

```
                for(j=0;j<HUNITS;j++)
                {
                        delta = error[k]*hout[j]*eta2;
                        htooweight[j][k] = htooweight[j][k] + delta;
                }
        }

        /* compute the error correction for itohweitht matrix elements *
        for(j=0;j<HUNITS;j++)    /* first find sigma(e(k)u(kj)) */
        {
                sigma[j] = 0;
                for(k=0;k<OUNITS;k++)
                {
                        sigma[j] = sigma[j] + error[k]*htooweight[j][k];
                }
                temp = (double)(1.0/cosh(netih[j]));
                fprime[j] = temp*temp;
        }

        for(i=0;i<IUNITS;i++)
        {
                for(j=0;j<HUNITS;j++)
                {

                        delta = eta1*fprime[j]*sigma[j]*invector[i];
                        itohweight[i][j] = itohweight[i][j] + delta;
                }
        }
d1 = pow((oout[0]-target[0]),2.0);
d2 = pow((oout[1]-target[1]),2.0);
miss = sqrt(d1 + d2);
d = d + (sqrt(d1 + d2))/FREQUENCY;
if( d>0.5)
{
        d = 0.5;
}
if(miss <= 0.01)
{
        percent = percent + 100/FREQUENCY;
}
counter = counter + 1;
if(counter == FREQUENCY)
{
        /* plot stuff here */
                /* error plot */
        _setcolor(0);
        _setpixel(exmin+iterate*(exmax-exmin)/TRMAX,
                        eymin+percent*(eymax-eymin)/ERMAX);
                /* neurons */
        _setcolor(3);
        _rectangle(_GFILLINTERIOR,nxmin,nymin,nxmax,nymax);
        _setcolor(1);
        for(u=0;u<10;u++)
        {
                _rectangle(_GBORDER,nxmin,nymin+u*(nymax-nymin)/10,
                                nxmax,nymin+(u+1)*(nymax-nymin)/10);
        }
        _setcolor(2);
        for(u=0;u<10;u++)
        {

        _rectangle(_GFILLINTERIOR,(nxmax+nxmin)/2,
                nymin+u*(nymax-nymin)/10,
                (nxmax+nxmin)/2 + (nxmax-nxmin)*hout[u]/2,
                nymin+(u+1)*(nymax-nymin)/10);
```

Fig. 6-25. Continued.

```
}
_setcolor(0);
_moveto((nxmax+nxmin)/2,nymin);
_lineto((nxmax+nxmin)/2,nymax);
           /* space data plot */
_setcliprgn(sxmin+3,symin-3,XOVER-WBORD,YDOWN+WBORD);
_setcolor(3);
_rectangle(_GFILLINTERIOR,sxmin+3,symin-3,XOVER-WBORD,
                                  YDOWN+WBORD);
oldxt=0;
oldyt=0;
_moveto(sxmin,symin);
for(u=0;u<51;u++)
{
        _setcolor(2);
        xo = 1.3 - u*(1.3 - oout[0])/50.0;
        yo = u*oout[1]/50.0;
        xt = vel*u*cos(theta)/5.0;
        yt = (vel*u*sin(theta)/5.0) - 0.5*a*u*u/25.0;
        _setpixel(sxmin+xo*(sxmax-sxmin),
                symin+yo*(symax-symin)/1.2);
        _setcolor(0);
        _moveto(sxmin+oldxt*(sxmax-sxmin),
                symin+oldyt*(symax-symin)/1.2);
        _lineto(sxmin+xt*(sxmax-sxmin),
                symin+yt*(symax-symin)/1.2);
        oldxt = xt;
        oldyt = yt;
}
if(miss <= 0.01)
{
        _setcolor(2);
        _moveto(sxmin+xt*(sxmax-sxmin),
                        symin+yt*(symax-symin)/1.2+3);
        _lineto(sxmin+xt*(sxmax-sxmin),
                        symin+yt*(symax-symin)/1.2-3);
        _moveto(sxmin+xt*(sxmax-sxmin)-3,
                        symin+yt*(symax-symin)/1.2);
        _lineto(sxmin+xt*(sxmax-sxmin)+3,
                        symin+yt*(symax-symin)/1.2);
        _moveto(sxmin+xt*(sxmax-sxmin)-2,
                        symin+yt*(symax-symin)/1.2-2);
        _lineto(sxmin+xt*(sxmax-sxmin)+2,
                        symin+yt*(symax-symin)/1.2+2);
        _moveto(sxmin+xt*(sxmax-sxmin)+2,
                        symin+yt*(symax-symin)/1.2-2);
        _lineto(sxmin+xt*(sxmax-sxmin)-2,
                        symin+yt*(symax-symin)/1.2+2);
}

_setcliprgn(0,0,XMAXSCREEN,YMAXSCREEN);




percent = 0;
        d = 0;
        counter = 0;


}

}
while(!kbhit());
_setvideomode(_DEFAULTMODE);
```

Fig. 6-25. Continued.

```
}

double rnd(idum)
long *idum;
{
        static long iy,ir[98];
        static int iff=0;
        int j;

        if(*idum < 0 || iff == 0)
        {
                iff=1;
                if((*idum=(IC-(*idum)) % M) < 0) *idum = -(*idum);
                for(j=1;j<=97;j++)
                {
                        *idum = (IA*(*idum)+IC) % M;
                        ir[j] = (*idum);
                }
                *idum=(IA*(*idum)+IC) % M;
                iy=(*idum);
        }
        j=1 + 97.0*iy/M;
        iy=ir[j];
        *idum=(IA*(*idum)+IC) % M;
        ir[j] = (*idum);
        return (double) iy/M;

}
```

The program continues by declaring several arrays. The array itohweight[IUNITS][HUNITS] is the weight matrix from the input units to hidden units. The array htooweight[HUNITS][OUNITS] is the matrix from hidden units to output units. After these declarations then an input vector, a net-input-to-hidden vector, an output vector, an error vector, and three more vectors are declared. These last three are discussed later. After main( ) starts there are many more declarations. The counting variables i, j, iterate, and counter are declared. Then d1, d2, and d, which are distances used later in the program, are declared. The variables eta1 and eta2 are the learning rates for the input units and the hidden units. The variable a is a pseudo acceleration for the projectile. The variables t1 and t2 are used in the input vector. The variables ve1 and theta are the initial random velocity and angle. The next series of declarations are for graphics.

The program then continues with a test of the rnd function and various setups. The first block of setups are for entering small random numbers in all the matrix positions, of the weight matrices. These small numbers are used to break symmetry and prevent the network from diverging. The network must start with random weights. The next large selection of the program sets up MicroSoft C graphics and could be modified for other computers or languages.

The program learning loop begins with the counter iterate. The first block of lines allows the user to interrupt the program by hitting any key. This clears the screen and returns to DOS. Random numbers chosen for velocity and angle are used to compute the target vector. The input vector is then set up from the same random numbers and the vector is fed forward into the hidden layer of neurons. Each hidden neuron has a hyperbolic tangent output. The output from the hidden layer is then fed forward into the output layer. The output layer neurons have a linear response. The error vector is also computed from the difference of the target and the output vectors.

The weight correction for the hidden-to-output weight matrix elements are computed using the algorithm outlined above. The formula for the correction is:

$$\Delta w_{ij} = \eta o_j \, \delta_j$$

$$\delta_j = (t_j - o_j) \, f_j' \, (net_j)$$

Also, using the above algorithm, the weight correction for the input-to-hidden matrix elements are computed from the relation

$$\Delta w_{ij} = \eta o_j \delta_j$$

$$\delta_j = f_j' \, (net_j) \sum_k \delta_k \, w_{jk}$$

An error vector or distance vector is then computed from the magnitude of the difference of the output vector and the target vector. This distance vector is used in the graphic update that is the next section of the program. Several counters are set back to zero and the learning loop continues with another random projectile.

Figure 6-26 is a sketch of the computer screen for a run of this program. The upper graph represents the learning curve. It is a function of the magnitude of the distance vector between the target and output points, and the iterations or learning cycles, and is a plot of the percent of correct guesses by the neural network. The graph on the bottom represents the projectile and the neural network prediction. The bargraph on the right represents the analog output of the ten hidden neurons. This emphasizes the fact that neural networks are parallel analog processing systems and not token processors.

As a second application/example program for back-propagation neural networks, I will discuss the strange attractor known as the Henon attractor. For more information on computer modeling of strange attractors and chaos, I recommend my earlier book (1989).

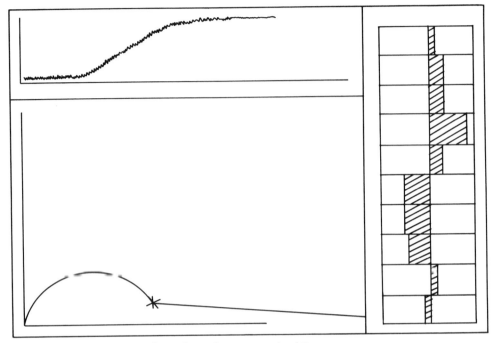

Fig. 6-26. Sketch of screen dump from the program back8.c.

The Henon attractor was introduced by Henon (1976) and has been studied by Curry (1979), Ruelle (1980), Thompson and Thompson (1980) and Devaney (1986). The Henon map is a two-dimensional relation and is given by:

$$x_{n+1} = y_n + 1 - ax_n^2$$
$$x_{n+1} = bx_n$$

The system is shown in Fig. 6-27. It is an area-contracting mapping of a strange attractor. Iterating to infinity will not cause the points to diverge; rather they will always wander on the chaotic attractor. Figure 6-28 shows the x and y plots as functions of time. (These chaotic time plots were made with the program henont.c, shown in Fig. 6-29.) It can clearly be seen that attempting to predict the value for the next iteration is almost impossible. Yet this task can be done reasonably well with a neural network. Incidentally neural networks can be used to discriminate real statistical noise from deterministic chaos. For a detailed discussion of this aspect of neural networks with respect to real analog processing hardware, I recommend Frye, et al (1989). The learning curve shown in Fig. 6-30 is an example of a neural network learning the Henon attractor prediction problem. This figure was prepared with the program henon1.c, shown in Fig. 6-31.

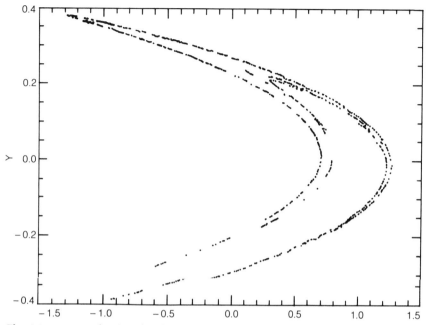

Fig. 6-27. Locus of points for the Henon attractor.

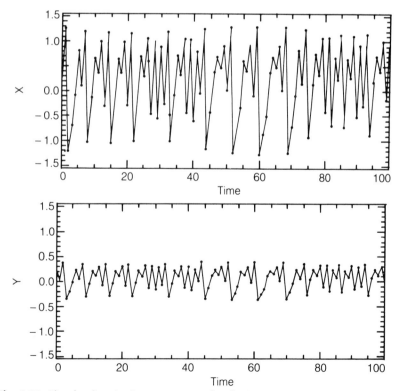

Fig. 6-28. Simple chaotic time sequences for the Henon attractor.

```
#include <float.h>
#include <stdio.h>
#include <graph.h>
#include <math.h>

struct videoconfig vc;
char error_message[] = "this video mode is not suported";
float xdata[1000],ydata[1000],tdata[1000];


void main()
{
        /* declarations */
        int i,t,count,n;
        float x0,y0;
        double xmax,ymax,xmin,ymin;
        int xmaxscreen=280,ymaxscreen=160;
        int ymaxtext=30;
        float xcoord,ycoord;
        float text[80];

        /* user input */
        printf("input number of data points\n");
        scanf("%d",&n);

        /* set mode of screen */
        if (_setvideomode(_MRESNOCOLOR) == 0)
        {
                printf("%s\n",error_message);
                exit(0);
        }
        _getvideoconfig(&vc);
        _setcolor(1);
        _clearscreen(_GCLEARSCREEN);

        /* computation here */
        xdata[0] = 0.05;
        ydata[0] = 0.05;
        count = 0;
        for(t=0;t<n;t++)
        {
                xdata[t+1] = ydata[t] + 1 - 1.4*xdata[t]*xdata[t];
                ydata[t+1] = 0.3*xdata[t];
                xdata[count] = xdata[t+1];
                ydata[count] = ydata[t+1];
                tdata[count] = count;
                count++;
        }



        /* find min and max of x and y
           (tdata is set as xdata)        */
        xmax= -1e+20;
        xmin= -xmax;
        ymax= -1e20;
        ymin= -ymax;
        for(i=0;i<n;++i)
        {
                if(ymin > ydata[i])
                        ymin=ydata[i];
                if(ymax < ydata[i])
```

Fig. 6-29. henont.c made the plots in Fig. 6-28.

Fig. 6-29. Continued.

```
                            ymax=ydata[i];
                if(xmax < tdata[i])
                            xmax=tdata[i];
                if(xmin > tdata[i])
                            xmin=tdata[i];
        }
        /* printf("xmin, xmax, ymin, ymax:%lf %lf %lf %lf\n",xmin,xmax,ymin,ymax


        /* draw axes */
        _setviewport(20,20,300,180);
        _moveto(0,0);
        _lineto(0,ymaxscreen);
        _moveto(0,ymaxscreen);
        _lineto(xmaxscreen,ymaxscreen);
        for(i=0;i<=ymaxscreen; i=i+ymaxscreen/10)
        {
                _moveto(0,i);
                _lineto(5,i);
        }
        /* tic marks */
        for(i=0;i<=xmaxscreen; i=i+xmaxscreen/10)
        {
                _moveto(i,ymaxscreen-5);
                _lineto(i,ymaxscreen);
        }

        /* plot data */
        _moveto(xmin,ymin);
        for(i=0;i<n;++i)
        {
                xcoord=((tdata[i]-xmin)/(xmax-xmin))*xmaxscreen;
                ycoord=ymaxscreen-((ydata[i]-ymin)/(ymax-ymin))*ymaxscreen;
                _lineto(xcoord,ycoord);
        }


        /* clear screen & return control hit enter */
        while(!kbhit());
        _clearscreen(_GCLEARSCREEN);
        _setvideomode(_DEFAULTMODE);




}
```

Now I begin a discussion of the program. Up to main( ) should be obvious, because it is similar to back8.c. After declarations and setups similar to the previous program, then an endless learning loop begins. The input vector is selected from random numbers and the target vector is computed. The input vector is fed forward to the hidden layer, and then through to the output layer. The error vector and weight changes are computed and finally a distance vector is computed. In this case the distance vector is simply the magnitude of the difference between the output vector and the target vector. As the network improves, this magnitude decreases as shown in Fig. 6-30.

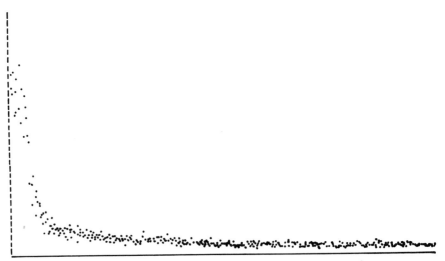

Fig. 6-30. Learning curve of the Henon attractor. Screen dump from henon1.c.

```
/* back propagation -- neural network simulation */

#include "\c\quick\include\stdio.h"
#include "\c\quick\include\math.h"
#include "\c\quick\include\float.h"
#include "\c\quick\include\stdlib.h"
#include "\c\quick\include\graph.h"
#include "\c\quick\include\conio.h"


#define IUNITS    3
#define HUNITS    10
#define OUNITS    2
#define XMAXSCREEN (double)(280)
#define YMAXSCREEN (double)(160)
#define YMAXTEXT (double)(30)
#define XMIN (double)(0)
#define XMAX (double)(10000)
#define YMIN (double)(0.0)
#define YMAX (double)(1.0)

static  double   itohweight[IUNITS][HUNITS];
static  double   htooweight[HUNITS][OUNITS];
static  double   target[OUNITS];
static  double   invector[IUNITS];
static  double   netih[HUNITS];
static  double   oout[OUNITS];
static  double   error[OUNITS];
static  double   sigma[HUNITS];
static  double   fprime[HUNITS];
static  double   hout[HUNITS];


struct videoconfig vc;
char error_message[] = "this video mode is not supported";


void main()
```

Fig. 6-31. henon1.c made the plot in Fig. 6-30.

Fig. 6-31. Continued.

```
{
        /* declarations */
        int     i,j,k;
        long int     iterate = 0;
        int counter = 0;
        double  d1,d2,d = 0;
        double  eta = 0.1;
        double  a = 3.95;
        double  deltat = 1.0;
        double  t1;
        double  temp,delta;
        double  rnd();
        short int  xcoord,ycoord;
        double xin=0.5,yin=0.5;


        /* set ups */
        for(i=0;i<IUNITS;i++)
        {
                for(j=0;j<HUNITS;j++)
                {
                        itohweight[i][j] = 0.1*rnd();
                }
        }

for(j=0;j<HUNITS;j++)
{
        for(k=0;k<OUNITS;k++)
        {
                htooweight[j][k] = 0.1*rnd();
        }
}

if(_setvideomode(_MRESNOCOLOR) == 0)
{
        printf("%s\n",error_message);
        exit(0);
}

_setviewport(20,20,300,180);
_moveto(0,0);
_lineto(0,YMAXSCREEN);
_moveto(0,YMAXSCREEN);
_lineto(XMAXSCREEN,YMAXSCREEN);

target[0]=0.5;
target[1]=0.5;

/* endless learning loop */
for(;;)
{

        if(kbhit())
        {
                _setvideomode(_DEFAULTMODE);
                exit(0);
        }

        /* select input numbers */
        xin = target[0];
        yin = target[1];

        /* compute the target vector using the model */
        target[0] = yin + 1.0 - 1.4*xin*xin;
```

Fig. 6-31. Continued.

```
target[1] = 0.3*xin;


/* select input vector */
invector[0] = xin;
invector[1] = yin;
invector[2] = 1.0;

/* feed forward  --  input to hidden */
for(j=0;j<HUNITS;j++)
{
        netih[j] = 0;
        for(i=0;i<IUNITS;i++)
        {
                netih[j] = netih[j] + itohweight[i][j]*invector[
        }
        hout[j] = tanh(netih[j]);

 }


/* feed forward  --  hidden to output */
for(k=0;k<OUNITS;k++)
{
        oout[k] = 0;
        for(j=0;j<HUNITS;j++)
        {
                oout[k] = oout[k] + htooweight[j][k]*hout[j];
        }
        error[k] = target[k] - oout[k];
}


/* compute the error correction for htooweight matrix elements *
for(k=0;k<OUNITS;k++)
{
        for(j=0;j<HUNITS;j++)
        {
                delta = error[k]*hout[j]*eta;
                htooweight[j][k] = htooweight[j][k] + delta;
        }
}

/* compute the error correction for itohweitht matrix elements *
for(j=0;j<HUNITS;j++)    /* first find sigma(e(k)u(kj)) */
{
        sigma[j] = 0;
        for(k=0;k<OUNITS;k++)
        {
                sigma[j] = sigma[j] + error[k]*htooweight[j][k];
        }
        temp = (double)(1.0/cosh(netih[j]));
        fprime[j] = temp*temp;
}


for(i=0;i<IUNITS;i++)
{
        for(j=0;j<HUNITS;j++)
        {

                delta = eta*fprime[j]*sigma[j]*invector[i];
                itohweight[i][j] = itohweight[i][j] + delta;
        }
```

Fig. 6-31. Continued.

```
}

d1 = pow((oout[0] - target[0]), 2.0);
d2 = pow((oout[1] - target[1]), 2.0);
d = d + (sqrt(d1 + d2))/25.0;

iterate = iterate + 1;
counter = counter + 1;
if(counter == 24)
{
        xcoord = (((double)(iterate) - XMIN)/(XMAX-XMIN))*XMAXSC
        ycoord = YMAXSCREEN - ((d-YMIN)/(YMAX-YMIN))*YMAXSCREEN;

                    _setpixel(xcoord,ycoord);


                    d = 0;
                    counter = 0;


        }

    }

}

double rnd()
{
        double result;
        result = (double)(rand())/(double)(32767.0);

        return (result);

}
```

COMMERCIAL NEURAL NETWORK SOFTWARE PACKAGES
With the advent of digital signal processing chips for fast vector-matrix multiplication, only applications requiring great speed will likely use analog neural network hardware. These analog systems could easily do computation in the teraflops range. This is about one million times faster than a Cray computer.

Many software packages are currently available for many types of computers. The chief advantage in using these is that you can begin to investigate the capabilities of neural networks, and with a DSP accelerator board it is possible to do neural computer at the equivalent of about one gigaflop. (These speed comparisons are very superficial because neural networks are non-token processing—it is like comparing apples and oranges.)

California Scientific Software
California Scientific Software, in Sierra Madre, CA, have a software package for neural network simulation called the BrainMaker. (I reviewed version 1.0.) This package is designed for IBM PC clones, and is easy to install. I created a directory, \neural\css, to which I copied all the programs on the disk provided. The package includes

six sample networks. All the networks use back-propagation and assume one hidden layer. The actual operation time of the program to settle to a learned state is quite fast. It is also one of the easiest packages to use. The executable program (no source code included) calls a file which contains all the appropriate information about the problem to be studied. The problems include Boolean logic, character recognition, speech recognition and pattern recognition. The net-file contains information such as the number of neurons in each layer, the number of layers, the input training set, the target vectors and the desired output display. The output display can be customized to include histograms of the synaptic values in each weight matrix. The network can manipulate pictures, numbers or symbols.

A very interesting feature of BrainMaker is that the neurons can be adjusted to have linear transfer functions, linear threshold functions, step functions, sigmoid functions, tanh or Gaussian transfer functions. This ability is unique to this software package. The Gaussian transfer function has no direct analogy to any biological function (nor does back-propagation) and is mostly useless except it does speed up learning of logic functions such as XOR.

The nettalk programs that are included are designed to demonstrate speech recognition. The input training set and target set must be included in an ASCII file with all the network parameters. This is called the net-file. There is some disadvantage to this because the program does not include source code. Nettalk is a particularly exciting application and it would be fun to interface the program with a D/A converter and amplifier and listen to the network as it learns to read from a data file, for example.

The only complaint I have about the software package was that the user customization interface (it allows the user to choose the appearance of the pull-down menus and screen) did not work for me. There might have been a bit error on the master disk.

The authors of the documentation have done an excellent job. I wish all computer hardware/software documentation was this good.

Explorations in Parallel Distributed Processing

The software package to accompany the two volumes by McClelland and Rumelhart (1986) includes a handbook and source code for C programs to study many of the neural networks discussed in the books. The software/handbook is sold as a separate package published by MIT press. *Explorations in Parallel Distributed Processing: A Handbook of Models, Programs and Exercises* by James L. McClelland and David E. Rumelhart.

The handbook with the source code is a real advantage if you are interested in writing your own neural network programs. Many of the actual examples, however, have a very biological flavor, and if your primary interests are in parallel processing it might be a little too far off the mark. I do wish to stress that the source code is useful for certain types of networks.

DAIR Computer Systems

DAIR Computer Systems, in Palo Alto, CA, has available a neural network package known as NETWURKZ. The package I tested was version 1.2. The system includes documentation on neural networks and a programming language called PL/D, which is the system language in which NETWURKZ is written. The neural networks are only feedforward networks without back-propagation learning. They are much like one-pass Hopfield networks. In other words, they are simple one-interation vector-matrix multiplication networks.

The most unique feature of the package is that the networks do not perform vector-matrix multiplication in loop processing, but rather in list processing. Individual lists represent the neurons and all the connections to it. This speeds up the processing greatly, because most of the matrices are sparse. For example the matrix:

```
0 1 0 0 1 0 0 0 0
0 0 1 0 0 1 0 0 1
0 0 0 0 0 0 0 0 0
0 0 0 0 1 0 0 1 0
0 0 1 0 0 1 0 0 1
0 0 0 0 0 0 0 0 0
0 0 0 0 1 0 0 1 0
0 0 1 0 0 1 0 0 1
0 0 0 0 0 0 0 0 0
```

can be represented by

Neuron	Connections
2	1
3	2, 5, 8
5	1, 4, 7
6	2, 5, 8
8	4, 7
9	2, 5, 8.

The chief disadvantage of NETWURKZ is that in order to do any experimentation with the package you must be prepared to write a lot of code on your own using the language PL/D.

DAIR Computer Systems also has available a package called CONNECTIONS for simulation of using neural networks to solve the traveling salesman problem and a package called CHAOS MANNER which plots the one-dimensional logistic equation. (It is out of place to review CHAOS MANNER here, but I was disappointed.)

Neural Systems Incorporated

Neural Systems Inc. in Vancouver, British Columbia has a neural network package called AWARENESS. The program is easy to install and to run. (I evaluated version 1.0.) This package contains four neural network architectures: back-propagation, categorization, optimization, and self-organization.

The back-propagation model is a fixed architecture of two inputs, eight neurons in one hidden layer and one output neuron. This is a disadvantage of this package. The example in the documentation is for the XOR problem. I had no trouble using this simulation.

The categorization model uses Hebbian learning for an associative network. This is fixed at eight neurons. Because of its small size little can be done with this network.

The optimization model, is a model of the Hopfield-Tank solution of the traveling salesman problem. I couldn't get this program to run. It only generated a frozen keyboard which necessitated a soft-boot of the system.

The self-organization model is a model by Kohonen and uses neurons operating in the linear regime. There is a threshold algorithm for determining which neuron will fire.

The four networks were very small and of a limited architecture. It was not possible to modify the system because source code was not included. I, however, might be too harsh of a critic for this package and the one from DAIR. The versions I evaluated were very early. I am sure these companies have new versions with upgrades and no bugs. The programs I have included in this chapter easily perform as well as these last two packages They also can easily be modified for larger or different architectures, and more complex problems can be studied.

Neural Ware Inc.

The largest software package for neural network simulation (that I evaluated) is NEURALWORKS PROFESSIONAL version 2.0 from Neural Ware Inc. in Sewickley, PA. This package, which includes five disks and a 500-page manual, allows one to experiment with over a dozen neural network paradigms. These include: adaline, BAM, back-propagation, brain-state-in-a-box, Hopfield, Madline, and perceptron.

It is not an easy package to use. It includes far too many pull-down menus, and too many key strokes to achieve a desired result. Networks can be built from pull-down menus, but the graphics resolution is poor. Rather than just show the network, which is of very little information value, you can show the Hinton diagram of the synaptic connections, but even this is low graphics. A better approach would be to show a histogram of the synaptic values or a realtime learning curve of the performance.

The clear winner of the neural network packages is BRAINMA-KER from California Scientific Software. Although the package does contain pull-down menus, there is less cut-and-pasting needed to build a network. The major disadvantage is that only one paradigm, the back-propagation learning algorithm, can be used in the experimentation. This is, however, a very minor point because back-prop is the most useful of the neural network paradigms.

DIGITAL SIGNAL PROCESSING AND NEURAL NETWORKS

The programs I have included in this chapter are, with minor modifications, general-purpose for neural network simulations. I have included three major paradigms: Hopfield, Boltzmann machines and back-propagation learning. These all are computationally intensive. The major computation bottleneck is caused by the vector-matrix operations being done in serial mode. With a digital signal processing board it is possible to achieve a factor of about 100 in speed over a floating point coprocessor chip.

The following is a list of third-party vendors of DSP products:

Ariel

Ariel Corporation has announced the DSP-32C card, a floating-point digital signal processing card for the IBM PC and compatibles, with complete dual-channel professional audio-quality analog I/O and advanced digital I/O. Because the DSP-32C card is interface compatible with AT&T's DSP32C-DS DSP Development System, all of AT&T's existing development tools can be used with Ariel's DSP-32C card.

For more imformation, contact Ariel Corporation, 433 River Road, Highland Park, NJ 08904. Phone (201) 249-2900.

Burr Brown

Burr Brown offers several hardware and software products. DSPeed is a family of PC plug-in cards (currently includes the 16-MHz ZPB32 and 25-MHz ZPB32-HS) based on a 160-ns version of the DSP32. It includes 64k bytes of static RAM, and a 10 Mbit/sec buffered serial data bus for interfacing multiple DSPeed boards and data acquisition boards such as the ZFB100, which is based on AT&T's T7520 Codec.

DSPlay XL/32 (ZPM32) is a graphically oriented, menu driven signal processing development package and code generator for the IBM PC XT/AT and DSPeed PC plug-in boards. It includes a graphics editor, text editor, function library, extensive display capabilities, assembler, disassembler, and debugger. It also supports Momentum Data System's Filter Design and Analysis System.

With DSPlay, designers develop applications by combining functional blocks using the FlowGrams language. The library's 60 + functions include correlation, signal sources, filters, windows, FFTs, math and transcendental functions. Using FlowGrams and its built-in editor, designers combine these blocks to create a flow diagram. Each block may contain a process function, its parameters, inputs, outputs, and connections to the next or previous function. Once designers have completed their application using FlowGRams, they can invoke a code generator, which automatically generates DSP32 code for the PC plug-in DSPeed accelerator board.

Burr Brown also supports the AT&T development tools, which include a C compiler, assembly language optimizer, and library of generic math and digital signal processing functions. Applications include signal processing, telecommunications, sonar, medical instrumentation, real-time control, and robotics.

For information, contact Burr-Brown Corporation, 6550 S. Bay Colony Drive, Tucson, AZ 85706. (602) 746-1111.

Communications Automation and Control

Communications Automation & Control (CAC) provides plug-in floating point array processor boards for the IBM PC, XT, and AT based on AT&T's DSP32 and DSP32C. The DSP32-PC is available in two versions: an 8-MFLOPS DSP32-based board for the IBM PC and PC XT that includes from 32k to 128k bytes of zero-wait-state static RAM: and a 25-MFLOPS DSP32C-based version for the PC AT that includes 64k bytes of zero-wait-state static RAM. Additional on-board sockets will allow the board to provide a total of 256k bytes of static RAM.

An 8-bit CODEC provides D/A and A/D conversion, as well as low pass and bandpass filtering for speech signals. To interface to higher precision off-board A/D and D/A boards, or to other DSP32-PC boards, the board provides an 8M bit/sec (16M bit/sec for the AT version) double-buffered DMA serial port. Software support includes a

C-callable applications library, C compiler, window-based emulator, and debugger. It also includes Hyperception's Hypersignal-Workstation software, Momentum Data System's Filter Design and Analysis software, and Sonitech's EDSP Workstation software.

Applications for the boards include signal processing, CAD/CAM, image processing, graphics, and even scientific computing.

For information, contact Communications Automation & Control. 1642 Union Blvd., Suite O, Allentown, PA 18103. (215) 776-6669.

Causal Systems

Causal Systems provides a family of array processors for the IBM PC/XT/AT, STD Bus, and Macintosh II (Nubus). Known as the THOR-AP, THOR-STD, and Nu-THOR, respectively, this family of boards is based on AT&T's floating point DSP32. All three boards feature a peak performance of 12.5 MFLOPS, IEEE 32-bit floating point compatibility, and 64k bytes of 45-nsec static RAM.

Software support for the boards includes an assembler, C and PASCAL compilers, C-, Fortran-, and Turbo Pascal-callable math and signal processing subroutine libraries, and a development system. It also includes an ICON-based development package known as the System Simulator (SysSim), which enables designers with little or no programming experience to generate applications by combining ICONS. Additional software support for the THOR family will include a graphics and image processing subroutine library. The programming environment for all three boards is seamless—programs written for one platform will run altered on either of the other two platforms.

The boards are targeted at computationally-intensive applications such as signal processing, image processing, graphics, and simulation, and scientific computing.

For information, contact Causal Systems Inc., Suite 300, 9227 6th Ave, Inglewood, CA 90305. Phone (213) 754-7157.

DSP Applications

The Dual-32 Board uses two AT&T DSP32 160-ns chips and includes 32k bytes of external memory. It also includes A/D and D/A daughter boards, which may be either mounted on the Dual-32 or outside of the PC for greater noise immunity. Software support includes the Athena Group Monarch DSP Applications Package, a menu-driven 2D and 3D graphics package. Applications for the Dual-32 include simulation, Ethernet, PC acceleration, graphics, and signal processing.

For information, contact DSP Applications, The Athena Group, Inc., 3424 N.W. 31st St. Gainesville, FL 32601, or call (904) 371-2567.

DSP Design Tools

Offers an extensive catalogue of DSP hardware and software products. In addition to manufacturing the IBM PC AT plug-in DSP32C board, the company offers design kits and a DSP16 plug-in board. The DSP32C PC AT board costs $1995.

For more information, contact DSP Design Tools. 4101 Green Pond Rd., Bethlehem, PA 18017. (215) 691-2413.

Eighteen Eight Laboratories

The PL800 is a full-size PC plug-in card based on a 250-nsec version of AT&T's DSP32. An auxiliary interface card for the PL800 known as the PL802 provides a 1M byte/sec I/O channel. An array processor based on a parallel combination of up to 8 boards is also available.

Software support includes an assembler and a large library of arithmetic, logical, vector, array, and signal processing routines. It also includes a wide variety of compilers, including FORTRAN, C, and Turbo Pascal. Applications include PC acceleration, graphics, and signal processing. The board costs $1995.

For information, contact Eighteen Eight Laboratories, 771 Gage Drive, San Diego, CA 92106. (619) 224-2158.

Ensigma

The PCT-32C is an IBM PC XT/AT plug-in telephony card based on the DSP32/DSP32C. Providing 512k bytes of static RAM, this full-length card includes a fully approved BABT telephony interface, giving developers direct access to either British, American, or French public switched telephone networks. The telephone interface provides PSTN isolation, 2 to 4 wire conversion, hook-switch and dial pulse control, and ring detection. The board also includes a Codec that provides 10-bit linearity at either 8 or 9.6 kHz.

The card is I/O mapped at a user-selectable address, enabling developers to configure multiple boards for multiple channels. The analog signals to and from the card can be connected to an audio interface (instead of the telephony interface), enabling the PCT-32C to be used with standard audio equipment.

Software support includes AT&T's development tools, as well as the company's own SRS-32 word recognition software. This software provides speaker independent recognition and playback over public lines in a wide range of ambient noise conditions, and is immune to line variations and frequency distortion.

The maximum number of words that can be simultaneously supported is 32, though the total vocabulary is unlimited. SRS-32 comes with a demonstration vocabulary of numbers 0-9 and control words such as Yes, No, and Next. Custom vocabularies and grammars can be built to suit the customer's application. Applications for the card include audio and speech processing, as well as modem development.

For more information, contact Ensigma Ltd., Archway House, Wlech St. Chepstow, Gwent, NP6 5LL, United Kingdom. Phone 0291 6254 22.

Loughborough Sound Images (LSI)

The DSP32C Board is a 25-MFLOPS IBM PC plug-in board that includes interfaces for data acquisition, multiprocessing, and host communications. Software support includes a window-based debug monitor and function library. Fortran and Ada compilers will be available in the third quarter.

Applications include scientific computing, signal processing, vibration and noise analysis, nuclear magnetic resonance and image processing.

For more information, contact Loughborough Sound Images, The Technology Center, Epinal Way, Loughborough. Leicesestershire, LE11, 0QE, England. Phone 44 509 231 843.

Micro K Systems

Micro K Systems offers an IBM PC XT plug-in board based on AT&T's DSP32. Known as the DSP32-8, the 8-MFLOPS board features full C language and Forth development software. This software includes assemblers, compilers, a Forth operating system and editor, math and DSP subroutine libraries, interactive debugger, and a host-to-target communications server.

Implemented on a PC XT half card, the development system includes 128k bytes of 70-nsec static RAM, and serial and parallel I/O with DMA options. The buffered serial I/O port provides an interface to external plug-in codec and data acquisition modules. The Codecs supported are AT&T's 8-bit T7500 and 15-bit T7522. Data acquisition modules incorporate 12-bit, as well as 16-bit audio A/D and D/A converters.

Applications include telecommunications, real-time processing, image analysis, spectral analysis, graphics, rasterization, ray tracing, and robotics.

For more information, contact Micro K Systems, 15874 E. Hamilton Place, Aurora, CO 80013. Phone (303) 693-3413.

Skalar GmbH

The TXP32 is an 8-MFLOPS DSP32-based plug-in board for the IBM PC XT/AT. It includes 48k bytes of on-board static RAM, as well as an optional I/O module (TXA12) that provides four analog input channels, a track/hold amplifier, and a multiplexor that supports simultaneous sampling. Applications include general-purpose signal processing, math acceleration, graphics, image processing, spectral analysis, and speech processing.

For more information, contact Skalar GmbH at Robert-Bosche-Breite 9, D-3400 Go, West Germany. Phone 05 51/6 50 68 /89.

Spectrum Signal Processing

The DSP32C System Board is an IBM PC/AT plug-in development board based on the 80-nsec DSP32C. The board contains 64k bytes of memory, a buffered serial port that supports, 8-, 16-, 24-, and 32-bit transfers, and a 16-bit 256-byte memory mapped expansion port. The analog interface includes a dual-channel 16-bit D/A converter, as well as a dual-channel 16-bit A/D converter with sampling rates up to 200 kHz (with sample and hold amplifier).

Development support includes a monitor/debugger and a library of C callable board drivers for the PC. Spectrum also supports AT&T's development software, which includes a C compiler, assembler, linker, and library of math and signal processing routines. Spectrum will also support Hyperception's Hypersignal Workstation Software.

Applications for the board include robotics, industrial control, image processing, sonar, radar, seismic analysis, instrumentation, speech recognition/synthesis, communications workstations, and vibration analysis. The board will cost $2995, with separate pricing for the AT&T and Hyperception software. Production boards will be available in June, 1989.

For information, contact Spectrum Signal Processing, Inc., Suite 301, Discovery park. 3700 Gilmore Way, Burnaby, B.C., V5G 4MI. Phone (604) 438-7266 or 1 (800) 663-8986.

Surrey Medical Imaging Systems, Ltd. (S.M.I.S.)

S.M.I.S. sells three DSP32-based PC plug-in boards: their 12.5-MFLOPS VECTOR 32, the VECTOR 32C/256, and Communications Automation and Control's DSP32-PC. They also offer compatible data acquisition cards that feature options such as 2-channel, multiplexed 12-bit A/D and D/A converters, a 16-bit parallel output, a 16-bit Codec with 100-kHz or 330-kHz sampling rate, and a dual 12-bit A/D converter with a 1-MHz sampling rate.

Software support includes AT&T's development tools, as well as C and Fortran libraries. Applications include scientific computing, signal processing, vibration and noise analysis, nuclear magnetic resonance and image processing.

7

Applications
and Algorithms

This chapter is a survey of applications and algorithms for parallel processing computer systems. There have been numerous conferences on parallel processing. Almost all of them have included papers about applications and algorithms. In addition, the IEEE has published several special volumes on parallel processing. In this chapter I review two of these IEEE volumes and several conference proceedings. I also review several other sources that discuss applications for parallel processing. The main body of this chapter will consist of short reviews of applications; most of the applications are taken from science and engineering.

SIGNAL PROCESSING

Reijns and Barton (1987) edited a conference proceeding on parallel processing. Most of the papers were about parallel architecture. Several, however, were about applications or algorithms. Maehle and Wirl (1987) reported on numerical and signal processing. The system they use is known as the DIRMU-25, a 25-processor machine. They used it to solve partial differential equations and speech preprocessing. The partial differential equation:

$$\frac{\partial^2 u}{\partial x^2} + \frac{\partial^2 u}{\partial y^2} = 0$$

is known as the Laplace partial differential equation. The problem is solved on an n × m grid, U, the boundary values are passed as messages. The second application discussed is speech preprocessing. This consists of low-pass filtering and computation of autocorrelation, frequency spectrum, and numerical parameters for classification. The autocorrelation is just the convolution of a function f(x) with its mirror image.

LINEAR SYSTEMS

Gao (1987) uses vector-matrix operations to solve linear systems of equations. Using a concurrent machine for vector-matrix operations is overkill and an inefficient use of computing power. Signal processing chips and signal processing cards can be used more efficiently for these types of mathematical operations. Quarmby (1985) has written an excellent introductory book on signal processing chips; I believe these devices will cause systolic arrays to become orphanware in the near future.

Houstis, et al (1988) edited the conference proceedings from the First International Conference on Supercomputers, held in June 1987. Almost all aspects of parallel and supercomputing were covered in 52 papers.

SPACE-MAPPING

Sadayappan and Ercal (1988) reported on approaches to mapping parallel programs onto a hypercube. Figure 7-1 is a task precedence graph, and Fig. 7-2 is a task interaction graph. In the task precedence the parallel program is represented as a graph whose vertices represent processes, and the directed edges represent execution dependencies. In the interaction graph the relative amount of data communication required between task a and task b is two. These are arbitrary units. The essence of the mapping problem can be described

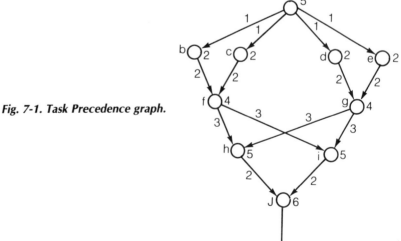

Fig. 7-1. Task Precedence graph.

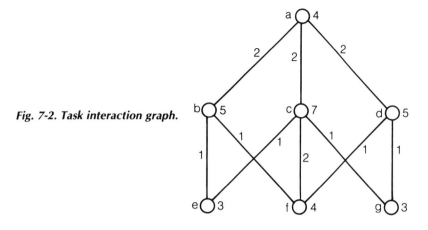

Fig. 7-2. Task interaction graph.

with Fig. 7-3. In this figure you have an irregular space. This space can be divided up into eight regions each with five cells. All nodes in the problem are assigned to processors, and each processor computes the same load. The communication load is also well balanced.

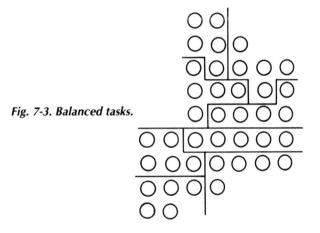

Fig. 7-3. Balanced tasks.

PARALLEL SPEEDUP

Brochard (1988) presented a paper on efficiency of parallel computers. He concluded that massively parallel, fine-grained systems can achieve nearly ideal speedup. Each problem must be considered for load and communication balancing.

Without going into any detail here, Chiricozzi and Damico (1988) and Jesshope (1987) edited conference proceedings on parallel processing. The interested reader should consult these sources.

ENGINEERING APPLICATIONS

A small book by Lord, et al (1983) discusses applications and architectures of parallel processors. The authors conducted a survey of many supercomputer centers and discuss some of the applications being pursued on parallel computers. These applications consist of nuclear reactor safety, nuclear fuel cycle studies, nuclear material safeguards (scenario evaluation), fusion energy studies, environmental study of pollution uptake, and atmosphere and ocean dynamics.

VECTOR AND MATRIX OPERATIONS

Vector and matrix operations have been discussed in the excellent book by Fox, et al (1988) and by McBryan and Van de Velde (1987). These workers used an MIMD - hypercube processor. As I pointed out earlier, doing vector-matrix operations, per se, are more efficiently done by signal processor chips like those discussed by Quarmby (1985).

To perform a matrix multiplication of the type

$$C = A \cdot B$$

where A, B and C are full M $\times$ M matrices, the matrices A and B are decomposed into sub-blocks.

$$\begin{bmatrix} A^{00} & A^{01} & A^{02} & A^{03} \\ A^{10} & A^{11} & A^{12} & A^{13} \\ A^{20} & A^{21} & A^{22} & A^{23} \\ A^{30} & A^{31} & A^{32} & A^{33} \end{bmatrix}$$

The elements in these sub-blocks may be single elements or small square sub-matrices. If the matrix of interest is an M $\times$ M matrix the sub-matrices A^{lk} contain the elements A_{ij} with

$$Ml/4 <= i < M(l+1)/4$$
$$Mk/4 <= j < M((k+1)/4$$

The sub-matrices can be manipulated as if they were single elements.

$$C^{lk} = \sum_{n} A^{ln} \cdot B^{nk}$$

All the processors in each row, i, receive a copy of A^{ii} sub-matrix by a message broadcast. The elements in each processor are then multiplied and stored in a C matrix. The B sub-blocks are then shifted up one processor. All the sub-blocks, one position to the right of the diagonal are now broadcast to all the processors in that row. The B submatrices are again shifted up one row. This shifting and multiplying is repeated until the B elements are in their initial configuration. The C matrix is now complete. I recommend Fox, et al (1988) for a more detailed description of the previous procedure.

FAST FOURIER TRANSFORM

The fast Fourier transform implemented on parallel processing computers has been described by Fox, et al (1988), Chamberlain (1988), Ashworth and Lyne (1988), and Cvetanovic (1987). Quarmby (1985) discusses using DSP chips for FFT solutions.

A signal waveform can be transformed from the time domain into the frequency domain with the Fourier transform. A complex waveform is considered to be represented by a series of sine and cosine terms. If you consider N input numbers:

$$x_0, x_1, x_2, \dots , x_k, \dots , x_{N-1}.$$

The output numbers are given by

$$X_0, X_1, X_2, \dots , X_k, \dots , X_{N-1}$$

and the transform is given by

$$x_l = \sum_{k=3}^{N-1} x_k \cdot w_{lk}$$

where w_{lk} is an array of complex constants given by

$$W_{lk} = \exp(-j \cdot 2\pi lk/N)$$

This is clearly a vector-matrix multiplication.

To perform a discrete Fourier transform, or DFT, the N values are split into two groups each with N/2 values.

$$x_0, x_1, x_2, \dots , x_{N-1}$$
$$x_0, x_2, x_4, \dots , x_{N-2}$$
$$x_1, x_3, x_5, \dots , x_{N-1}$$

These two groups are relabeled

$$y_0, y_1, y_2, \dots , y_{(N/2)-1}$$
$$z_0, z_1, z_2, \dots , z_{(N/2)-1}$$

The Fourier transform on these new sequences is then performed to give:

$$Y_0, Y_1, Y_2, \ldots, Y_1, \ldots, Y_{(N/2)-1}$$
$$Z_0, Z_1, Z_2, \ldots, Z_1, \ldots, Z_{(N/2)-1}$$

So

$$X_l = y_l + w_l \cdot z_l$$

and

$$X_{l+N/2} = Y_l - W_l \cdot Z_l$$

where W_l is given by

$$W_l = \exp(-j \cdot 2\pi l/N)$$

The above operations can be represented schematically in Fig. 7-4. MIMD processors with butterfly switches or message passing can be used to implement the FFT. Systolic arrays and DSP chips can also be used to perform the FFT.

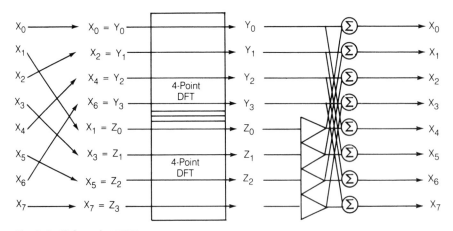

Fig. 7-4. Eight point DFT.

IMAGE PROCESSING

Video image processing is an important application for parallel processing architecture. Feature extraction is the most primitive image processing operation. This consists of edge detection from shadows, for example. Two sources for image processing are Kent, et al (1985) and Rohrbacher and Potter (1977).

A common image enhancement technique is called *convolution*.

This involves the modification of each pixel as a function of the sum of the products of its near neighbors and an a priori weighting matrix. Other image processing techniques include pseudocolor assignment, gray code manipulation, and fast Fourier transform.

PARALLEL OPTIMIZATION

Lootsma and Ragsdell (1988) discusses the state-of-the-art in parallel non-linear optimization. Typical optimization involves searches in phase-space for a minimum. This searching can be conducted in parallel by traversing several paths simultaneously. The Newton-Rapson method of minimizing a function f over the n-dimensional vector space E_n starts from an arbitrary point $x^o \epsilon E_n$. At the beginning you calculate the gradient

$$\nabla f(x^k)$$

and the Hessian matrix

$$\nabla^2 f(x^k)$$

At the current iteration point x^k. (I recommend String, 1986, for a discussion of the gradient method and the Hessian matrices.) The search direction s^k is solved from the relation

$$\nabla^2 f(x^k) \, S^k = -\nabla f(x^k)$$

The search direction is explored by seeking an approximation λ^k to a local minimum of the function

$$\phi_k(\lambda) = f(x^k + \lambda S^k)$$

The next iteration χ^{k+1} is compared with χ^k in the relation

$$x^{k+1} = x^k + \lambda_k S^k$$

If x^{k+1} and x^k are close to some tolerance, the procedure can be terminated.

MOLECULAR DYNAMICS

In performing molecular dynamics calculations on a parallel processing computer, it is necessary to partition the space such that each processor has a balanced load of molecules. The calculation consists of computing the velocity, acceleration, and forces on all the molecules at each time step. Message passing between processors occurs when a molecule leaves its space and drifts to another processor's space. I would guess that cellular automata could be used for molecular dynamics modeling.

LATTICE GAUGE THEORY OF QUARK CONFINEMENT

Nuclear matter is made up of protons and neutrons. These subatomic particles are built up from quarks. Quarks have never been observed or isolated, yet there is strong evidence for their existence. The proton, for example, is made up from three quarks bound together by flux tubes with the energy density of the tubes providing much of the mass of the system.

In the computation of the energy of quark confinement the space-time continuum is replaced with a four-dimensional hypercube lattice. A Monte Carlo method is then applied to solve relations of the type

$$<q^n> = \frac{\int dq\ q^n e^{-s(q)}}{\int dq\ e^{-s(q)}}$$

where q is one degree of freedom. The lattice spacing, a, must be much smaller than the diameter of a proton, R. And the spatial extent L of the lattice must be large. This means that this problem is best solved by a massive parallel computer. The memory requirements grow as L^4 and the CPU time grows as $R_p^2 L^4$. Lattice-gauge Monte Carlo simulation often contains 10^7 degrees of freedom.

Figure 7-5 is a sketch of quark potential computed by Monte Carlo methods on a hypercube parallel processor. The increasing potential corresponds to the formation of a flux tube between quarks leading to quark confinement.

Rebbi (1983) and Taylor (1989) give readable accounts of the methods of lattice-gauge theory of quarks. Kogut (1988) gives an account of these type of computations on a high-speed computer.

BIOMOLECULAR DESIGN

There are two powerful techniques used in the design of biomolecules. The first is a quantitative structure-activity analysis. This method correlates activity with physicochemical properties of molecules. A second technique is to design a molecular structure using potential energy functions and molecular dynamics. This technique can be used to study the interaction between a drug and its protein receptor site, for example. Lerner (1983) has published an article on synthetic vaccines designed with the aid of a computer.

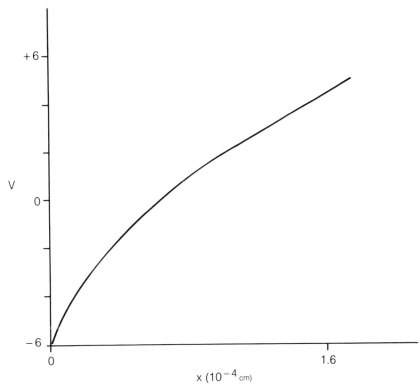

Fig. 7-5. Quark potential.

CONCLUSION

In this chapter I have sketched several scientific applications and algorithms for parallel computers. Loard, et al (1983) have discussed many applications in engineering ranging from aircraft design, nuclear reactor design, and earthquake modeling. Fox, et al (1988) is a very good source for scientific and engineering algorithms for parallel processors.

8

SIXTH GENERATION AND BEYOND

In this chapter I describe some fifth-generation supercomputers and a sixth-generation computer. These descriptions are of systems that are marketed today. The main sections of the chapter cover advanced technologies that might have an impact on future computing for the sixth generation and beyond. Much of this chapter will be speculations founded on hard research.

STATE OF THE ART

In this section I review some (certainly not all) of the current fifth-generation computers available. I classify fifth-generation computers as small parallel computers. These could have from a few to a few hundred processors. By this classification the PC plug-in-boards with several processors make the system a fifth-generation machine.

Intel, the maker of the 80×86 processors also assembles and markets parallel processing computer systems. These systems are configured as hypercubes of 8, 16, 32, 64, or 128 nodes. Each node consists of a microcomputer with local memory, communication and a vector processor. The prices are far beyond what a computer hacker could afford.

A company by the name of NCUBE in Beaverton, OR markets a hypercube architecture. They have available a 4-node hypercube on a PC-AT card. The cost is just beyond the hacker market. They also have systems up to 1024 nodes. The nodes are custom VLSI chips.

Chopp Computer Corporation in La Jolla, CA manufactures and markets parallel computer systems with up to 16 nodes. Their custom design and high price are designed for the high performance market. They claim that each node is more powerful than a conventional supercomputer.

BBN Advanced Computer, in Cambridge, MA markets a parallel processing system with 256 nodes. The system uses a butterfly switch to configure the system. There is a processor at each node and all the nodes share the same memory.

The Connection Machine, from Thinking Machines Corporation, is clearly a sixth-generation machine. It has 65,535 processing nodes. Each node is a one-bit processor with its own memory and communication links. There are 16 such nodes in a single custom VLSI package and 4096 such packages in the entire machine. These 64K of nodes are configured as a 16-dimensional hypercube. Hillis (1987, 1984), the developer of the machine, has written some very good descriptions of the computer. This machine can clearly outperform anything now available and could transform many fields, including artificial intelligence. Hillis (1985) has referred to this machine as a cellular automata machine. As a cellular automata machine the cells can have long-range interaction.

GALLIUM ARSENIDE

In this section I will discuss gallium arsenide (GaAs) as a potential material for advanced computers. First I'll look at the properties of GaAs that might result in the use of this material for faster computers. Then I will explore the structure of a few GaAs transistors, and problems and successes in GaAs digital IC devices. The last part of this section will concern electrooptical and integrated optical circuits. A good introductory book on GaAs technology is by Sclater (1988). An excellent book is by Ferry (1985).

Properties of GaAs

Gallium arsenide is known as a III-IV compound. It is a semi-insulating material, and when doped with appropriate donor or acceptor atoms becomes a semiconductor. In GaAs the effective mass of the electron is about seven percent less than that of silicon. This means that the GaAs electron mobility is about five to seven times higher than that of silicon. For similar power requirements the GaAs transistor can switch about five times faster than a silicon transistor.

Other major properties of GaAs are higher radiation resistance, and a wider working temperature range. Silicon chips can withstand about 10^3 to 10^4 rads of radiation, and GaAs chips can withstand 10^7 to 10^8 rads. This property is due to a higher band gap. More energy is required to ionize the GaAs than that required to ionize Si. The working temperature range is -200 to $+200$ degrees Celsius and, by special processing, GaAs transistors can operate as hot as 300-400 degrees Celsius. These two properties alone mean that device development will continue for space probes and robots to be used in a harsh environment.

Another major property of GaAs is that it is a direct energy gap material. As a result, GaAs can be used in electrooptic emitters and detectors. Silicon is an indirect gap material and is therefore a poor photonic emitter.

Crystal Growth

Gallium arsenide crystals are grown by a technique known as liquid-encapsulated Czochralski. The method consists of slowly pulling a seed crystal from a melt of pure, zone-refined GaAs. The top layer of the liquid GaAs is covered by a layer of molten B_2O_3. The B_2O_3 is a glass encapsulation for the GaAs. This glass layer suppresses the loss of arsenic from the molten GaAs. Crystals are typically three inches in diameter, and wafers are cut from these large boules.

Another very attractive technique to obtain wafers is to use a molecular beam machine to epitaxially grow atomic layers of GaAs on pure Si wafers. Panish (1989) has described molecular beam epitaxy and Morkoc, et al (1988) have described the problems in MBE growth of GaAs on Si.

GaAs Transistors

In this section I describe the structure of a simple transistor of the type found in gallium arsenide integrated circuits. The most common type of transistor in GaAs integrated circuits is the metal-semiconductor, field-effect transistor (MeSFET). A rough sketch of such a transistor is shown in Fig. 8-1.

The gate length is the distance electrons must travel from the source to the drain. Gate lengths as low as 0.5 microns have been fabricated for research purposes. The device consists of a semi-insulating substrate layer of GaAs. By ion implantation, n^+ layers are built up. The ohmic contacts are deposited followed by metal contacts for the source, gate and drain.

Digital GaAs Integrated Circuits

In this section I discuss some of the problems, advantages, and disadvantages in integrated digital gallium arsenide circuits. An excellent review on the subject is given by Gilbert (1985). Two very important concepts in integrated circuits are gate delay and power dissipation. As the gate count increases on a chip, the power dissipation per gate should drop to prevent the chip from overheating. As

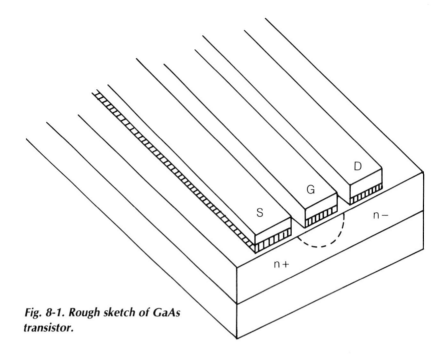

Fig. 8-1. Rough sketch of GaAs transistor.

transistors become smaller, the gate delay decreases. This presents an apparent dilemma. High gate count of GaAs transistors on an integrated circuit will not be possible (at least in the forseeable future).

Figure 8-2 is a rough sketch of the power dissipation versus gate delay for several families of chips. Silicon CMOS is one of the most common chip families. It has a good power dissipation. With electron-beam and x-ray lithography it is possible to decrease the gate size until the CMOS family is overlapping with GaAs chips. This doesn't imply that GaAs will become obsolete before it is used. Actually GaAs and Si chips will most likely be used together in hybrid systems. The two types of materials complement each other.

Applications for GaAs Chips

From the above mentioned limitations and advantages of GaAs several applications are apparent. High-speed, high-bandwidth array and signal processing are obvious applications. It should be possible to design pipelined data-flow, data-driven computers from GaAs. High-speed, high-bandwidth vector processors and systolic arrays are also good possibilities. Wafer-scale integration and advanced VLSI packaging should alleviate some of the chip-to-chip interconnection delays and avoid terminated transmission line interconnects.

With GaAs grown by MBE on Si wafers, it should be possible to build hybrid GaAs-Si devices on the same chip. This idea was dis-

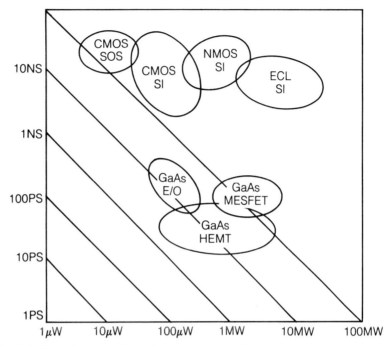

Fig. 8-2. Plot of power dissipation versus gate delay.

cussed by Morkoc, et al (1988). Using this technique it should be possible to build hybrid electronic-photonic devices. Recall that GaAs is a direct gap semiconductor and is therefore useful for photon emission and detection. Dautremount-Smith, et al (1989) and Alles and Brady (1989) have discussed fabrication and packaging for high-speed, high-bandwidth fiberoptic transmitters and receivers integrated on chip with electronics. This entire device is no larger than a typical 16-pin DIP. These devices are currently manufactured by AT&T and marketed for use in connecting computers to LANs.

These ideas of electronic-photonic devices integrated in one package naturally bring to mind the new integrated optic technology. Dutta (1989) briefly discussed these ideas and Hunsperger (1984) has written a complete review of the technology of integrated optics. It is possible to build complete micro-optical benches integrated on a single wafer of hybrid superlattice material. The small optical bench (SOB) would contain prisms, mirrors, lenses, lasers of several wavelengths, detectors, photonic switching devices and electronic devices all integrated in one small package. These ideas bring to mind the possibility of building not only electronic-photonic computers, but also pure optical computers as well. This is the subject of the next section.

Gallium arsenide grown by molecular beam epitaxy opens up a whole range of new device physics. Because atoms are placed on the crystal lattice one at a time, it is possible to engineer specific lattices known as superlattices. This allows what is known as bandgap engineering. Multi-state transistors for multiple-valued logic is a possibility. The physics of these submicron and ultra-submicron devices are discussed by Iafrate (1985). Quantum dots and quantum well devices are possible. The electrostatic Aharonov-Bohm effect discussed by Webb and Washburn (1988) is another possibility for advanced computing with gallium arsenide, bandgap-engineered materials.

OPTICAL COMPUTING

In this section I discuss in some depth the principles of digital optical computing. This is followed by discussion of current technology in integrated optis and speculations on future optical computers. Much of the following is from an early paper I wrote (1986).

Design for a General-Purpose Optical Computer

All modern computers are derived from a so-called classical finite state machine (see Chapter 2). In a finite state machine the memory units are latches and the CPU is a combinatoric logic unit. This circuit is completely parallel and has no von Neumann bottleneck (Fig. 8-3).

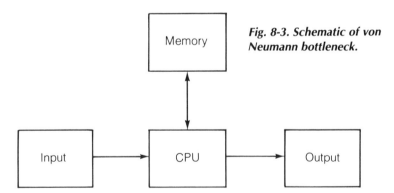

Fig. 8-3. Schematic of von Neumann bottleneck.

If more state variables are needed, then the number of data lines increases. To reduce the number of lines a binary encoding technique is used to reduce N to $\log_2 (N)$. This is the source of the von Neumann bottleneck.

A finite state machine is shown in Fig. 8-4, and a modified finite state machine is shown in Fig. 8-5. Notice that only one latch at a time can be addressed. To remove the bottleneck N channels must be connected in parallel to the CPU. An obvious choice would be an optical computer, but there are several difficulties in constructing such a sys-

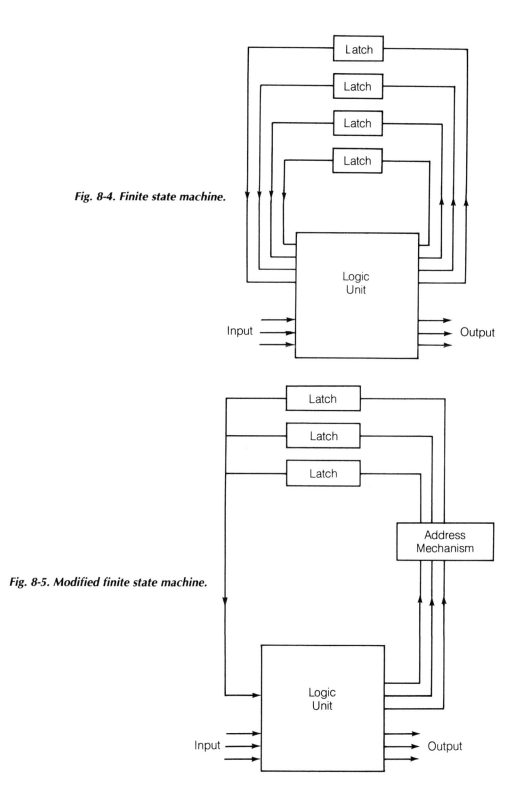

Fig. 8-4. Finite state machine.

Fig. 8-5. Modified finite state machine.

tem: memory elements; detection and regeneration of optical signals; and fast optical logic. Each of these problems I will discuss in more detail.

The problem of optical memories seems to be a problem of materials—specifically for memory addressing and storage. To implement the modified state machine, a material for long term storage is needed. For the classical finite state machine the storage medium need only delay the information one clock cycle.

Detection and restimulation also seem to be a problem in materials science. It is very difficult to get one optical signal to affect another optical signal. If pn junctions are used to stimulate and detect the light, why use light at all? An optical computer must be almost purely optical because any hybrid approach will suffer from the limitation of an electronics interface.

One approach to an optical computer is an optical NOR gate array, which can be constructed in the following manner. Two checkerboard images are projected onto a common surface to give an OR resulting image. After inverting in contrast and threshold the intensity is the NOR of the inputs. The output of these NOR gates is used as the inputs of other NOR gates. The interconnection is performed with a hologram. The reference point source (x,y) is associated with three object point sources at $(x,y-1)$, $(x+1,y-1)$, $(x+2,y-1)$. Such a distribution system would distribute the outputs of any number of inputs in parallel. This type of computer will be discussed in the next section on residue arithmetic and liquid crystal light valves.

Residue Arithmetic Computing

The problem of detection and regeneration of the optical signal can be avoided with a computer based on the residue number system. With the system that Huang (1975) has proposed, parallel optical processing is possible, but conversion from residue to standard is awkward. Before I discuss the residue arithmetic unit I will discuss the residue number system. Then I will discuss methods of doing residue arithmetic by optical means. In particular I will discuss the use of the liquid crystal light valve as a component of the optical computer.

The residue number system was described by Szabo and Zanka (1967). The system is based on a N-tuple of integers $m_1, m_2, m_3 \ldots, m_n$, called the *moduli*. The residue of moduli m_i is the least positive integer of the division of x by m_i where x is the number to be converted and M is the product of the moduli. Between 0 and M-1 the answer is unique. As an example, the moduli are 5, 7, 9. Therefore $M = 315$ and calculations are unique between 0 and 314. Consider addition of 87 and 49.

$$
\begin{array}{rcccc}
87 & \rightarrow & 2 & 3 & 6 \\
+49 & \rightarrow & 4 & 0 & 4 \\
136 & \leftarrow & 1 & 3 & 1
\end{array}
$$

In the residue system, 87 is 2, 3, 6. The 2 is a residue of 87 moduli 5. Similarly for 3 and 6 from moduli 7 and 9. The 49 is translated in the same way. Each column is added and the result written as a residue of that particular modulus. A look-up table could be used for conversion from residue to decimal system. Subtraction is done in a similar manner. Division and multiplication are done by subtraction and addition of logs which are found in a look-up table. A look-up table is essentially a mapping operation and can be done quickly by an optical computer by representing the residue number by spatial position.

Tai (1980), has discussed the advantages of residue arithmetic and has implemented some techniques. One major advantage is very high throughput with parallel computation. It is possible to Fourier transform 10^6 data samples in a few microseconds once the data is entered in the optical computer. However, present optical techniques lack flexibility and programmability. An advantage of the residue system for optical computers is that no carry is needed. Therefore a computation can be done in a single clock cycle.

A simple residue optical computer could now be built. The phase of polarization of a coherent monochromatic beam might be used to implement a residue encoder-adder. A separate beam would be used to represent each of the moduli. Residues would be denoted as various phase shifts relative to a reference beam at various angles of polarization. Phase shift steps would be implemented by Kerr cells and rotation of polarization could be done by the Faraday effect. The cycle of the Faraday effect could be divided into equal parts to represent each of the residues of a particular modulus.

A simple design concept is based on directional coupler waveguide switches. Two waveguides are placed close enough to each other so that with no applied field the waveguides are synchronous.

When a voltage V_t is applied to the electrode, the synchronism between the waveguides is broken and the propagation will remain in the first waveguide as shown in Fig. 8-6.

A modulo 5 adder using waveguide switches is shown in Fig. 8-7 and a multipurpose module is shown in Fig. 8-8.

Another method of implementing residue arithmetic on an optical computer is given by Huang, et al, (1978). The residue can be represented by spatial positions of light spots and the residue operation becomes a spatial permutation of possible spot positions. To represent the residue of a number of modulus 5, for example, would

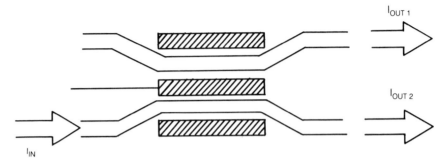

Fig. 8-6. Directional coupler wave guide switch. Reproduced with permission from: Tai, A. "Design Concept for an Optical Numerical Computer Based on the Residue Number System", IEEE 1980 Optical Computing Conference.

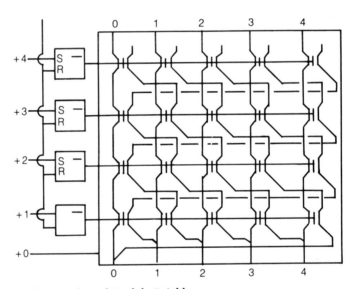

Fig. 8-7. Implementation of Modulo 5 Adder.
Reproduced with permission from:
Tai, A. "Design Concept for an Optical Numerical Computer Based on the Residue Number System", IEEE 1980 Optical Computing Conference.

require five spatial positions to be allocated, and one of these would contain a spot of light to indicate the number being represented. The various fundamental mathematical operations may be viewed as mappings of the set of possible input residues onto itself, but with a reassignment of values. The maps must be capable of performing spatial permutation. Figure 8-9 illustrates the residue operation: addition by 3 and multiplication by 3 as maps for the particular modulus 5. There are two types of maps for residue operations: fixed maps and changeable maps.

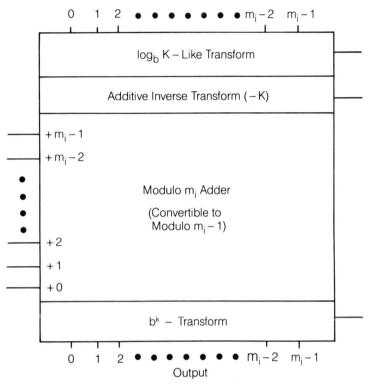

Fig. 8-8. Conceptual design of Programmable multi-purpose computation module. Reproduced with permission from: Tai, A. "Design Concept for an Optical Numerical Computer Based on the Residue Number System", IEEE 1980 Optical Computing Conference.

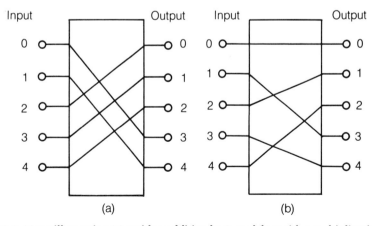

Fig. 8-9. Maps illustrating (a) residue addition by 3, and (b) residue multiplication by 3. Reproduced with permission from: Huang, A.; Tsunoda, Y.; Goodman, J.W. and Ishihara, S., "Some Optical Methods for Performing Residue Arithmetic Operations" IEEE 1978, Optical Computing Conference.

A fixed map always performs the same operation. Figure 8-10 illustrates four permutation devices. These methods use mirrors, prisms, optical waveguides and gratings. All four of these approaches can be integrated, as will be discussed in the next section. Another method, shown in Fig. 8-11, uses a spatial matrix mask.

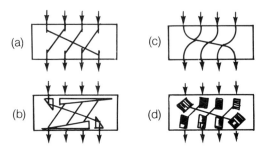

Fig. 8-10. Possible approaches to constructing fixed maps using (a) mirrors, (b) prisms, (c) optical waveguides or fibers, and (d) gratings. Reproduced with permission from: Huang, A.; Tsunoda, Y.; Goodman, J.W. and Ishihara, S., "Some Optical Methods for Performing Residue Arithmetic Operations" IEEE 1978, Optical Computing Conference.

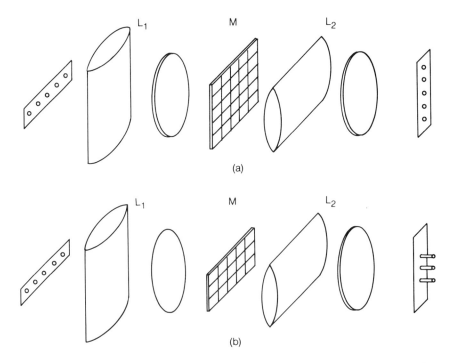

Fig. 8-11. (a) Spatial permutations by means of a permutation matrix. (b) residue multiplication with a binary output. Reproduced with permission from: Huang, A.; Tsunoda, Y.; Goodman, J.W. and Ishihara, S., "Some Optical Methods for Performing Residue Arithmetic Operations" IEEE 1978, Optical Computing Conference.

Light incident on any one of the input ports is spread vertically to fill the height of the matrix mask M. In the horizontal direction lens combination L_1 images the input port to form a vertical column of light incident on the matrix mask. Lens combination L_2 images the matrix mask in the vertical direction onto the vertically stacked output ports, while integrating or adding the light transmitted across horizontal rows of the mask. Yet another method is shown in Fig. 8-12. In this optical adder the incoming signal M_1 is represented in binary form. Each bit controlling a selector that addresses one of two possible maps. A series of $M = \log_2 M_i$ map pairs is required. Each map has M_i input and output ports.

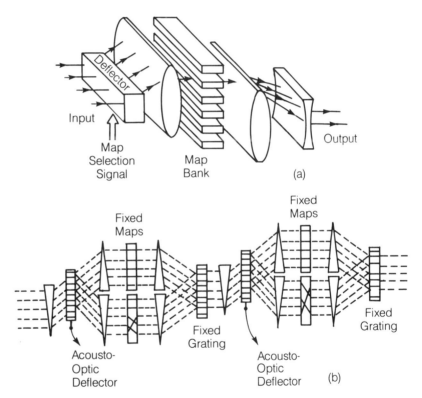

Fig. 8-12. Optical realization of a changeable map by means of (a) a single deflector addressing many maps, and (b) multiple deflectors addressing only two maps each. Reproduced with permission from: Huang, A.; Tsunoda, Y.; Goodman, J.W. and Ishihara, S., "Some Optical Methods for Performing Residue Arithmetic Operations" IEEE 1978, Optical Computing Conference.

A changeable map with modulus of 5 is shown in Fig. 8-13. This map has five inputs and outputs and is made up of 10 subunits, each consisting of a planar waveguide with three switching channels. A light beam incident on a switching channel is either transmitted or

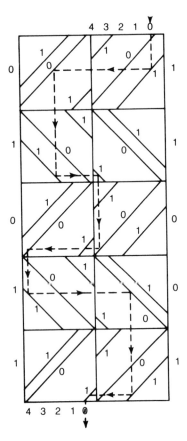

Fig. 8-13. Changeable map realized by a series of integrated optic switches. Reproduced with permission from: Huang, A.; Tsunoda, Y.; Goodman, J.W. and Ishihara, S., "Some Optical Methods for Performing Residue Arithmetic Operations" IEEE 1978, Optical Computing Conference.

reflected depending on the electrical signal applied to the switch. If the binary number applied to a subunit is zero, then the diagonal channel is activated and is reflected. If the binary number applied is one then the diagonal channel is transmissive. The first subunit corresponds to the most significant bit. After reflection of the diagonal or off-diagonal channels, the beam enters the second subunit. Finally the beam will emerge from the tenth subunit. The number of this port will be the residue of the sum of the incoming residue and the input binary for a modulus of 5.

Collins, et al, (1978) devised what they call a spatial light modulator for residue arithmetic computations. They used a Hughes liquid crystal light valve (LCLV) as shown in Fig. 8-14. This figure shows a birefringent mirror. The incident beam is polarized at 45 degrees to the axis. After reflection it is resolved into two components along the two axes. The component parallel to the slow axes undergoes a phase delay relative to that along the fast axis. The phase delay is cyclic modula 360 degrees and provides the variable needed to implement residue arithmetic. With respect to a base P, phase delays of 360n/p

Spatial Light Modulator:
Liquid Crystal Light Valve
(Hughes)

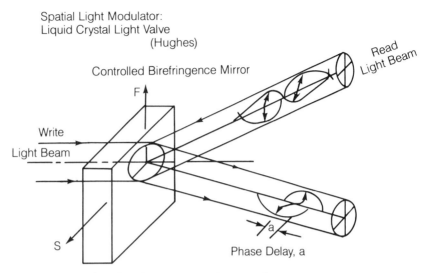

Fig. 8-14. Reproduced with permission from: Collins, S.A., Jr., Ambuel, A., and Damon, E.K. "Numerical Optical Data Processing" IEEE 1978, Optical Computing Conference.

are allowed. If a beam of light is reflected several times off this controlled birefringent mirror the relative phase delays add modulo p. The liquid crystal light valve has been discussed in a paper by Bleka (1978). The major interest in the LCLV is that light beams can be used to control other light beams. (In the next section I will discuss another method for light to control light.)

Sequential Optical Logic Processor

Chavel, et al, (1983) has described some of the architecture and techniques for sequential optical logic processors. The two basic elements needed are a non-linear device to provide the gate function and an interconnection element as shown in Fig. 8-15. For sequential logic the interconnection path must include feedback for generating clock signals and for obtaining information from memory elements.

The Hughes LCLV, as pointed out earlier, produces pointwise non-linear behavior that can, to some extent, be modified and in particular can be used to implement the NOR function as shown in Fig. 8-16.

This graph is a sketch of the non-linear input/output relationships for the LCLV. Each element or pixel on the LCLV acts as an independent gate so $10^5 - 10^6$ pixels can be used in parallel.

A general interconnection system would provide for connecting any gate output to the input of any gate or combination of gates. The interconnection system images the gate output array plane into the

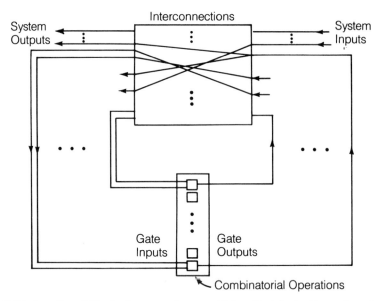

Fig. 8-15. Functional block diagram of sequential optical logic. Reproduced with permission from: Chavel, P., Forchheimer, R., Jenkins, B.K., Sawehuk, A.A., and Strand, T.C. "Architectures for a Sequential Optical Logic Processor" IEEE 1983 Optical Computing Conference.

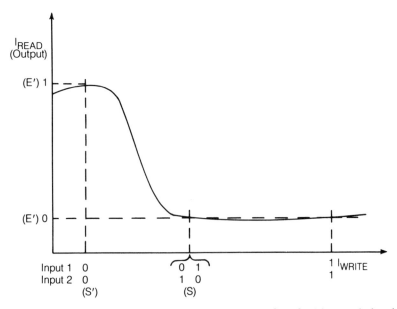

Fig. 8-16. LCLV input/output characteristics. Reproduced with permission from: Chavel, P., Forchheimer, R., Jenkins, B.K., Sawehuk, A.A., and Strand, T.C. "Architectures for a Sequential Optical Logic Processor" IEEE 1983 Optical Computing Conference.

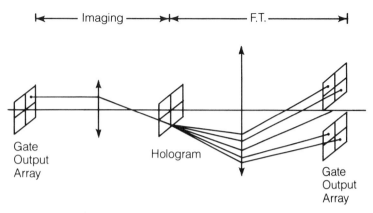

Fig. 8-17. Space-Variant interconnection system. In general the hologram produces multiple diffraction orders, only one of which is used. Reproduced with permission from: Chavel, P., Forchheimer, R., Jenkins, B.K., Sawehuk, A.A., and Strand, T.C. "Architectures for a Sequential Optical Logic Processor" IEEE 1983 Optical Computing Conference.

gate input array plane. This represents a space-variant imaging system, and is sketched in Fig. 8-17.

The gate outputs are imaged onto the interconnection hologram. This computer-generated hologram (CGH) consists of an array of subholograms, one for each output. The subhologram reconstructs an image on the gate input side of the LCLV. The reconstructed image is a simple dot pattern with each bright spot illuminating a gate input. The reconstructed images can illuminate any combination of gate inputs. This interconnection scheme allows complete generality, but at the expense of space bandwidth requirements on the CGH. Given an N × N array of subholograms on the CGH and a N × N array of gates on the LCLV, each subhologram must be able to address any of the N^2 gate inputs. The number of addressable points in the reconstruction of a subhologram is equal to the number of complex valued sample points in the subhologram. The space bandwidth produced (SBWP) by each hologram is

$$S_s = P^2Q^2N^2$$

where P^2 is the number of resolution elements in the hologram, Q^2 is a factor representing the amount of oversampling in the hologram plane, and N^2 is the number of subholograms. The total SBWP is therefore

$$S_T = N^2S_s = P^2Q^2N^4$$

Let the cross-talk be X. Then the ratio between gate inputs of the worst case zero value I_0 and the worst case one value I_1 is:

$$X = I_0/I_1$$

In order to distinguish all possible zero and one states, X must be less than one. The hologram coding parameter P has a minimum value of three for square cells, and Q will be in the range of two-three. The maximum number of gates corresponding to a value of PQ is on the order of ten. Because SBWP is on the order of 10^{10} then N is about 100. The computer-generated hologram is the limiting element.

If one compromises on the arbitrariness of gate interconnections, a substantial increase in the number of gates results. This system is implemented with a space-invariant filter as shown in Fig. 8-18. The filter has an impulse response such that every gate output and gate input is addressed relative to the position of the gate output. Because the holographic element used in this system is simple, a very large number of gates can be interconnected. If full SBWP with the computer generated hologram could be exploited, and $P^2Q^2 = 100$, then about 10^8 gates could be interconnected.

The point of the above analysis is that optical computing is a real possibility in the near future. In the following sections I will describe a different approach to optical computing.

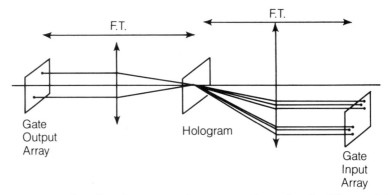

Fig. 8-18. Space-invariant interconnection system. Reproduced with permission from: Chavel, P., Forchheimer, R., Jenkins, B.K., Sawehuk, A.A., and Strand, T.C. "Architectures for a Sequential Optical Logic Processor" IEEE 1983 Optical Computing Conference.

The Transphasor

An interesting recent development reported by Abraham, et al (1983) is a device known as a transphasor. This is the optical analog of the transistor. The transphasor uses what is known as non-linear optical materials. A transistor switches an electrical signal by use of a small control signal. The transphasor operates in a similar manner. A laser beam switches another laser beam. This could be a key component of an optical computer.

The non-linear optical material has the property that a light beam of increasing intensity causes a change in the refractive index of the material. This non-linear material is placed in the cavity of a Fabry-Perot interferometer. If the length of the cavity is changed it can result in interference of the light waves in the cavity, and near-total reflection or near-total transmission.

Figure 8-19 is a diagram of the Fabry-Perot interferometer transphasor switch. By means of the control beam it is possible to change the net intensity of light in the cavity. This allows the refractive index of the material to be adjusted by the control beam. Because the refractive index of the material can change by the control beam, then the effective cavity length can change and the transmitter beam can be modulated by the control beam.

This device could be a key component in an optical computer. Abraham and his coworkers have constructed OR gates and AND gates using transphasors. Incorporating these devices in integrated optical circuits might result in more rapid advances in the development of the optical computer.

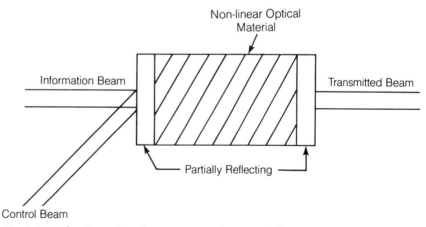

Fig. 8-19. Fabry-Perot interfermeter transphasor switch.

Integrated Optics

A very interesting development in optics is the integrated optical circuit. Early hybrid integrated optics were made from a combination of materials such as zinc oxide, organic polymers, lithium niobate, and magnetooptic garnets. Hull (1987) has proposed a silicon-based

Table 8-1.

Integrated Optical Components from GaAs
Lasers
Couplers
Detectors
Switches
Modulators
Filters
Amplifiers
Lenses
Acoustic Transducers
Polarizers
Reflectors
Diffraction Gratings
Charged Coupled Devices

monolithic integrated optics. It is doubtful that this scheme will be very successful because silicon is an indirect bandgap material and is a poor photon emitter and detector. Also it cannot be bandgap engineered as readily as GaAs. Table 8-1 is a list of all the integrated optics components that have been fabricated with GaAs. In the remainder of this section I discuss what an integrated optics circuit is and how some of the devices listed in Table 8-1 can be integrated into a monolithic circuit.

Sluss, et al (1987) have written an excellent introduction to integrated optics. Figure 8-20 is a sketch of the basic element of an integrated optic circuit. The thin film waveguide is used to pipe the light beam from one optical element to another. By Snell's law, if the refractive index of the waveguide material is higher than the surrounding material, then all light rays below a critical angle of reflectance with the wall of the waveguide will be confined to the waveguide.

These waveguides can be deposited, or ion implanted, into the GaAs substrate. They can also be assembled by molecular beam epitaxy. Two waveguides can be coupled as shown in Fig. 8-21. The angle of cutoff is appropriate for the refractive index to allow the light to escape from one waveguide and enter into another. Prisms and lenses can also be coupled to waveguides in order to modify the light beam.

Another type of coupler is the dual-channel directional coupler shown in Fig. 8-22. This type of coupler consists of two waveguides placed in close proximity so the optical field profiles in the two waveguides overlap, causing a coupling between the two. Coupling effi-

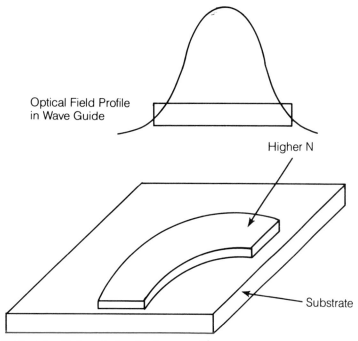

Optical Field Profile
in Wave Guide

Higher N

Substrate

Fig. 8-20. Sketch of integrated optical waveguide.

Fig. 8-21. Waveguide coupling device.

Substrate

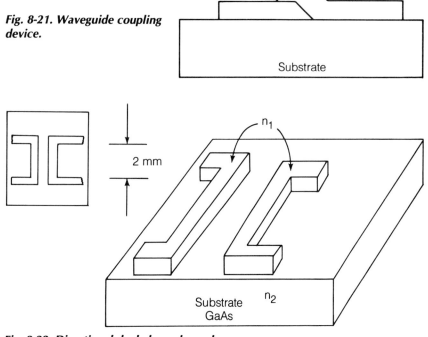

2 mm

n_1

Substrate
GaAs

n_2

Fig. 8-22. Directional dual-channel coupler.

ciency between 10% and 100% can be achieved by this technique. The actual coupling length must be on the order of millimeters.

Another interesting device for integrated optics is the electrooptic modulator shown in Fig. 8-23. In this device the waveguide is a material in which the refractive index can be changed by an electric field. By modulating a voltage signal, the light beam in the waveguide can be modulated to impress information on the carrier signal. With a dual channel electrooptic modulator, it is possible to build switches as complex as a butterfly switch of the type discussed in Chapter 2.

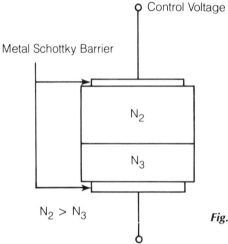

Fig. 8-23. Electrooptic modulator.

With gallium arsenide as the substrate, it is possible to build all these devices including lenses and photodetectors all on the same chip. Several systems such as spectrum analyzers, optical multiplexers, analog-to-digital converters, and telecommunication devices with fiberoptic waveguides have been described by Hunsperger (1985).

Conclusion and Comments

Optical computing is potentially very fast. If the number of electronic components in the system can be minimized, the processing speed can increase to nearly the speed of light.

Another advantage of optical computing is the massive parallelism inherent in optics. Spatial-light-modulators can be used to interconnect computers. They could also act as optical crossbar networks. Optics will become competitive in applications where communication overhead is intensive.

As a last comment, I should point out that the Journal of Applied Optics often publishes papers on optical computing and optical neural networks.

QUANTUM DEVICES

When I talked about gallium arsenide, I mentioned the possibility of using molecular beam epitaxy to bandgap engineer materials and grow quantum wells and quantum dots. These quantum devices are so small that the wavelength of an electron is about the same size (0.1 micron). An electron confined to a well will have several discrete, well-defined energy levels. If a quantum well is connected to a quantum line of appropriate width, it is possible for the electron to tunnel out of the well and enter the quantum wire at the same energy level. At this size, waveguide relationships are more relevant than the ideas of electrons in wires. If two dots of different size are in close proximity, there will be an energy barrier between them. Each dot will have electrons confined at different energy levels. By applying a bias to a dot, it will be possible to cause the electron to tunnel to a neighboring dot. These ideas could be extended to constructing a quantum dot, cellular automata machine. A good reference on the physics of these submicron devices is Iafrate (1985).

MOLECULAR ELECTRONIC DEVICES

Far below the quantum devices in scale are molecular electronic devices. (Some of the principles of electron tunneling apply to these devices.) At this level single molecules are the individual electronic elements in a circuit. Forrest Carter developed many of these ideas and held a workshop in 1981. Carter (1982) was the editor of the proceedings. Many of the ideas presented here are from a paper by Carter (1983).

Electrons shifting from one atom to another can change the state of a molecule. This state change can affect, for example, the ability to conduct electricity or absorb light of a certain wavelength. Aviram and Ratner (1974) assembled a molecule of the type shown in Fig. 8-24. They used this material in the construction of a molecular rectifier. Devices of this type can be assembled by using Langmur-Blodgett films, thin films only one molecule thick. Mobius (1978) has written a good review of this technique with potential applications to molecular electronics.

The shift of an electron in a molecule can change the properties of the molecule as was shown above for the molecular rectifier. Another molecular electronic device is the soliton switch. A soliton is a pseudoparticle that is able to travel through a medium without dissipating any energy. In a conjugated system like that shown in Fig. 8-25 it is possible to have a traveling soliton wave.

A molecule known as the push-pull olefin can be used as a source or trigger for sending a soliton down a conjugated chain of carbon

CN
CN
S
S
S
S
CN
CN

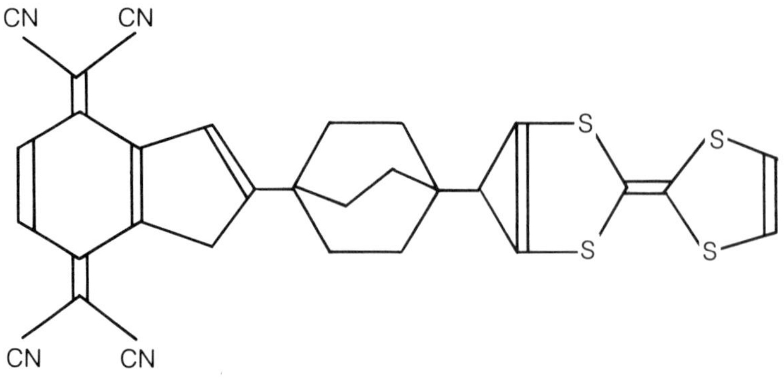

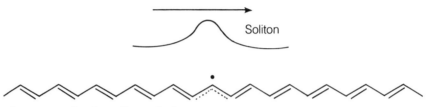

Fig. 8-24. Molecular diode, ala Aviram and Ratner (1974).

Soliton

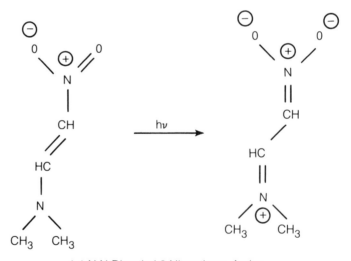

Fig. 8-25. Molecular soliton, ala Carter (1983).

hν
1,1-N,N-Dimethal-2-Nitroethene Amine

Fig. 8-26. Molecular soliton, ala push-pull olefin.

atoms. Figure 8-26 is a schematic diagram of the push-pull olefin. In the presence of light there is an electron shift. If a conjugated system is attached in place on one of the $-CH_3$ groups then the shifting would continue and a soliton would be propagated down the $(CH)_x$ chain. Carter (1983) has proposed ganged switches and soliton valves based on these principles. These soliton switches would operate at less than the speed of sound, since the soliton travels at less than this speed.

Solitons can also be generated in an electric field as indicated in Fig. 8-27. As a result of this reaction, a proton is shifted and two solitons of opposite charge will be traveling in opposite directions. When the solitons are far from the shifted proton, then the proton will shift again and generate two more solitons of opposite charge. Carter has also shown how molecular laser generated photons can operate from traveling solitons.

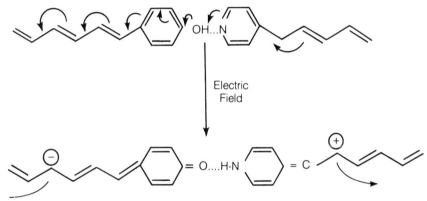

Fig. 8-27. Molecular soliton generator, ala Carter (1983).

In the above section I discussed quantum wells and quantum dots. Quantum wells also can occur in molecular systems. Figure 8-28 is a schematic of several quantum wells. These could be formed in a conjugated system, for example.

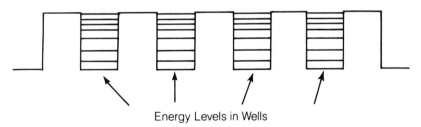

Fig. 8-28. Quantum energy wells.

If an electron approaching a well has the same energy as the electron in the well, then it is possible for the electron to tunnel through the barrier. In other words, the approaching electron's energy is equal to one of the energy levels in the quantum well. If the height of the wells can be controlled, then switching can occur.

A molecular electronic, quantum-well, cellular automata computer might be assembled. Each element (or cell in the machine) needs to only communicate with its nearest neighbors. The initial state might be set optically with a holographic mask, or chemically with a chemical-dynamic of the type proposed by Conrad (1985).

How might you construct one of these molecular computers? There are two proposed methods for constructing these systems: one is known as the Merrifield method and the second is self organization. The Merrifield method is, in some respects, an extension of current lithographic techniques for making integrated circuits.

The Merrifield method is specifically designed for precise atomic assembly of polypeptides or proteins. The method has been extended to polynucleotides or synthetic DNA. The technique is simple in concept. A plastic bead substrate is prepared such that an amino acid will bond. This bond is later broken. By using computer-controlled valves, reagents and other amino acids are passed over the beads in the proper sequence to assemble the desired polypeptide. After the final amino acid has reacted, the linkage with the substrate is broken and the polypeptide is released.

A similar technique might be used to grow a molecular computer. In this case the bonds to the substrate might not be broken. X-ray or electron lithography or molecular beam epitaxy may be used in conjunction with the wet chemical methods to assemble the molecular computer.

The second major technique of assembling a molecular computer is self-organization. Within living organisms there are hundreds of examples of molecular recognition and self-assembly. Enzymes must interlock at certain sites for various biochemical reactions. This is an example of molecular recognition. Stillinger and Wasserman (1978) have suggested a synthetic approach to molecular recognition and self-organization. Saenger (1984) discusses the structural aspects of cyclodextrin. These materials are often used as model compounds for molecular recognition and self-assembly. They have also been studied as model enzymes and are similar to compounds studied by Penderson, Crum and Lehn, who received the Nobel Prize in chemistry in 1987 for their work.

Cyclodextrin is an interesting compound. Its molecular structure is shown in Fig. 8-29. From this computer-generated plot it can be seen that there is a large open space in the center of the molecule. This has a major advantage. Small molecules can enter this hole or cage and become trapped. These types of compounds are therefore known as *inclusion* compounds. The cyclodextrin molecule can form an inclusion complex with metal iodides, for example. These com-

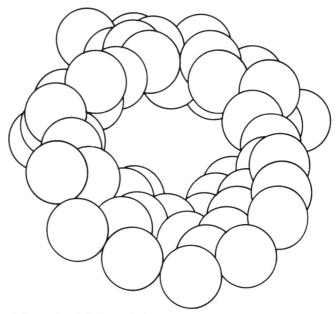

Fig. 8-29. Schematic of alpha-cyclodextrin.

pounds can then be crystallized to form chains of iodine and metal atoms as shown in Fig. 8-30. The side view of the cyclodextrin is similar to a rounded trapezoid. These stack to form channels with the iodine atoms trapped inside and the metal atom trapped in the interstitial region of the crystals. These could be thought of as atomic-size wires. By extending these ideas of molecular self-assembly, it might be possible to build a molecular computer.

Both the Merrifield technique and molecular self-assembly might take advantage of genetically engineered polymers as discussed by Ulmer (1982).

Drexler (1981, 1986) has proposed an entire technology, not just computing machines, based on molecular-scale devices. These molecular devices could be small robots that are smaller than a living cell. They could be used to grow complex structures from exotic materials. The structures could grow similarly to the way a tree grows from a small seed. The seed contains all the information and molecular machinery to grow a tree. The same ideas could be used to grow far more complex structures when you have the ability to assemble the appropriate molecular devices or assemblers.

BEYOND MOLECULAR ELECTRONICS

Fredkin and Toffali (1982) have designed a reversible logic element, Feynman (1987) has devised quantum mechanical computers

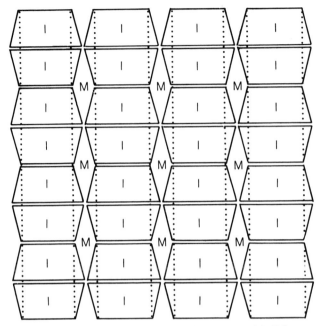

Fig. 8-30. Schematic of crystals of alpha-cyclodextrin metal iodide complex.

using this reversible or conservative logic. He has shown that it is possible to build logic elements with the laws of quantum mechanics, and therefore computing elements on atomic scale. The NOT gate is an example of a reversible logic element where no information is lost. One of the logic gates suggested by Fredkin and Toffali is the controlled NOT gate, which is shown in Fig. 8-31. They also discuss the controlled NOT gate shown in Fig. 8-32.

Feynman gives extensive design principles for these quantum mechanical computers, but he does not give a hint how to assemble

Fig. 8-31. CONTROLLED NOT gate and truth table.

a	b	a'	b'
0	0	0	0
0	1	0	1
1	0	1	1
1	1	1	0

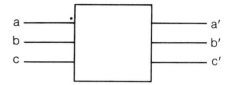

**Fig. 8-32. CONTROLLED CONTROLLED
NOT gate and truth table.**

a	b	c	a'	b'	c'
0	0	0	0	0	0
0	0	1	0	0	1
0	1	0	0	1	0
0	1	1	0	1	1
1	0	0	1	0	0
1	0	1	1	0	1
1	1	0	1	1	1
1	1	1	1	1	0

them. What type of materials are required? It might require new forms of matter. Hansen (1974) edited a conference proceeding on the physics of dense matter. This is an unusual state of matter like neutron star stuff. Farhi and Jaffe (1984) discuss the properties of quark matter and show that it may be stable! Mann and Primakoff (1980) show how to produce this strange matter in nucleon collisions and Donaldson (1986) has done paper engineering for accelerators needed to make these strange materials, like quark matter and neutron star stuff. These ideas are clearly speculative and might remain that way for some time to come. The point is that there isn't any fundamental physics to block our assembly of massively parallel computers based on molecular or quantum-size logic elements.

References

Aarts, E., and Korst, J., *Simulated Annealing and Boltzmann Machines: A Stochastic Approach to Combinatorial Optimization and Neural Computing,* John Wiley, New York, 1989.

Abraham, E., Seaton, C. T. and Smith, S. D., "The Optical Computer," SCI. AM., February, 1983.

Agrawal, D.P., Janakiram, V.K. and Pathak, G.C., "Evaluating the Performance of Multicomputer Configurations," *IEEE Computer,* pp. 23 – 37, May, 1986.

Alles, D.S. and Brady, K.J., "Packaging Technology for III-V Photonic Devices and Integrated Circuits," *AT&T Technical Journal*, p. 83, Vol. 68, No. 1, Jan./Feb., 1989.

Ashworth, M and Lyne, A.G., "A Segmented FFT Algorithm for Vector Computers," *Parallel Computing*, pp. 217 – 224, Vol. 6, 1988.

Askew, C.R., Carpenter, D.B., Chalker, J.T., Hey, A.J.G., Moore, M., Nicole, D.A., and Pritchard, D.J., "Monte Carlo Simulation on Transputer Arrays," *Parallel Computing*, pp. 247 – 258, Vol. 6, 1988.

Aviram, A. and Ratner M.A., "Molecular Rectifiers," *Chem. Phys. Lett.,* pp. 277 – 283, Vol. 29, No. 2, 1974.

Basu, A., "Parallel Processing Systems: A Nomenclature Based on Their Characteristics," *IEEE Proceedings*, Vol. 134, Pt. E, No. 3, May, 1987.

Beizer, B., *The Frozen Keyboard: Living with Bad Software*, TAB BOOKS, Blue Ridge Summit, PA, 1988.

Berlekamp, E.R., Conway, J.H., Guy, R.K., *Winning Ways for Your Mathematical Plays Vol 2: Games in Particular*, Academic Press, New York, 1982.

Bernstein, J. *Three Degrees above Zero: Bell Labs in the Information Age*, Mentor Books, 1984.

Bleha, W.P. *Laser Focus/Electro Optics*, pp. 111, October, 1978.

Bogoch, S. and Bason, I., "Parallon Message Passing: Using MS-DOS and C to Communicate in Parallel," *Microcornucopia*, #39, pp. 58 – 60, Jan./Feb., 1988.

Booth, T.L. and Chien, Y., *Computing: Fundimentals and Applications* Hamilton Pub, Santa Barbara, CA, 1974.

Boyce, W.E. and Diprima, R.C., *Elementary Differential Equations* Wiley, New York, 1977.

Boyle, J., Butler, R., Disz, T., Glickfeld, B., Lusk, E., Overbeek, R., Patterson, J. and Stevens, R. *Portable Programs for Parallel Processors*, Holt, Rinehart and Winston, New York, 1987.

Brochard, L., "Communication and Control Costs of Domain Decomposition on Loosely-Coupled Multiprocessors," *Supercomputing*, Houstis, E.N. (editor), Springer-Verlag, New York, 1988.

Brown, F.R. and Christ, N.H., "Parallel Supercomputers for Lattice Gauge Theory," *Science*, Vol 239, pp. 1393 – 1400, 1988.

Carriero, N. and Gelernter, D., "Applications Experience with LINDA," *Proceedings SIPLAN Symposium on Parallel Processing*, 1988.

Carriero, N. and Gelernter, D., "Linda in Context," Yale University Research Report, *YALEU/DCS/RR-622*, April, 1988.

Carriero, N. and Gelernter, D. "How to Write Parallel Programs: A Guide to the Perplexed," Yale University Research Report, *YALEU/DCS/RR-628*, May, 1988.

Carter, F.L. (editor), *Molecular Electronic Devices*, Marcel Dekker, New York, 1982.

Carter, F.L., "The Chemistry of Molecular Computers," *Computer Applications in Chemistry*, Heller, S.R. and Potenzone, R., Jr. (editors), Elsevier Science Publishers, Amsterdam, 1983.

Carter, F.L., "The Molecular Device Computers: Point of Departure for Large Scale Cellular Automata," *Physica*, Vol. 10D, pp. 175 – 194, 1984.

Chamberlain, R.M., "Gray Codes, Fast Fourier Transforms and Hypercubes," *Parallel Computing*, Vol. 6, pp. 225 – 233, 1988.

Chavel, P., Forchheimer, R., Jenkins, B.K., Sawchuk, A.A. and Strand, T.C., "Architectures for a Sequential Optical Logic Processor," *IEEE Proceedings 1983 Optical Computing Conference*, pp. 6 – 12.

Cheney, W. and Kincaid, D., *Numerical Mathematics and Computing*, Brooks/Cole Publishing, Monterey, CA, 1980.

Chiricozzi, E. and Damico, A. (editors), *Parallel Processing and Applications*, North-Holland, New York, 1988.

Codd, E.F., *Cellular Automata*, Academic Press, New York, 1968.

Collins, S.A., Ambuel, J. and Damon, E.K., "Numerical Optical Data Processing," *Proceedings 1978 International Optical Computing Conference*, pp. 194–197, IEEE Computer Society, 1978.

Condon, J.H. and Ogielski, A.T., "Fast Special-Purpose Computer for Monte Carlo Simulations in Statistical Physics," *Review of Scientific Instruments*, Vol. 56, p. 1691, 1985.

Conrad, M., "On Design Principles for a Molecular Computer," *Comm. of the ACM*, Vol. 28, No. 5, May, 1985.

Crookes, D., Morrow, P.J., Millingan, P., Kilpatrick, P.L. and Scott, N.S., "An Array Processing Language for Transputer Networks," *Parallel Computing*, Vol. 8, pp. 141–148, 1988.

Curry, J.H., *Comm Math. Phys.*, 68, 129, 1979.

Cvetanovic, Z., "Performance Analysis of the FFT Algorithm on a Shared Memory Parallel Architecture," *IBM J. of Research & Development*, Vol. 31, pp. 435–451, July, 1987.

Danby, J.M.A., *Computing Applications to Differential Equations*, Prentice-Hall, Englewood, NJ, 1985.

Dautermount-Smith, W.C., McCoy, R.J., Burton, R.H. and Baca, A.G., "Fabrication Technologies for III-V Compound Semiconductor Photonic and Electronic Devices," *AT&T Technical J.*, Vol. 68, No. 1, p. 64, Jan./Feb., 1989.

Desrochers, G.R., *Principles of Parallel and Multiprocessing*, McGraw Hill, New York, 1987.

Devany, R.L., *An Introduction to Chaotic Dynamical Systems*, Benjamin Commings Company, 1986.

Dewney, A.K., *Scientific American*, May, 1985.

Dewney, A.K., *Scientific American*, Aug., 1985.

Dewney, A.K., *The Armchair Universe: An Exploration of Computer Worlds*, W.H. Freeman & Co., New York, 1988.

Donaldson, T., "New Matters," *Analog Science Fiction/Science Fact*, pp. 48–63, Dec., 1986.

Drexler, K.E., "Molecular Engineering: An Approach to the Development of General Capabilities for Molecular Manipulation," *Proc. Natl. Acad. Sci.*, U.S.A., Vol. 78, No. 9, pp. 5275–5278, 1981.

Drexler, K.E., *Engines of Creation*, Doubleday, Garden City, New York, 1986.

Ducksbury, P.G., *Parallel Array Processing*, Ellis Horwood Ltd., West Sussex, England, 1986.

Dura, S., "Special Report: Complex Tasks Signal Change for High-Speed Processing," *Research & Development*, pp. 101–110, Feb., 1984.

Dutta, N.K., "III-V Device Technologies for Lightwave Applications," *AT&T Technical, J.*, Vol 68, No. 1, p. 5 Jan./Feb., 1989.

Farhi, E. and Jaffe, R.L., "Strange Matter," *Physical Review*, Vol. 30D,

No. 11, pp. 2379–2390, (1984).

Fathi, E.T. and Krieger, M., "Multiple Microprocessor Systems: What, Why and When," *IEEE Computer*, pp. 23–32, March, 1983.

Ferry, D.K. (editor), *Gallium Arsenide Technology*, Howard W. Sams Inc., Indianapolis, IN, 1985.

Feynman, R.P., "Tiny Computers Obeying Quantum Mechanical Laws," *New Directions in Physics*, Metropolis, N., Kerr, D.M. and Gian-Carlo, R. (editors), Academic Press, New York, 1987.

Flynn, M.J., "Some Computer Organizations and Their Effectiveness," *IEEE Transactions on Computers*, Vol. C-21, No. 9, pp. 948–960, Sept., 1972.

Fogg, L., *Microcornucopia*, #39, Jan./Feb., 1988.

Forrest, B.M., Roweth, D., Stroud, N., Wallace, D.J. and Wilson, G.V., "Implementing Neural Network Models on Parallel Computers," *The Computer Journal*, Vol. 30, No. 5, pp. 413–419, 1987.

Forrest, B.M., Roweth, D., Stroud, N., Wallace, D.J. and Wilson, G.V., "Neural Network Models," *Parallel Computing* Vol. 8, pp. 71–83, 1988.

Fox, G., Johnson, M., Lyzenga, G., Otto, S., Salmon, J., and Walker, D., *Solving Problems on Concurrent Processors Volume 1 General Techniques and Regular Problems*, Prentice-Hall, NJ, 1988.

Fredkin, E. and Toffoli, T., "Conservative Logic," *International Journal of Theoretical Physics*, Vol. 21, No. 3/4, pp. 219–253, 1982.

Frye, R.C., Rietman, E.A. and Wong, C.C., Submitted for publication, 1989.

Gao, G.R., "A Pipelined Code Mapping Scheme for Tridiagonal Linear Equation Systems," *Highly Parallel Computers*, Reijns, G.L. and Bargon, M.H. (editors), pp. 59–80, North-Holland Pub., New York, 1987.

Gelernter, D., "Getting the Job Done," *Byte*, pp. 301–308, Dec., 1988.

Gilbert, B.K., "GaAs Digital Integrated Circuits," *Gallium Arsenide Technology*, Ferry, D.K. (editor), Howard W. Sams Inc., Indianapolis, IN, 1985.

Goles, E., and Vichniac, G.Y., *Neural Networks for Computing*, AIP #151, Denker, J.S. (editor), American Institute of Physics, New York, 1986.

Hansen, C.J. (editor), *The Physics of Dense Matter*, Reidel Pub., Boston, 1974.

Harel, D., *Algorithmics: The Spirit of Computing*, Addison Wesley Pub., Reading, MA, 1987.

Henon M., *Commun. Math. Phys.*, Vol. 50, p. 69, 1976.

Hilhorst, H.J., Bakker, A.F., Fruin, C., Compagner, A., and Hoogland, A., "Special Purpose Computers in Physics," *J. Stat. Physics*, Vol. 34, No.

5/6, pp. 987–1000, 1984.

Hillis, W.D., "The Connection Machine," *Sci. Am.*, pp. 108–115, June, 1987.

Hillis, W.D., *The Connection Machine*, MIT Press, Cambridge, MA, 1985.

Hinton, G.E. and Sejnowski, T.J., "Learning and Relearning in Boltzmann Machines," *Parallel Distributed Processing: Explorations in the Microstructure of Cognition Volume 1 Foundations*, Rumelhart, D.E., McClelland, J.L., and the PDP Research Group (editors), MIT Press, Cambridge, MA, 1986.

Hoare, C.A.R., "Communicating Sequential Processes," *Communications of the ACM*, Vol. 21, No. 8, pp. 666–677, 1978.

Hoare, C.A.R., *Communications Sequential Processes*, Prentice-Hall, Englewood-Cliffs, NJ, 1985.

Hopfield, J.J., *Proc. Natl. Acad. Sci.*, U.S.A., Vol. 79, p. 2554, 1982.

Hopfield, J.J., *Proc. Natl. Acad. Sci.*, U.S.A., Vol. 81, p. 3088, 1984.

Houstis, E.N., Papatheodorou, T.S., and Polychronopoulos (editors), *Supercomputing*, Springer-Verlag, New York, 1988.

Huang, A., "An Implementation of a Residue Arithmetic Unit via Optical and Other Physical Phenomina," *IEEE Proceedings of the 1975 International Optical Computing Conference*, pp. 14–18, IEEE Computer Society, 1975.

Huang A., Tsunoda, Y., Goodman, J.W., and Ishihara, S., "Some Optical Methods for Performing Residue Arithmetic Operations," *Proceedings 1978 International Optical Computing Conference*, pp. 185–193, IEEE Computer Society, 1978.

Hull, D.G., "Survey of Silicon-Based Integrated Optics," *IEEE Computer*, Vol. 20, No. 12, pp. 25–32, Dec., 1987.

Hunsperger, R.G., *Integrated Optics: Theory and Technology*, Second Edition, Springer-Verlag, New York, 1985.

Hwang, K. and Briggs, F.A., *Computer Architecture and Parallel Processing*, McGraw-Hill, New York, 1984.

Iafrate, G.J., "The Physics of Submicron/Ultrasubmicron Dimensions," *Gallium Arsenide Technology*, Ferry, D.K. (editor), Howard W. Sams Publishing, Indianapolis, IN, 1985.

Inmos, *Transputer Reference Manual*, Prentice-Hall, New York, 1988.

Inmos, *The Transputer Instruction Set—A Compiler Writer's Guide*, Prentice-Hall, New York, 1986.

Inmos, *OCCAM 2 Reference Manual*, Prentice-Hall, New York, 1988.

Jesshope, C., "Transputers and Switches as Objects in OCCAM," *Parallel Computing*, Vol. 8, pp. 19–30, 1988.

Jesshope, C. (editor), *Parallel Processing*, Pergman Press, 1987.

Jones, G., *Programming in OCCAM*, Prentice-Hall, Englewood Cliffs, NJ, 1987.

Kent, E.W., Shneier, M.O., and Lumia, R., "PIPE: Pipelined Image-Processing Engine," *J. of Parallel and Distributed Computing*, Vol. 2, pp. 50 – 78, 1985.

Klerer, M. and Korn, G.A. (editors), *Digital Computer Users Handbook*, McGraw-Hill, New York, 1967.

Knuth, D.E., *The Art of Computer Programming Volume 2 Seminumerical Algorithms*, Addison-Wesley, Reading, MA, 1969.

Kogge, P.M., *The Architecture of Pipelined Computers*, McGraw-Hill, New York, 1981.

Kogut, J.B., "Simulating Gauge Theories of Nature: Present Problems and Future Goals," *High-Speed Computing: Scientific Applications and Algorithm Design*, Wilhelmson, R.B. (editor), U. of Illinois Press, Chicago, 1988.

Kung, H.T., "Why Systolic Architectures," *Computer*, pp. 37 – 46, January, 1982.

Kung, S.Y., "On Supercomputing with Systolic/Wavefront Array Processors," *Proceedings of the IEEE*, Vol. 72, No. 7, pp. 867 – 884, July, 1982.

Landers, P.M., "A Generalized Message-Passing Mechanism for Communicating Sequential Processes," *IEEE Transactions on Computers*, Vol. 37, No. 6, pp. 646 – 651, June, 1988.

Langton, C.G., "Self-Reproduction in Cellular Automata," *Physicia*, Vol. 10D, pp. 135 – 144, 1984.

LeCun, Y., "Learning Processes in an Asymmetric Threshold Network," *Disordered Systems and Biological Organization*, Bienenstock, E., Fogelman-Soulie, F., and Weisbuch, G. (editors), NATO ASI Series F, Vol. 20, Springer-Verlag, Berlin, 1986.

Leeds, H.D. and Weinberg, G.M., *Computer Programming Fundamentals*, McGraw-Hill, New York, 1961.

Legendi, T., Parkinson, D., Vollmar, R., and Wolf, G. (editors), *Parallel Processing by Cellular Automata and Arrays*, Proceedings of the Third International Workshop on Parallel Processing by Cellular Automata and Arrays, Berlin, Sept. 9 – 11, 1986, Published by North Holland, New York, 1987.

Lerner, R.A., "Synthetic Vaccines," *Scientific American*, p. 66, Feb., 1983.

Lin, S.Y. and Lin, Y.F., *Set Theory: An Intuitive Approach*, Houghton Mifflin, Boston, MA, 1974.

Little, M.J. and Grainberg, J., "The Third Dimension," *Byte*, Vol. 13, No. 12, pp. 311 – 319, 1988.

Liu, C.L., *Elements of Discrete Mathematics*, Second Edition,

McGraw-Hill, New York, 1985.

Loard, N.W., Girogosiam, P.A., Ouellette, R.P., Clerman, R.J. and Cheremisinoff, P.N., *Advanced Computers: Parallel and Biochip Processors*, Ann Arbor Science, Ann Arbor, MI, 1983.

Lootsma, F.A. and Ragsdell, K.M., "State of the Art in Parallel Nonlinear Optimization," *Parallel Computing*, Vol. 6, pp. 133–155, 1988.

Loucks, W.M., Snelgrove, M., and Zaky, S.G., "A Vector Processor Based on One-Bit Microprocessors," *IEEE Micro*, pp. 53–62, Feb., 1982.

Machle, E. and Wirl, K., "Parallel Programs for Numerical and Signal Processing on the Multiprocessor System Dirmu 25," *Highly Parallel Computers*, Reijns, G.L. and Barton, M.H. (editors), pp. 29–39, North Holland, New York, 1987.

Mandelbrot, B.B., *The Fractal Geometry of Nature*, W.H. Freeman, San Francisco, CA, 1977.

Mann, A.K. and Primakoff, H., "Possible Production of Collapsed Hadronic Matter in Very-High-Energy Nucleon-Nucleon Collisions," *Physical Review*, Vol. D22, No. 5, pp. 1115–1119, 1980.

Marcus, M., *Discrete Mathematics: A Computational Approach Using BASIC*, Computer Sci. Press, Rockville, MD, 1983.

Margolus, N., "Physics-Like Models of Computation," *Physicia*, Vol. 10D, pp. 81–95, 1984.

Markoc, H., Unlu, H., Zabel, H. and Otsuka, N., "Gallium Arsenide on Silicon: A Review," *Solid State Technology*, pp. 71–76, March, 1988.

Maxwell, L. and Reed, M., *The Theory of Graphs: A Basis for Network Theory*, Pergamon Press, New York, 1971.

McBryan, O.A. and Van de Velde, E.F., "Matrix and Vector Operations on Hypercube Parallel Processors," *Parallel Computing*, Vol. 5, pp. 117–125, 1987.

McCanny, J.V. and McWhirter, J.G., "Some Systolic Array Developments in the United Kingdom," *Computer*, Vol. 20, No. 7, pp. 51–63, 1987.

McEliece, R.J., Posner, E.C., and Rodemich, E.R., *Twenty-Third Annual Allerton Conference on Communication, Control, and Computing*, Oct., 1985.

Metropolis, N., Rosenbluth, A.N., Rosenbluth, M.N., Teller, A.H., and Teller, E., "Equations of State Calculations by Fast Computing Machines," *J. Chem. and Physics*, Vol. 21, pp. 1087–1091, 1953.

Mobius, D., "Monolayer Assemblies," *Topics in Surface Chemistry*, Kay, E. and Bagus, P. (editors), Plenum Press, New York, 1978.

Packard, N.H., "Complexity of Growing Patterns in Cellular Automata," *Dynamical Systems and Cellular Automata*, Demongeot, J., Goles, E., and Tchuente, M. (editors), Academic Press, Inc., New York, 1985.

Panish, M.B. "Molecular Beam Epitaxy," *AT&T Technical Journal*, Vol. 68, No. 1, p. 43, Jan./Feb., 1989.

Peitgen, H.O., Saupe, D., and Haesler, F.V., *Mathematical Intelligencer*, Vol. 6, No. 2, p. 11, 1984.

Peitgen, H.O., and Richter, P.H., *The Beauty of Fractals: Images of Complex Dynamical Systems*, Springer-Verlag, New York, 1986.

Potter, D., *Computational Physics*, Wiley, New York, 1973.

Poundstone, W., *The Recursive Universe: Cosmic Complexity and the Limits of Scientific Knowledge*, Contemporary Books, Chicago, 1985.

Pountain, D. and May, D., *A Tutorial Introduction to OCCAM Programming*, Inmos, 1987.

Press, W.H., Flannery, B.P., Teukolsky, S.A., and Vetterling, W.T., *Numerical Recipes in C: The Art of Scientific Computing*, Cambridge Univ. Press, Cambridge, MA, 1988.

Quarmby, D. (editor), *Signal Processor Chips*, Prentice-Hall, Englewood Cliffs, NJ, 1985.

Rabbi, C., "The Lattice Theory of Quark Confinement," *Scientific American*, p. 54, Feb., 1983.

Rector, R. and Alexy, G., *The 8086 Book*, Osborne/McGraw-Hill, Berkley, CA, 1980.

Reijns, G.L. and Barton, M.H. (editors), *Highly Parallel Computers*, Proceedings of the IFIP WG 103 Working Conference, North-Holland, New York, 1987.

Rietman, E.A., "Digital Optical Computing," *Journal of the British American Scientific Research Association*, Sept., 1986.

Rietman, E.A., *Experiments in Artificial Neural Networks*, TAB BOOKS, Blue Ridge Summit, PA, 1988.

Rietman, E.A., *Exploring the Geometry of Nature: Computer Modeling of Chaos, Fractals, Cellular Automata and Neural Networks*, Windcrest Books, Blue Ridge Summit, PA, 1989.

Robert, F., *Discrete Interations: A Metric Study*, Springer-Verlag, New York, 1986.

Rohrbacher, D. and Potter, J.I., "Image Processing with the Staran Parallel Processors," *Computer*, Vol. 10, No. 8, pp. 54–59 1977, Reprinted in: *Tutorial on Parallel Processing*, edited by Kuhn, R.H. and Padua, D.A., IEEE Computer Society Press, Piscataway, NJ, 1981.

Ruelle, D., *Mathematical Intelligencer*, Vol. 2, No. 3, p. 126, 1980.

Rumelhart, D.E., Hinton, G.E., and Williams, R.J., "Learning Internal

Representations by Error Propagations," *Parallel Distributed Processing: Explorations in the Microstructure of Cognition Vol. 1,* Rumelhart, D.E. and McClelland, J.L. (editors), MIT press, Cambridge, MA, 1986.

Rumelhart, D.E., McClelland, J.L. and the PDP Research Group, *Parallel Distributed Processing: Explorations in the Microstructure of Cognition Vol. 1,* MIT press, Cambridge, MA, 1986.

Sadayappan, P. and Ercal, F., "Cluster-Partitioning Approaches to Mapping Parallel Programs onto a Hypercube," *Supercomputing,* Houstis, E.N. (editor), Springer-Verlag, New York, 1988.

Saenger, W., "Structural Aspects of Cyclodextrines and their Inclusion Complexes," *Inclusion Compounds Vol. 2,* Atwood, J.L., Davies, J.E.D. and MacNicol, D.D. (editors), Academic Press, London, 1984.

Sclater, N., *Gallium Arsenide IC Technology: Theory and Practice,* TAB Books, Blue Ridge Summit, PA, 1988.

Shastri, L., "Massive Parallelism in Artificial Intelligence," *Applied Optics,* Vol. 26, No. 10, pp. 1829–1844, May 15, 1987.

Shoup, T.E., *Numerical Methods for the Personal Computer,* Prentice-Hall, Englewood Cliffs, NJ, 1983.

Sluss, J.J., Veasey, D.L., Batchman, T.E. and Parrish, E.A., "An Introduction to Integrated Optics for Computing," *IEEE Computer,* Vol. 20, No. 12, pp. 9–23, Dec., 1987.

Stillinger, F.H. and Wasserman, Z., "Molecular Recognition and Self-Organization in Fluorinated Hydrocarbons," *J. Phys. Chem.,* Vol. 82, No. 8, pp. 929–940, 1978.

Stone, H.S., *High-Performance Computer Architecture,* Addison-Wesley Publishers, Reading, MA, 1987.

Strang, G., *Introduction to Applied Mathematics,* Wellesley-Cambridge Press, Wellesley, MA, 1986.

Szabo and Tanaka, *Residue Arithmetic and Its Applications to Computer Technology,* McGraw-Hill, New York, 1967.

Tai, A., "Design Concept for an Optical Numerical Computer Based on the Residue Number System," *Proceedings 1980 International Optical Computing Conference, Book II,* Vol. 232, pp. 137–150, IEEE Computer Society, 1980.

Taylor, R., "Transputer Communication Link," *Microprocessors and Microsystems,* Vol. 10, No. 4, pp. 211–215, 1986.

Thompson, J.M.T. and Thompson, R.J., *The Insi. of Math and Its Appl.,* Vol. 16, p. 150, April, 1980.

Toffoli, T., "Cellular Automata as an Alternative to (Rather than an Approximation of) Differential Equations in Modeling Physics," *Physica,* Vol. 10D, pp. 117–127, 1984.

Toffoli, T., "CAM: A High-Performance Cellular-Automata Machine," *Physica*, Vol. 10D, pp. 195–204, 1984.

Toffoli, T. and Margolus, N., *Cellular Automata Machines: A New Environment for Modeling*, MIT Press, Cambridge, MA, 1987.

Ulmer, K.M., "Biological Assembly of Molecular Ultracircuits," *Molecular Electronic Devices*, Carter, F.L. (editor), Marcel Dekker, New York, 1982.

Vannimenus, J., Nadal, J.P. and Derrida, B., "Stochastic Models of Cluster Growth," *Dynamical Systems and Cellular Automata*, Demongeot, J., Goles, E., and Tchuente, M. (editors), Academic Press, New York, 1985.

Vaughan, J., Brookes, G., Chalmers, D., and Walts, M., "Transputer Applications to Speech Recognition," *Microprocessors and Microsystems*, Vol. 11, No. 7, pp. 377–382, 1987.

Vichniac, G.Y., "Simulating Physics with Cellular Automata," *Physica*, Vol. 10D, pp. 96–116, 1984.

Walker, P., "The Transputer," *Byte*, pp. 219–235, May, 1985.

Wasserman, P.D., *Neural Computing: Theory and Practice*, Van Nostrand Reinhold, New York, 1989.

Webb, R.A. and Washburn, S., "Quantum Interference Fluctuations in Disordered Metals," *Physics Today*, p. 46, Dec., 1988.

Widrow, B. and Hoff, M.E., "Adaptive Switching Circuits," *IRE WESCON*, Convention Record IRE, New York, pp. 96–104, 1960.

Widrow, B. and Hoff, M.E., "Associative Storage and Retrieval of Digital Information in Networks of Adaptive Neurons," *Biological Prototypes and Synthetic Systems*, Vol. 1, Bernard, E.E., and Kare, M.R. (editors), Plelnum Press, New York, 1962.

Williams, T., "Software Machine Model Blazes Trail for Parallel Processing," *Computer Design*, pp. 20–26, Oct. 1, 1988.

Wilson, P., "Parallel Processing Comes to PCs," *Byte*, pp. 213–218, Nov., 1988.

Wolfram, S., *Rev. Mod. Phys.*, Vol. 55, No. 3, p. 601, 1983.

Wolfram, S., "Some Recent Results and Questions about Cellular Automata," *Dynamical Systems and Cellular Automata*, Demongeot, J., Goles, E. and Tchuente, M. (editors), Academic Press, New York, 1985.

Index

265